OXFORD LATIN COURSE
COLLEGE EDITION
Grammar, Exercises, Context

OXFORD LATIN COURSE

COLLEGE EDITION

Grammar, Exercises, Context

Maurice Balme

James Morwood

New York   Oxford

OXFORD UNIVERSITY PRESS

Oxford University Press, Inc., publishes works that further Oxford University's
objective of excellence in research, scholarship, and education.

Oxford   New York
Auckland   Cape Town   Dar es Salaam   Hong Kong   Karachi
Kuala Lumpur   Madrid   Melbourne   Mexico City   Nairobi
New Delhi   Shanghai   Taipei   Toronto

With offices in
Argentina   Austria Brazil   Chile   Czech Republic   France   Greece
Guatemala   Hungary   Italy   Japan   Poland   Portugal   Singapore
South Korea   Switzerland   Thailand   Turkey   Ukraine   Vietnam

For titles covered by Section 112 of the US Higher Education Opportunity Act,
please visit www.oup.com/us/he for the latest information about
pricing and alternate formats.

Published by Oxford University Press, Inc.
198 Madison Avenue, New York, New York, 10016
http://www.oup.com

Oxford is a registered trademark of Oxford University Press

Library of Congress Cataloging-in-Publication Data
Balme, Maurice.
    Oxford Latin course / Maurice Balme, James Morwood—College edition.
        volumes cm.
        ISBN 978-0-19-986296-2 (volume 1)—ISBN 978-0-19-986297-9 (volume 2)   1.
Latin language—Textbooks.   2. Latin language—Grammar.   I. Morwood, J.   II.
Title.
    PA2087.5.M674 2012
    478.2'421—dc23
                        2011044996

About the Cover: This is a section of the beautiful wall paintings in the Villa of the Mysteries at Pompeii in
Southern Italy. The subject of the paintings is disputed but they may well illustrate the initiation of a woman into
the mystery cult of the god Dionysus. They date from the first century BC and are therefore contemporary with
Horace, the subject of our Readings. The figures in the paintings are life-size.

Printing number: 9 8 7 6 5 4

Printed in the United States of America
on acid-free paper

Contents

Introduction

This book is written to be used in tandem with *The Oxford Latin Course, College Edition: Readings and Vocabulary*. In it will be found:

1. Chapter-by-chapter grammatical explanations and exercises to support the reading of the 31 chapters of the Readings. Our recommendation is that the readings should be completed before the students learn the relevant grammar, but they may well wish to consult the language notes on the readings as they go through them.

2. Word-building and (later) post script (P.S.) activities to consolidate vocabulary, draw attention to English derivations from the Latin, and enhance knowledge of Latin grammar and Roman civilization.

3. Notes and essays on the social, political and cultural context of the Readings. These are intended bit by bit to build up a rounded picture of Rome in the first century BC. We believe that a vital ingredient of learning a language is to have some understanding of the world in which it was spoken. With this end in view, we also include notes on the illustrations.

4. Appendices covering aspects of grammar not dealt with elsewhere.

5. A glossary of grammatical terms.

6. A metrical appendix to explain the scansion of the poetry we have included.

7. A reference grammar, which brings together all the grammar met in the course.

8. A vocabulary for the English–Latin exercises.

9. An index to the grammar, referring to chapters in this volume.

10. Three review (comprehension) exercises to be done after the completion of Chapters 9, 17 and 31.

If you do not understand any of the grammatical terms, they are explained in the glossary on pages 284–90.

Grammar: verbs: transitive & intransitive; 1st conjugation, 3rd singular; *est* + complement
nouns & adjectives: 1st declension sing. nominative & accusative

COMMENTARY

Scintilla in casā labōrat

l.2: **Scintilla Horātiam uocat**: the names so far have been in the nominative as is shown by the fact that they end in **-a**; they have been the subjects of the verbs. Now **Horātiam** is in the accusative, ending in **-am**, and is therefore the object of **uocat**: Scintilla calls Horatia.

R̄V̄ **Argus:** this famous mosaic of a dog is from the floor of a
doorway in Pompeii. (National Archaeological Museum, Naples).
See page 3 in Oxford Latin Course, College Edition: Readings and
Vocabulary.

Word-building
A very large number of English words are derived from Latin. What is (a) a *laborious* task (b) *puerile* behavior (c) *feminine* intuition? From which Latin words is each of the English words in italics derived?

GRAMMAR

1. Note that Latin has no definite article (the), nor indefinite article (a); so, **Quīntus est puer Rōmānus.** = Quintus is a Roman boy. **Scintilla in casā labōrat.** = Scintilla is working in the house.

2. Note that verbs usually come at the end of their clauses, though **est** often comes earlier.

3. For the earlier chapters of this course only the present tense of verbs is used; Latin has only one form for the present tense, English has three, e.g. **Scintilla labōrat** = either "Scintilla is working" or "Scintilla does work."

4. Latin does not express the subject of the verb if the context makes it clear, e.g. **Scintilla in casā labōrat; fessa est.** = Scintilla is working in the house; she is tired.

5. In English the meaning of a sentence is determined largely by word order; in Latin it is determined by inflexion, i.e. by changes in the endings of nouns and adjectives, and word order is flexible, e.g.
   Horātia Scintillam iuuat. = Horatia helps Scintilla.
   Horātiam Scintilla iuuat. = Scintilla helps Horatia.
   Ending **-a** indicates the subject of the verb; ending **-am** indicates the object. It is therefore always vital to pay close attention to word endings.

6. This chapter introduces the three types of sentence which form the skeletons of all Latin sentences:
   (a) subject + intransitive verb (an intransitive verb is a verb which does not require an object), e.g. **Scintilla labōrat.** = Scintilla is working.
   (b) subject + transitive verb + object (a transitive verb is verb which requires an object), e.g. **Horātia Scintillam iuuat.** = Horatia is helping Scintilla.
   (c) subject + joining word + complement (complement = completing word) e.g. **Horātia est puella Rōmāna**. Note that the complement is in the same case as the subject. This structure almost always occurs with the verb "to be" (e.g. "is," "are").

7. Cases: the inflexions of nouns and adjectives (changes in their endings) are called cases:
   -a nominative case (indicating the subject of a verb or the complement of the verb "is")
   -am accusative case (indicating the object of a transitive verb). The accusative case is also used after many prepositions, e.g. **in casam** = into the house.

There are in all five cases, which are introduced in successive chapters:

Case	1st Declension Endings	Usage
nominative	**-a**	subject of sentence
genitive	**-ae**	of
dative	**-ae**	to, for
ablative	**-ā**	by, with, from*
accusative	**-am**	object of sentence

*At present the ablative case is used only after certain prepositions, e.g. **in casā** = in the house; note that **in casam** (accusative) = into the house; **in casā** (ablative) = in the house.

EXERCISE 1.1

Translate the following
1. fēmina festīnat.
2. puella cēnat.
3. Scintilla intrat.
4. Horātia nōn labōrat.

EXERCISE 1.2

Translate the following
1. Scintilla fessa est.
2. puella laeta est.
3. cēna nōn parāta est.
4. Scintilla est fēmina.

EXERICISE 1.3

In each of the following give the correct Latin form for the word in parentheses and translate the whole sentence, e.g.
Scintilla ad casam (walks): **ambulat** Scintilla walks to the house
1. puella casam (enters).
2. fēmina (is working).
3. cēna nōn parāta (is).
4. Scintilla (is hurrying).

5. mox (dinner) parāta est.
6. Horātia (glad) est.

EXERCISE 1.4

Copy out the following sentences in Latin. Fill in the blanks with the correct endings and translate

1. Horāti– in casā labōrat.
2. puella Scintill– uocat.
3. Scintill– cas– intrat.
4. filia Scintill– salūtat.
5. puella cēn– parat
6. Scintilla fīli– laudat.
7. Argus casam intrat et cēn– dēuorat.
8. Scintilla īrat– est; cēnam iterum (*again*) par– .

EXERCISE 1.5

In each of the following give the correct Latin form for the word in parentheses; then translate the whole sentence

1. Scintilla filiam (calls).
2. Horātia casam (enters) et (Scintilla) salūtat.
3. Horātia Scintillam (helps).
4. Scintilla Horātiam (looks at).
5. Horātia (happy) est.

EXERCISE 1.6

Translate into Latin

1. Horatia is carrying water into the house.
2. She is tired but she hurries.
3. She enters the house and calls Scintilla.
4. Scintilla praises (her) daughter.

QUINTUS

Our story traces the life of Quintus Horatius Flaccus, who rose from humble beginnings to become the friend of the great and one of the most famous of the Roman poets. He tells us a significant amount about his life in his writing but what he says should probably be approached with caution. He creates a poetic persona for himself which is clearly stylized in some ways, but he would have made himself ridiculous if his portrait of himself had not had some foundation in reality. And so, while we have filled in the picture with many details of our own, we have basically taken him at his word.

This mountainous landscape is characteristic of southeast Italy.

He was born on December 8, 65 BC in Venusia, a large town in the wild area of Apulia in southeast Italy. His father, whom he loved and admired, was an ex-slave, a freedman who was an auctioneer's agent and a provider of banking services as well as running a small farm (Horace, *Satires* 1.6.6, 71, 86). We know nothing at all about any other relatives. We have invented the name Scintilla for his mother and given him a sister called Horatia.

His father did not send him to the local school—though in our story we pretend that he did go there for a while—but "dared to take me to Rome as a boy to be taught the arts which any father from the top levels of society would have his sons taught" (*Satires* 1.6.76–8). In Rome, Flaccus sent him to what was perhaps the best school, that of Orbilius. After this, he may have studied rhetoric, the art of public speaking, which was the usual form of tertiary education. Finally, when he was about 20, he went to the Academy in Athens, the most famous university in the ancient world, where he studied philosophy (*Epistles* 2.2.43–5).

At the age of 21, he ended his student career and joined the army of Marcus Brutus, the leading assassin of Julius Caesar. Thus when he was 22 he fought as a military tribune, a surprisingly high rank, and even commanded a legion on the losing side in one of the bloodiest battles of the ancient world, at Philippi in northeast Greece in the autumn of 42 BC (*Satires* 1.6.48, *Epistles* 2.2.47–9).

After this humiliation, he returned to Rome, became a clerk in the Treasury and started to write poetry (Suetonius, *Vita Horatii*; *Epistles* 2.2.51–2). This led him to move in literary circles where he met Virgil, usually regarded as the greatest of the Roman poets. Virgil introduced him to Maecenas, one of the most powerful men of the time and a great patron of the arts. Maecenas became a close friend and presented him with a farm in the Sabine hills near Rome, and his support allowed Horace to devote himself to writing poetry (*Satires* 1.6.54–62, 2.6.1–5). Through his patron, he became a friend of Augustus, the first Roman emperor, who admired his poetry and may even have asked him to become his private secretary (Suetonius, *Vita Horatii*). If he did, Horace refused the position but remained on good terms with Augustus.

This relief may be the single possibly identifiable ancient portrait of Horace. The wine mug suggests a pleasure-lover and the receding hairline suggests Horace! (Museum of Fine Arts, Boston)

Horace did not write a vast number of poems: in fact they fit into one slim volume. But they are highly original—they include four books of *Odes*, which he modeled on Greek lyric poetry, two books of *Satires*, in which he laughs either at himself or at the follies of his fellow men, and two books of *Epistles*, letters to friends in poetic form. At the end of the first set of *Odes*, he proudly claims:

> I have raised a monument more lasting than bronze and higher than the ruins of the royal pyramids. Neither biting rain nor the wild north wind nor the innumerable procession of the years nor the flight of time can destroy it … Not all of me shall die … a man who became powerful from humble beginnings.
>
> (*Odes* 3.30.1–6, 12)

He died not long after Maecenas on November 27, 8 BC, at the age of 56.

Further Reading

An important ancient source for Horace's life is Suetonius' *De Viris Illustribus*. For a full modern account of Horace's life, see Robin Nisbet, "Horace: Life and Chronology," pp. 7–21 of *The Cambridge Companion to Horace*, ed. Stephen Harrison (Cambridge, 2007). An excellent, attractively presented selection from his work (in English) is Keith Maclennan, *Horace: A Poet for a New Age* (Cambridge, 2010).

Chapter 2
Quīntus Flaccum iuuat

Grammar: nouns & adjs 2nd declension: nominative & accusative sing. & plural; gender: masc., fem. and neuter; agreement of adjectives; verbs: 3rd plural—all conjugations

---

CARTOONS AND PATTERN SENTENCES

These introduce the concept of the plural and the masculine gender. You will be exercising these in the three passages in this chapter. Full explanations are given below, but see how much you can work out on your own.

COMMENTARY

(a) Quīntus Flaccum iuuat

Vocabulary 2a: the prepositions **ā** and **ē** change form to **ab** and **ex** if they are followed by a vowel, e.g. **ē casā** (out of the house) but **ex agrō** (out of the field).

R V **Gathering olives:** this illustration from a sixth century Attic vase (British Museum) shows two men beating the branches of an olive tree to shake down the fruit; a boy has climbed the tree to pick the olives while another gathers up the fallen fruit. Olives, harvested in October and November, formed a vital part of the rural economy; olive oil was used for cooking, lamp-lighting, washing (soap) and scent. *See page 6 in* Oxford Latin Course, College Edition: Readings and Vocabulary.

(b) Flaccus ad tabernam exit

R V **A tavern at Pompeii:** As in modern Italy, so in ancient, there were numerous drinking shops scattered round the town. The illustration on page 7 shows one in Pompeii on the Via

8

dell'Abbondanza. (For full comment, see p. 70.) Hot and cold drinks were served from the counter. *See page 7 in* Oxford Latin Course, College Edition: Readings and Vocabulary.

The names of Flaccus' friends and the tenor of their conversation are taken from Petronius, *Satyrica* 42 ff. The *Satyrica* is an immensely long novel, much of it lost, centering round the escapades of two disreputable undergraduates; the best-preserved section tells of a dinner party given by the millionaire Trimalchio; at one point the guests are discussing the price of corn: "No one cares how the price of corn hurts. My god, I've not been able to find a mouthful of bread today. And how the drought goes on and on! There's been a famine now for a year. Curse the aediles, who are in league with the bakers." (The aediles were officials in charge of the supply and price of grain.)

l.7 *domum redit*: "he returns home"; note that the preposition *ad* is omitted before *domum*.

RV **An election poster:** this poster is inviting support for Cnaeus Heluius Sabinus. (**V** is a capital **u**.) What case is his name in? *See page 8 in* Oxford Latin Course, College Edition: Readings and Vocabulary.

(c) Scintilla et Horātia ad fontem festīnant

The wealthier houses in Pompeii had a piped water supply but most had none. And so it was a daily chore for the women of the family to go to one of public fountains dotted round the town to collect water. The same was true of ancient Greece, a scene often represented on Greek vases.

RV **Women filling urns at the spring:** this black-figure vase from Vulci dates from about 530 BC. It shows some women coming to a spring with a lion-head spout to fill their vases. The central figure is leaving after filling hers. There is an element of humor since the jar on which the scene is painted is itself a water jar. (Villa Giulia, Rome) *See page 9 in* Oxford Latin Course, College Edition: Readings and Vocabulary.

RV **A scene from twentieth-century Italy:** it was also true of modern Italy until quite recently. *See page 9 in* Oxford Latin Course, College Edition: Readings and Vocabulary.

l. 6 *eam*: it (feminine because it refers to *urna*)

l.9 *surge...portā*: "get up!...carry!" These are imperative forms of the verb, used in giving orders (see Chapter 4).

Word-building

It is often possible to guess the meaning of Latin words from the English words which come from them. What do the following Latin words mean?

VERBS	NOUNS	ADJECTIVES
dēfendit	familia	ānxius
dēscendit	flamma	dēsertus
repellit	memōria	timidus

Since many words can easily be guessed from their similarity to English words, e.g. **cōnsūmit** = he/she consumes, eats; and **dēuorat** = he/she devours, we do not always gloss them in the passages. But all such words are included in the General Vocabulary.

GRAMMAR

Nouns

1 Cases

All nouns consist of a stem, which shows the meaning of the word, and an ending, which shows its case. The cases indicate the relation of the nouns to the rest of the sentence. There are five cases, the uses of which may be summarized as follows:

Nominative: subject of clause and complement after the verb "to be": **puell-a, colōn-us,**
Genitive: = "of" **puell-ae, colōn-ī**
Dative = "to" or "for" **puell-ae, colōn-ō**
Accusative: object of a transitive verb and after certain prepositions: **puell-am, colōn-um**
Ablative = "by," "with," or "from" **puell-ā, colōn-ō**

There is a sixth case—the Vocative—used in calling to or addressing someone; this is the same in form as the nominative for all nouns except for 2nd declension nouns (see below) ending **-us** in the nominative; the vocative of these nouns ends -**e**; thus **"quid facis, Flacc-e?"** = "What are you doing, Flaccus?"

The uses of these cases will be introduced and more fully explained in successive chapters.

2 Declensions

Nouns fall into groups called declensions; Chapter 1 introduced only nouns of the first declension characterised by the case ending **-a**, e.g. nominative **Horāti-a,** accusative **Horāti-am,** ablative **Horāti-ā** (N.B. in the nominative the **-a** sounds short, in the ablative **-ā** sounds long; in this book all long vowels are marked by a macron—**Horātiā.**)

1st declension plurals end in **-ae** in the nominative and **-ās** in the accusative.

This chapter introduces nouns of the second declension, which have nominative **-us** or **-er,** accusative **-um,** ablative **-ō,** e.g.

colōn-us, colōn-um, colōn-ō,
puer, puer-um, puer-ō,
ager, agr-um, agr-ō

2nd declension masculine plurals end in **-ī** in the nominative and **-ōs** in the accusative

First and second declensions, nominative and accusative singular and plural			
		singular	plural
nominative	1st decl. (fem.)	**puell-a**	**puell-ae**
	2nd decl. (masc.)	**colōn-us**	**colōn-ī**
		puer	**puer-ī**
accusative	1st decl. (fem.)	**puell-am**	**puell-ās**
	2nd decl. (masc.)	**colōn-um**	**colōn-ōs**
		puer-um	**puer-ōs**

3 Gender

All nouns are either masculine or feminine or neuter (i.e. neither masculine nor feminine) in gender.

Nearly all nouns of the 1st declension are feminine (a few are masculine because of their meaning, e.g. **nauta** = a sailor).

Most nouns of the 2nd declension are masculine; some are neuter (neuter nouns of 2nd declension have nominative and accusative singular **-um,** plural **-a**), e.g. **colōnus** and **puer** are masculine; **bellum** (war) is neuter.

Adjectives

Adjectives agree with their nouns, i.e. they have the same case and gender, e.g. **puella bona; puellam bonam. multī colōnī; multōs colōnōs.**

They are given in the vocabulary with all three genders, e.g.

masc.	fem.	neuter	
magn-us	**magn-a**	**magn-um**	big

These are abbreviated to **magn-us, -a, -um.**

EXERCISE 2.1

Give the gender (masculine or feminine or neuter) of the following words (which are all in the nominative case)

terra, puer, uia, saxum, fābula, colōnus, bellum

EXERCISE 2.2

Correct the following Latin sentences
1. fīlia fessus est. *fīlia fessa est*
2. fīliī laetae sunt. *fīlliī laetī sunt*
3. cēna nōn parātum est. *cena non parata est*
4. puer īrāta est. *puer iratus est*
5. Horātia multum aquam portat. *Horatia multam aquam portat*

EXERCISE 2.3

Give the plural of the following noun plus adjective phrases (notice that some are in the nominative, others in the accusative case)

fēmina laeta, colōnum īrātum, puer fessus, puellam miseram, agrum magnum

---

GRAMMAR

Verbs

1 Conjugations
Latin verbs fall into four classes, called conjugations, which differ in the endings of their stems:

1st conjugation: stem ending -A, e.g. **parA-t**
2nd conjugation: stem ending -E, e.g. **monE-t**
3rd conjugation: stem ending in consonant e.g. **caD-it**
4th conjugation: stem ending -I e.g. **audI-t**

In Chapter 1 all verbs belong to the first conjugation, the ending **-at** (**intrA-T, uocA-T** etc). In Chapter 2 all four conjugations are used (see vocabulary).

Conjugation	3rd person singular		3rd person plural	
1st	**para-t**	he/she prepares	**para-nt**	they prepare
2nd	**mone-t**	he/she warns	**mone-nt**	they warn
3rd	**reg-it**	he/she rules	**reg-unt**	they rule
4th	**audi-t**	he/she hears	**audi-unt**	they hear
Note 1: Note the change in the vowel in the 3rd person plural of the 3rd and 4th conjugations.				
	es-t	he/she is	**su-nt**	they are
Note 2: Note irregular forms above for the verb "to be."				

EXERCISE 2.4

Put into the plural and translate; for instance:

puer puellam uocat: **puerī puellās uocant**   The boys call the girls.

1. puella puerum monet.
2. puer fēminam audit.
3. fēmina fīlium laudat.
4. puella fessa est.
5. puer labōrat.
6. colōnus fīlium dūcit.
7. illa fēmina eum iuuat.
8. puella urnam magnam portat.
9. puer in casā sedet.
10. puella puerum uocat.

EXERCISE 2.5

Pick out from the English translations below the ones that fit each of the following Latin words. What conjugation does each one of them belong to?

1. festīnant
2. audit
3. manent
4. audiunt
5. adsunt (This verb is a special case. Why?)
6. parant

7. uocat
8. ascendunt
9. currunt
10. sedet
11. accēdit
12. laudant

they are preparing, he is sitting, they run, they hear, he is approaching, he hears, they climb, they are present, they praise, they stay, they are hurrying, she is calling

EXERCISE 2.6

Translate into Latin
1. The anxious girls are now looking at the boy.
2. Horatia goes into the house and calls Scintilla.
3. (The) angry Flaccus warns (his) daughter.
4. The boy and the girl are running to the house.
5. Scintilla and (her) daughter are at last preparing dinner.

WOMEN

Ancient Rome was very much a man's world, and the most important function of women was to produce children and bring up a new generation of Romans. The main emphasis was on the boys, but girls could go to school at least in its early stages (Plautus, *The Persian* 171–5; Livy 3.44.4–7; Martial, *Epigrams* 9.68, *CIL* 10.3969, *CIL* 5.5262; M. Joyal, I. McDougall & J.C. Yardley, *Greece and Roman Education: A Sourcebook* (Routledge, 2009) pp.152–3, 176–7, 185). After that, they might be taught at home by their mother or a gifted slave. If there was a private tutor in a household, it is likely that daughters could have joined the sons in their studies in grammar, literature and possibly Greek as well as music and philosophy.

Marriages were arranged by the parents of the bride and bridegroom and sometimes took place at an early age. Tullia, the daughter of the famous lawyer and politician Cicero, was betrothed at nine and when she died at the age of 30, she had been married three times. Cicero's friend Atticus started looking for a husband for his daughter Attica by the time she was six (Cicero, *ad Atticum* 13.21a.4); and she married a man old enough to be her father at the age of about 14. Though the average female was married by the age of 20, within the social elite the expected age for marriage was 15.

The ideal wife, we discover from epitaphs, was beautiful, chaste, devoted to her husband, a good mother, pious, modest, stay-at-home, accomplished at wool-working and economical. But if her life sounds dull and restricted, she was not necessarily downgraded as a human being or without influence. For one thing, she managed the house. And couples expected to live in harmony with each other, and many did. An inscription on one gravestone reads:

> To Urbana, the sweetest, chastest and rarest of wives, who certainly has
> never been surpassed, and deserves to be honoured for living with me
> to her last day in the greatest friendliness and simplicity. Her affection
> was matched by her industry. I added these words so that readers should
> understand how much we loved each other.
>
> (CIL 6.29580)

Another, set up by a freedman in Rome on the tomb of his wife, reads:

> This woman, who died before me, was my only wife; of chaste body, she
> loved me and was mistress of my heart; she lived faithful to her husband
> who was faithful to her, and never failed in her duty at any time of trouble.
>
> (Cl. Etr. 2.959)

If a marriage broke down, divorce was easy, and the fact that the husband had to give back her dowry with the divorced wife put a wealthy woman in a strong position.

Funeral monuments often show family groups in which husband and wife are represented with their children: the nuclear family was the norm, and most women appear to have found fulfillment in caring for their husband and children. Nor was their work all dull. Weaving is a skilful and creative craft, and managing a household a responsible and often challenging job. The talking that women do together during these and other activities has often been dismissed as gossip; but women are also exchanging information, some of it very useful, and giving mutual support and practical help.

Black-figure lekythos (vase) by the Amasis painter, dating from 550–540 BC. Here we see some of the processes of wool-making, including the loom with two women working at it. To the right of it a woman is holding scales in which the raw wool (almost out of the frame) is being weighed. On the left a woman draws a "snake" of wool from a basket. The unrelated scene on the rim shows a goddess or priestess to whom young men and dancing girls are paying homage. (Metropolitan Museum of Art, New York)

And women could by and large go where they wanted. Provided that they were escorted by men (a slave would do), they could go to shops and temples and to the festivals and public entertainments which were such a feature of Roman life. They were present at dinner parties with their husbands. In fact, despite the laws which restricted certain areas of their lives and which were gradually lifted in Horace's time, they did not live all that differently from other women in the Western world up to the women's liberation movement in the twentieth century.

This beautiful scene of hairdressing from a wall-painting by a Campanian painter of the first century BC shows a girl being prepared for initiation into the rites of Bacchus. (Villa of the Mysteries, Pompeii)

Further Reading

Women's Life in Greece and Rome: A Source Book in Translation, by Mary R. Lefkowitz and Maureen B. Fant (Duckworth, 2005). This is an update of the classic source book which appeared in 1982; also *The Roman Household: A Source Book*, by J. F. Gardner and T. Wiedemann (Routledge, 1991). Also valuable are the relevant passages from *Growing Up and Growing Old in Ancient Rome*, by Mary Harlow and Ray Laurence (Routledge, 2002). A good, well-illustrated introduction to the topic is *Roman Women*, by Eve D'Ambra (Cambridge, 2007).

Chapter 3

Nūndinae

CARTOONS

The cartoons introduce us to the 1st and 2nd persons (I, we, you) in the singular and plural.

COMMENTARY

Nūndinae

Markets were held every eighth day and were public holidays. (For further details see p. 23.) In country towns they would be held in the forum, the town center.

l.1 *nūndinae sunt*: *nūndinae* is plural in form but singular in meaning, compare, e.g. *epulae* = a feast, and a number of place names, e.g. *Athēnae* = Athens.

l.6 *tabernae* = stalls; these would be flimsy constuctions erected for the day.

l.8 *mercēs*: wares (accusative feminine plural 3rd declension)

l.9 *quantī?* "for how much," genitive, expressing value; *ūnō dēnāriō*: "for one denarius," ablative expressing price. (The prices demanded by Flaccus and family are unrealistically high; there were 18 *asses* to the *denarius* and a basket of figs would scarcely cost one *as*—Martial says, no doubt with exaggeration, that one could buy a chick-pea dinner <u>and</u> a woman for an *as* each (*Epigrams* 1.103.10), but we wished to avoid 3rd declension forms). For Roman money, see J. Morwood, *A Latin Grammar* (Oxford, 1999), p. 147.

ll.11–12 *illās ficōs*: though *ficus* (fig) has masculine endings, it is usually feminine. Although it refers to the fruit here, it is worth remarking that in Latin all trees are feminine.

ll.14–15 *uēndidimus*: "we have sold"; the sense demands a perfect form. *cēnābimus*: "we shall dine"; the sense demands a future form. This tense will not be learned until Chapters 10 and 15, but note that the person endings are the same as for the present tense.

Fābella

This word means a story or, as here, a play. You are encouraged to read out as much Latin as possible and this will give you a chance to enact some.

l.15 *cēnābimus:* "we shall dine"; the sense demands a future form. This tense will not be learned until Chapter 15; but note that the person endings are the same as for the present tense.

R V **Fish mosaic:** in this mosaic from Pompeii there can be seen a pattern consisting of more than 20 species of fish, crustacea and other marine creatures including an extremely realistic octopus. (National Archaeological Museum, Naples) *See page 13 in* Oxford Latin Course, College Edition: Readings and Vocabulary.

GRAMMAR

Verbs: Present Tense, All Persons

Latin changes the verb endings to show which person (I, you, he/she/it, we, you, they) is performing the action of the verb (Old English did the same, e.g. I come, thou comest, he cometh.)

The person endings are the same for all types of verb:

person	singular		plural	
1st	**-ō**	I	**-mus**	we
2nd	**-s**	you	**-tis**	you
3rd	**-t**	he/she	**-nt**	they

These endings are attached to the verb stem.

1st conjugation (stem ends -a)			
singular		plural	
par-ō	I prepare	**parā-mus**	we prepare
parā-s	you prepare	**parā-tis**	you prepare
para-t	he/she prepares	**para-nt**	they prepare
2nd conjugation (stem ends -e)			
mone-ō	I warn	**monē-mus**	we warn
monē-s	you warn	**monē-tis**	you warn
mone-t	he/she warns	**mone-nt**	they warn
3rd conjugation (stem ends in consonant)			
reg-ō	I rule	**reg-imus**	we rule
reg-is	you rule	**reg-itis**	you rule
reg-it	he/she rules	**reg-unt**	they rule

4th conjugation (stem ends -i)			
audi-ō	I hear	**audī-mus**	we hear
audī-s	you hear	**audī-tis**	you hear
audi-t	he/she hears	**audi-unt**	they hear

Note 1. In the 3rd conjugation (where the stem ends in a consonant) vowels **i/u** are inserted before the person ending.

2. In the 3rd and 4th conjugations the 3rd person plural ends **-unt** (not **-int**).

sum (I am)

Present tense of sum (stems su- /e- /es-)					
sum	I am	**su-mus**	we are	*infinitive*	**esse**
e-s	you are	**es-tis**	you are		
es-t	he is	**su-nt**	they are		

Since the verb endings indicate the person, there is no need to give a separate subject pronoun; thus, **par-ō** = I prepare, **monē-mus** = we warn, **audī-tis** = you hear.

Note that **sum** does not take an object. We call the word that follows it (in English) a complement: "I am bad" = **malus sum**. The complement is in the same case and number as the subject of **sum**.

EXERCISE 3.1

Translate

1. Flaccum iuuāmus.
2. ad casam festīnō.
3. Quīntum uidet.
4. in uiā manētis.
5. in casā sedent puerī.
6. ad agrum currō.
7. puellās monēmus.
8. cūr puellam ad agrum mittis?
9. laetī sumus.
10. miserī estis.

EXERCISE 3.2

Pick out from the English translations below the ones that fit each of the following Latin verb forms

1. spectāmus
2. trādit
3. regimus
4. clāmātis
5. currimus
6. maneō
7. respondent
8. dīcimus
9. estis
10. festīnō
11. audīs
12. pōnis

we run, he hands over, I am hastening, you are, we are watching, I am staying, you hear, we rule, they reply, you place, we say, you are shouting

EXERCISE 3.3

In each of the following give the correct Latin for the words in parentheses, then translate the whole sentence

1. quid (are you doing), puellae? cēnam (we are preparing).
2. cūr nōn (are you hurrying), Quīnte? nōn sērō (I am coming).
3. cūr in uiā (are you sitting), amīcī? in uiā (we are sitting), quod fessī (we are).
4. Argus malus (is); eum (I call) sed ille nōn (come back).
5. cūr nōn (are you working)? nōn labōrō quod īrāta (I am).
6. quid colōnī (are saying)? nōn (they are) laetī.

EXERCISE 3.4

In the following sentences make the complement agree with the subject and translate

1. cūr (miser) estis, puerī? puellae (laetus) sunt.
2. Scintilla (īrātus) est; nam puerī nōn (parātus) sunt.
3. (fessus) sumus, quod diū labōrāmus.
4. cūr (ānxius) es, Scintilla?
5. (ānxius) sum quod Horātia (miser) est.

GRAMMAR

Cases

The Ablative Case

This case expresses the meanings "by," "with," "from," "at," "on."

At present it is used only after certain prepositions, e.g. **in agr-ō** = in the field, **in cas-ā** = in the house, **ex agrīs** = from the fields.

	abl. singular	abl. plural
1st declension (**puella**)	puell-ā	puell-īs
2nd declension (**colōnus**)	colōn-ō	colōn-īs
(**ager**)	agr-ō	agr-īs

Note that 1st declension nouns end in a short **-a** in the nominative but a long **-ā** in the ablative.

EXERCISE 3.5

Give the ablative of the following noun/adjective phrases

1. puer fessus
2. magna casa
3. multae fēminae
4. puella laeta
5. colōnī miserī

EXERCISE 3.6

Fill in the blanks and translate

1. Flaccus et fīlius in agr– labōrant.
2. puellae in ui– lūdunt; Scintilla eās in cas– uocat.
3. Flaccus puerōs ad agr– dūcit.
4. multae puellae cum fēmin– ad fontem ambulant.
5. puer cum amīc– ad lūd– festīnat.

GRAMMAR

Prepositions

Prepositions govern nouns, forming a prepositional phrase which expands the action of the verb:

in casam festīnat She hurries into the house.
in agrō labōrat He is working in the field.

Vocabulary lists tell you which case (accusative or ablative) each preposition takes, e.g. **per** (+ acc.) = through, **cum** (+ abl.) = with.

Note that prepositions expressing motion towards are followed by the accusative, e.g. **in agrum** = into the field, **ad casam** = to the house.

Prepositions expressing place where and motion from are followed by the ablative, e.g. **in agrō** = in the field, **ex agrō** = from the field.

EXERCISE 3.7

Translate into Latin
1. The farmer calls the boys into the field.
2. They stay in the field and work for a long time.
3. The boy is tired and soon returns from the field.
4. The women are walking to the house.
5. The girls are hurrying with their friends.
6. You (*sing.*) are sitting in the house; I am working in the forum.
7. We are looking at the girls but they do not answer.

NŪNDINAE AND FARMING

Every eighth day there were market days. These were called *nūndinae* ("ninth-day affairs") because of the Romans' inclusive way of counting (1+7+1). After seven days of hard work, people smartened themselves up and hurried to the market with their families. Nūndinae were regular school holidays, eagerly looked forward to by the children. The farmers would bring their produce to town to sell it to the townspeople and go home with money and tools for their farms, while their wives might buy pots and pans, etc. Most farmers would have lived in outlying villages and farms. Virgil describes such a farmer, a peasant called Simylus who grew cabbages, beet, sorrel, mallow and radishes for sale: "Every market day he carried on his shoulder bundles of produce for sale to the city; and returned home from there, his neck relieved of its burden, but his pocket heavy with money." (*Moretum* 78–81) Market day was also a good chance to visit a lawyer and do some business. And the townsmen might entertain some of their friends from the country at a celebratory lunch.

This scene of two satyrs—note their tails—treading grapes probably dates from the second century AD. (Archaeological Museum, Venice)

At the time when our story is set, Italy contained many vast country estates. On these, large-scale agricultural enterprises such as cattle ranching and the cultivation of vines and olives would be carried out. A fabulously wealthy freedman called Caecilius had 4,116 slaves on his estate. Many slaves who worked on such estates had a grim life. When not engaged in backbreaking work in chain gangs, they were housed in dreadful barracks. The vital aim was to bring in as much money as possible for the usually absentee owners. Varro talks about three types of farm equipment: "the kind that speaks (i.e. slaves), the kind that cannot speak (i.e. cattle) and the voiceless (i.e. agricultural tools)." (*De re rustica* 1.17.1.5–7) These huge estates, which used slaves as machines, had originally caused massive unemployment among the peasant farmers. But by Horace's day slave labor had become more expensive and the *colōnus* had made a comeback. Alongside the vast estates there were smallholdings of just a few acres, and it was one of these that we have represented Horace's father as working.

On the farm: in this scene from a mosaic of farming actvities, the man to the left is ploughing while the man to the right is sowing. (Cherchell, Algeria)

Further Reading
For more detailed discussion of these topics, see "Production and consumption" by Andrew Wallace-Hadrill in *The World of Rome*, ed. Peter Jones and Keith Sidwell (Cambridge, 1997), pp. 185–93.

Grammar: infinitives and imperatives; vocative; *possum, eō*; compound verbs (*adeō, ineō, abeō, exeō, redeō*); adverbs; questions

Lūdus Flāuī: Flāuī is the genitive case—"of Flavius." The genitive of names ending in *-ius* was regularly *-ī* (not *-iī*) until the end of the first century BC. (The same applies to words such as *filius* and *ingenium,* but since the *-iī* ending is allowable, we have thought it more helpful to keep it.)

CARTOONS

These demonstrate the imperative (giving commands) and illustrate uses of the infinitive.

COMMENTARY

(a) Quīntus et Gāius ad lūdum sērō adueniunt

[R][V] **magister clāmat: "cūr sērō uenīs? malus puer es!":** in this marble relief from Gaul dating from about 200 AD two boys sit on either side of the teacher with papyrus scrolls partly unrolled; a third arrives late, carrying his satchel. (Rheinisches Landesmuseum, Trier) *See page 16 in* Oxford Latin Course, College Edition: Readings and Vocabulary.

(b) Flāuius litterās docet

Horace says (*Satires* 1.6.72–5): "My father refused to send me to the school of Flavius, where the big boys, sons of big centurions, went with their satchels and tablets slung over their left shoulders, taking their eight asses on the Ides of each month." We take the liberty of making Flaccus send Quintus to Flavius' school for his elementary education but he removes him later to take him to the best school in Rome (see Chapter 10). Flavius' school was cheap; the children took the fee themselves to Flavius and had no tutor to carry their satchels and tablets. Venusia, Horace's home town, had recently received a colony (i.e. a settlement of army veterans), amongst them centurions, who would have been the "big men" of a country town.

We make Flavius' school coeducational; there is evidence that girls sometimes attended elementary schools (see p. 14). The Roman educational system (as in the USA) had three stages: primary, in which the "litterātor" taught reading, writing and arithmetic; secondary or "grammar," in which the "grammaticus" taught mainly Greek and Roman literature; and further, in which students learned rhetoric, the art of public speaking, the essential preparation for public life. (For a more detailed account of Roman education, see pp. 33–4 below.) Some continued to university, where the principal subject was philosophy. There is no evidence that Horace studied rhetoric but he did proceed to Athens to complete his education at the Academy (see Chapter 17).

R V **Writing implements:** back row: four leaves of a wooden writing tablet; inkpots in faience, pottery and bronze; front row: a letter in Greek on papyrus; (from the front) a reed pen, a bronze pen, an ivory stylus and a bronze stylus. *See page 17 in* Oxford Latin Course, College Edition: Readings and Vocabulary.

Word-building

Give English words derived from the following Latin words in our story: **magister, exit, īrātus, scrībunt, spectat, benignē**. What part of speech are the English words you choose?

GRAMMAR

The Infinitive

1st conjugation	parō	**parā-re**	to prepare
2nd conjugation	moneo	**monē-re**	to warn
3rd conjugation	regō	**rege-re**	to rule
4th conjugation	audiō	**audī-re**	to hear

Note that besides the four regular conjugations listed above a few common verbs belong to a "mixed" conjugation which in some forms behave like 3rd conjugation verbs and in other forms like fourth, e.g. **capiō**, infinitive **cap-ere**, **cupiō**, infinitive **cup-ere**. (For their full conjugation, see the Reference Grammar section on pages 306–13.)

The infinitive is used, as in English, with verbs such as:

cupiō	I desire to, I want to
lūdere cupimus	we want to play
dēbeō	I ought to, I must:
labōrāre dēbētis	you ought to work.
iubeō	I order x to
magister puerōs iubet labōrāre	the master orders the boys to work.

EXERCISE 4.1

Translate

1. in uiā lūdere cupimus.
2. ad lūdum festīnāre dēbētis.
3. magister puerōs iubet celeriter intrāre.
4. puerī labōrāre nōn cupiunt.
5. magister cupit puerōs dīmittere.
6. nōlīte in uiā manēre, puerī.

GRAMMAR

The Imperative

The imperative is the form of the verb used to give orders, e.g.

ad agrum festīnā	hurry to the field!
in casā manē	stay in the house!
magistrum audī	listen to the master!

Orders may be given to one or more persons and so Latin has both a singular and a plural form:

infinitive	1 **parāre**	2 **monēre**	3 **regere**	4 **audīre**
imperative sing.	**parā** prepare!	**monē** warn!	**rege** rule!	**audī** hear!
imperative pl.	**parāte**	**monēte**	**regite**	**audīte**

mixed conjugation	
infinitive	**capere**
imperative sing.	**cape** take!
imperative pl.	**capite**

Prohibitions, i.e. negative commands (don't) are expressed by **nōlī** (sing.), **nōlīte** (plural) + infinitive, e.g.

nōlī manēre, Horātia   Don't stay, Horatia!
nōlīte clamāre, puerī   Don't shout, boys!

Note the four irregular imperatives below:

	dīcō (I say)	**dūcō** (I lead)	**ferō** (I bring)	**faciō** (I do, make)
singular	dīc	dūc	fer	fac
plural	dīcite	dūcite	ferte	facite

EXERCISE 4.2

Translate
1. lūdum intrāte, puellae, et sedēte.
2. festīnā, Quīnte, et litterās disce.
3. Flāuium audīte, puerī. nōlī clamāre, magister.
4. nōlīte in uiā manēre, Gāī et Quīnte, sed in lūdum īte.
5. dūc Argum in agrum, Quīnte.
6. fer cēnam ad Flaccum, Horātia.

GRAMMAR

Irregular Verbs

1 eō = I go: stem i-

present
eō
īs
it
īmus
ītis
eunt

infinitive **ī-re**
imperatives **ī, īte**

All forms of the verb start **i-** except for **eō** and **eunt** (and also the present participle: nom. **iēns**, gen. **euntis**).

2 possum (pot + sum) = I can, am able

present

possum (for **pot-sum**)   *infinitive* **posse**

potes   *no imperatives*

potest

possumus (for **pot-sumus**)

potestis

possunt (for **pot-sunt**)

You can see that if the present tense of **sum** starts with a vowel, a **t** is inserted before it.

The imperatives of **sum** are **es** or **estō** (sing.) and **este** (plural).

3 Compound Verbs

Many verbs may be compounded with a preposition which is placed before the simple verb, e.g. **eō** = I go, **ineō** = I go into, **adeō** = I go towards, **exeō** = I go out, **abeō** = I go away.

Note also the prefix **re-/red-** = back, so **redeō** = I go back, return.

EXERCISE 4.3

Translate

1. nōn possumus in uiam exīre.
2. exī ē casā, Horātia. ad lūdum adīre dēbēs.
3. puerī ē lūdō exeunt et ad casās redeunt.
4. Flaccus ad casam redit. nōn diūtius (*any longer*) in agrō labōrāre potest.
5. litterās bene scrībere potes, Horātia? Decimus id (*this*) facere nōn potest.
6. nōlīte in agrō manēre, colōnī. ad casās redīre potestis.

GRAMMAR

Nouns

The Vocative Case

This case is used only in calling or addressing someone; it has the same form as the nominative in all nouns except for the singular of 2nd declension nouns ending **-us**: these end **-e** in the vocative, so:

quid facis, Quīnt-e? (but **quid facis, Horātia?**)

Nouns ending **-ius** in the nominative, e.g. **fīlius** (son), have vocative **-ī**, not **-ie**, e.g. **quid facis, fīlī?** Compare the vocative of **Gāius** in our story: **Gāī**.

Adverbs

Adverbs are usually attached to verbs and tell you how the action of the verb is performed, e.g.

We are walking <u>slowly</u>   **lentē ambulāmus**

Adverbs never change their form.

Many adverbs are formed from adjectives; from **bonus** type adjectives, they are formed by changing **-us** to **-ē**, e.g. **lent-us** slow   **lent-ē** slowly

mal-us bad   **mal-e** badly

(N.B.: **bon-us** good but **ben-e** well).

3rd declension adjectives usually form adverbs by adding **-ter** to the stem:

fortis brave   **fortiter** bravely

celer quick   **celeriter** quickly

There are many adverbs which are not formed from adjectives, such as:

diū for a long time	**numquam** never	**semper** always
mox soon	**subitō** suddenly	**hūc** hither, (to) here
uix scarcely	**iam** now, already	**cūr?** why?
umquam ever	**tandem** at last	**quandō?** when?

EXERCISE 4.4

In the following sentences fill in the blank with an appropriate adverb from the box above and translate

1. — pugnāte, amīcī, urbemque capite.
2. uenī —, Quīnte; pater tē — exspectat.
3. labōrāte —, puerī; magister nōs spectat.
4. Decimus litterās — scrībit; asinus est.
5. cūr — ambulās, Quīnte? — nōn festīnās?

EXERCISE 4.5

Translate

1. amīcī ad lūdum lentē ambulant. sērō adueniunt.
2. ubi lūdum ineunt, magister īrātus est.
3. "cūr sērō aduenītis?" inquit; "malī puerī estis."

4. puerī sedent et magistrum audiunt; ille litterās docet.
5. tandem puerōs dīmittere cupit; "puerī," inquit "domum currite."
6. puellae cum Scintillā ad fontem prōcēdunt.
7. Horātia magnam urnam portāre potest sed lentē ambulat.
8. Scintilla Horātiam festīnāre iubet. "cūr lentē ambulās?" inquit, "festīnā!"
9. ubi ad fontem adueniunt, aquam dūcunt.
10. Horātia fessa est; "iam domum redīre possumus?" inquit.

GRAMMAR

Questions

You have already met many sentences in Latin which are questions; their form is not unlike that of English questions.

They are usually introduced by an interrogative (question-asking) word, such as

cūr? why?, **quōmodo?** how?, **ubi?** where (adverbs);
quis? who?, **quid?** what? (pronouns); **quantus?** how big? (adjective).

Sometimes the interrogative particles **-ne** (attached to the first word of the sentence) or **nōnne** (used in questions expecting the answer "yes") are used, e.g.

uenīsne ad lūdum? Are you coming to school?
nōnne ad lūdum uenīs? Aren't you coming to school? *or* You are coming to school, aren't you?

num introduces a question expecting the answer "no," e.g.
num ad lūdum īs? You aren't going to school, are you? Surely you're not going to school?

EXERCISE 4.6

Translate
1. cūr nōn festīnās, Quīnte?
2. quis Scintillam iuuat?
3. quid facis, fīlī?
4. quantus est ager?
5. domumne mē dūcis?

6. nōnne domum mē dūcis?
7. num ē casā exit Argus?
8. qūomodo hoc (*this*) facere potest Quīntus?

EXERCISE 4.7

The following Latin words occur in connection with Roman education. What do you think each word means?

1. ēdūcāre
2. schola
3. scientia
4. litterae (*also spelled* literae)
5. historia
6. grammatica

EXERCISE 4.8

Translate into Latin

1. Can you hear the master, Quintus?
2. Listen to the master, Quintus and Gaius.
3. You can write letters well, Horatia, but I cannot.
4. "Go home, children," says Flaccus. "I cannot teach you (**uōs**) any more (**diūtius**)."
5. Flaccus is going to the field slowly with Quintus.
6. He does not want to work but he cannot stay in (his) house.
7. Neither he nor Quintus is ever happy.
8. "Hurry up, Quintus!" he says. "You must walk with me."
9. "Don't be angry," says Quintus. "I can run if (**sī**) you want."

EDUCATION

A significant number of Roman citizens were literate, and their children received a primary education at the local schools from the ages of 6 or 7 to 11 or 12. Here they were taught reading, writing and elementary arithmetic. As we have said (see p. 26), the evidence suggests that girls as well as boys attended these schools, though they did not, as far as we know, go on to the secondary or "grammar" schools.

In primary education, i.e. the first three or four years, the three "R"s were hammered into boys and girls by a *litterātor* with a syllabus of reading and writing in both Latin and Greek. The pupils would write their lessons on tablets (*tabulae*) using a stylus. They would also learn elementary arithmetic using an abacus. Horace poked fun at math lessons in his poetry:

> Roman boys learn how to divide a penny by a hundred with long calculations. "Tell us, son of Albinus, what do you end up with if a twelfth is taken away from five twelfths? Can you say?" "A third." "Well done! You'll end up a millionaire. What does it come to if you add a twelfth?" "A half." Is it any surprise that when we drag our children through these off-putting financial calculations they can't find the inspiration for poetry?
>
> (*Ars Poetica* 325–31)

For the most part, the lessons were boring and unpleasant. Pupils sat on uncomfortable benches or chairs, often in noisy surroundings. They endlessly recited the alphabet both forwards and backwards, as well as chanting their multiplication tables again and again. Teaching started very early, soon after dawn, and the poet Martial complained violently—and doubtless with satirical exaggeration—at being woken up by the noise:

> Why can't you stay out of our lives, you cursed schoolmaster, a man hateful to boys and girls alike? The crested cocks have not yet broken the silence of the night. Already you are making a noise with your cruel voice and your thwacks.
>
> (*Epigrams* 9.68.1–4)

And thwackings were very much part of the scene (Cicero, *Tusculan Disputations* 3.64). Adults' nostalgic recollections of childhood games can be contrasted with the vivid memory of the beatings which teachers inflicted (St. Augustine, *Confessions* 1.9 & 14). It is significant that Horace praised his father for teaching him by examples of good and bad behavior, not by force (*Satires* 1.4.105–29).

After a break for lunch, lessons probably started up again. There would be a holiday every eighth day, short breaks in the winter and spring, and a very long holiday in the summer.

A marble relief from the second century AD. From left to right: suckling the baby; the father holds his child, accepting him into the family; the boy at play rides a toy chariot drawn by a goat; he receives instruction from his father. The (incomplete) inscription lists the names of the monument's dedicator and dedicatees. (Louvre Museum, Paris)

Boys would move on to another school around the age of 11 or 12 for their secondary education. Here they would learn grammar and literature from a *grammaticus*. Greek and Greek literature were an important part of the syllabus. All educated Romans aimed at being bilingual. Though they had conquered Greece, they still recognized the greatness of Greek literature. As Horace himself wrote, "Conquered Greece conquered its wild conqueror and brought the arts to rustic Italy." (*Epistles* 2.1.156)

At the secondary stage, arithmetic, geometry, music and astronomy were studied as minor subjects. The curriculum was not wide. There were medical schools in Greece, but in Italy there was no scientific education at all. When they were about 16, upper-class Roman boys went on for their tertiary education to a teacher of rhetoric (a *rhētor*) who would teach them through public lectures. From him they received a thorough training in speaking and arguing, and this was a good preparation for a career in politics.

Further Reading

An up-to-date collection of essays on this subject can be found in *Education in Greek and Roman Antiquity*, ed. Yun Lee Too (Brill, 2001). Especially valuable is Anthony Corbeill's contribution, "Education in the Roman Republic: Creating Traditions," pp. 261–88 (with excellent bibliography). Also recommended is W. A. Johnson and H. N. Parker, *Ancient Literacies: The Culture of Teaching in Greece and Rome* (Oxford, 2009).

Chapter 5

Flāuius fābulam nārrat

> **Grammar:** 3rd declension, nouns and adjs.; genitives of 1st three declensions; some uses of genitive and ablative

PATTERN SENTENCES

These introduce the genitive and 3rd declension endings.

COMMENTARY

a) Agamemnōn Graecōs in urbem Trōiam dūcit

Flavius tells the story of the *Iliad* of Homer in this and the following chapter. The *Iliad* is the oldest, and some consider the greatest, poem of European literature. Its story would have been known to all children in Italy and Greece and a knowledge of it is essential to an understanding of much Roman poetry.

[R][V] **The Lion Gate at Mycenae:** these gateposts are 10.5 feet high; on top of these is a massive lintel, 15 feet long, 6.5 feet thick and 3.25 feet high in the center. A huge triangular slab of grey limestone (12 feet wide at the base, 10 feet high and 2 feet thick) shows a pillar supported by two lionesses which rest their feet on the altars that are the base of the column. Their heads are missing. *See page 19 in* Oxford Latin Course, College Edition: Readings and Vocabulary.

title: *in urbem Trōiam*: against Troy (*in* can have a hostile sense.)
l.1 *Mycēnārum*: of Mycenae (genitive plural in form): according to tradition Mycenae was the richest and most powerful of the kingdoms of late Bronze Age Greece. This tradition is supported by archaeology, which has revealed an immensely strong and powerful fortress complex.

l.2 *Menelāus* was king of Sparta and married to Helen, who was abducted by the Trojan prince Paris; this was the cause of the war.

l.3 *Achillēs...fortissimus*: *fortis* = brave, *fortissimus* (superlative form) bravest. So also *sapientissimus* = wisest.

Ulixēs is the Latin name for Odysseus. Since the Latin capital u is V, the name should be given as Vlixes, but we feel that the spelling we give will prove more user-friendly at this stage.

l.9 *rixam*: Agamemnon had taken from Achilles a slave girl who had been given to Achilles by the army as a prize. He had thus insulted the honor of Achilles, who was implacable.

l.11 *quī*: relative pronoun = who. The relative is used freely in the nominative in early chapters and is learned fully in Chapter 8.

[R][V] **Agamemnon and Achilles:** this fine wall painting from Pompeii shows Achilles quarrelling with Agamemnon over the captive girl Briseis (on the right). Because of the intervention of Athena, goddess of wisdom, Achilles does not go through with his intention of killing Agamemnon. (National Museum of Archaeology, Naples) *See page 20 in* Oxford Latin Course, College Edition: Readings and Vocabulary.

l.18 *inuītus*: unwilling(ly): Latin uses an adjective where English would use an adverb.

b) Mors Hectoris

l.4 *stantem*: standing: present participle of *stō, stāre*. The present participle is a verbal adjective (third declension); we use it freely in Part 1, always glossed.

l.7 *fīlī*: vocative of *filius*.

l.9 *nōn audit*: does not listen to.

nōn uult: is unwilling, refuses (*uolō* is irregular—*uolō, uīs, uult,* etc., see Chapter 8).

l.15 *sē uertit*: "turns himself" = turns (*sē* is the reflexive pronoun, see Chapter 8).

l.16 *ille*: "that man," "he": *ille* indicates a change of subject.

[R][V] **Achilles and Hector:** on the neck of this red-figure vase of about 490–480 BC by the Berlin Painter, Achilles (on the left) and Hector (on the right) carry the arms of Greek hoplites of the fifth century BC, not of Homeric warriors; and neither hoplites nor Homeric warriors would have fought naked. As Achilles moves in for the kill, the already-wounded Hector appears to have given up the struggle and exposes his body to death. The contrasting angling of the spears and positioning of the shields are deeply poignant. (British Museum) *See page 22 in* Oxford Latin Course, College Edition: Readings and Vocabulary.

l.21 *facinus*: 3rd declension accusative singular (there are several 3rd declension neuter nouns ending *-us* in the nominative singular that must be distinguished from 2nd declension nouns, e.g. *colōnus*, gen. *colōnī*; *facinus*, gen. *facinoris*).

R̲V̲ **Achilles dragging Hector's body:** this mosaic dates from the third century AD. (Vatican Museums) *See page 23 in* Oxford Latin Course, College Edition: Readings and Vocabulary.

R̲V̲ **The ransom of Hector:** this Attic red-figure cup of about 490–480 BC gives a rather different account of the ransom of Hector from that of Homer. To the left, Priam, with attendants carrying Hector's ransom (one of them is just visible), approaches an arrogant Achilles who reclines on a couch above Hector's body. The danger latent in Achilles is shown by the hanging armor and the dagger he holds. In Homer's version, Achilles takes great care that Priam and he should not be together with Hector's corpse. He presumably feels that this would arouse emotions dangerously. (Kunsthistorisches Museum, Vienna) *See page 23 in* Oxford Latin Course, College Edition: Readings and Vocabulary.

Word-building

You can build up your Latin vocabulary by seeing how words you have not met are formed from those you have learned, e.g.

cēn-a = dinner   **cēnō** = I dine

What do the following pairs of words mean?

NOUNS	VERBS
pugn-a	pugn-ō
uōx, uōc-is	uoc-ō
rēx, rēg-is	reg-ō
laus, laud-is	laud-ō
dux, duc-is	dūc-ō
labor, labōr-is	labōr-ō

GRAMMAR

The Genitive Case (= of)

The endings for the genitive case are:

1st declension singular **-ae**	plural **-ārum**
2nd declension singular **-ī**	plural **-ōrum**

e.g.

puell-ae māter	the mother of the girl, the girl's mother
puer-ī pater	the father of the boy, the boy's father
ager colōnī	the farmer's field
agrī colōnōrum	the fields of the farmers, the farmers' fields

Note that in Latin, as in English, the genitive can come before or after the noun to which it is attached.

EXERCISE 5.1

Translate the following phrases

Horātiae māter, Quīntī pater, Graecōrum prīncipēs, mūrī urbis, nāuēs rēgum, prōrae (prows) nāuium, multī Trōiānōrum, fortissimī Graecōrum

(All these are possessive genitives except for the last two: they are partitive genitives. All can be translated by "of.")

GRAMMAR

The 3rd Declension

1 Nouns

The nominative of 3rd declension nouns has various forms, e.g. **rēx, urbs, nāuis**.
    The endings of the other cases are:

	singular	plural
nom.	(varies)	**-ēs**
gen.	**-is**	**-um/ium**
dat.	(the dative is to be learned in Chapter 6)	
acc.	**-em**	**-ēs**
abl.	**-e/-ī**	**-ibus**

These endings are added to the noun stem, which is usually a consonant but in some nouns is the vowel **i**.
    Thus: **rēx** (m.) (king) stem **rēg-**: **nāuis** (f.) (ship) stem **nāui-**

	singular	plural	singular	plural
nom.	rēx	rēg-ēs	nāuis	nāu-ēs
gen.	rēg-is	rēg-um	nāu-is	nāu-ium
acc.	rēg-em	rēg-ēs	nāu-em	nāu-ēs/īs
abl.	rēg-e	rēg-ibus	nāu-e/ī	nāu-ibus

	nōmen (n.) (name) nōmin-		mare (n.) (sea) mari-	
	singular	plural	singular	plural
nom.	nōmen	nōmin-a	mare	mari-a
gen.	nōmin-is	nōmin-um	mari-s	mari-um
acc.	nōmen	nōmin-a	mare	mari-a
abl.	nōmin-e	nōmin-ibus	marī	mari-bus

Note 1. Most 3rd declension nouns with stems ending **-i** regularly drop the **-i** except in the genitive plural but have less common alternative forms in **-i**, e.g. abl. sing. **nāuī**, acc. plural **nāuīs**.

Note 2. The vocative case is the same as the nominative in all 3rd declension nouns.

Note 3. The nominative and accusative plural have the same endings.

Note 4. Genitive plural: the general rule is that nouns with stems ending in **-i** have genitive plural **-ium**, while those with stems ending in consonants have genitive plural **-um**. Apart from nouns ending in two consonants (e.g. **mōns** (mountain), **urbs** (city) and **pōns** (bridge)), if a 3rd declension noun gets longer in the genitive singular it does not get any longer in the genitive plural (which therefore ends in **-um**); and if it does not get any longer in the genitive singular, its genitive plural ends in **-ium**: unfortunately there are exceptions to the latter rule, **canis** (dog), **iuuenis** (young man), **senex** (old man), **pater** (father), **māter** (mother), **frāter** (brother), all of which have genitive plurals in **-um**.

Note 5. The 3rd declension contains masculine, feminine and neuter nouns; the gender of each noun must be learned.

2 Adjectives

Most 3rd declension adjectives have stems in **-i** and keep the **-i** in ablative singular and genitive plural; they have the same endings for masculine and feminine, e.g.

omnis (all) stem **omni-**

	singular		plural	
	m. & f.	**neuter**	**m. & f.**	**neuter**
nom.	omnis	omne	omnēs	omnia
gen.	omnis	omnis	omnium	omnium
acc.	omnem	omne	omnēs	omnia
abl.	omnī	omnī	omnibus	omnibus

A few adjectives have stems in consonants, e.g. **pauper** (= poor), gen. **pauper-is**. These have ablative singular **-e (pauper-e)** and genitive plural **-um (pauper-um)**; see Reference Grammar p. 298.

N.B.: The ending of the adjective is not always the same as that of the noun with which it agrees in case, gender and number, e.g.

bon-us rēx, bon-um rēg-em, bonō rēg-e
omn-ēs fēmin-ae, omn-ēs feminās, omn-ibus fēmin-īs.

These nouns and adjectives are from different declensions.

EXERCISE 5.2

Put the words in parentheses (at present all in the nominative) into the genitive case and translate

1. puella fābulam (māter) laeta audit.
2. magister tabulās (puerī) spectat.
3. Quīntus ad (pater) agrum celeriter currit.
4. colōnus clāmōrēs (fēminae) audīre nōn potest.
5. multī (rēgēs) in urbem fugere cupiunt.
6. paucī (Trōiānī) fortiter pugnant.
7. Hector ter (*three times*) fugit circum mūrōs (urbs).
8. omnēs Trōiānī (Hector) mortem lūgent (*mourn*).

EXERCISE 5.3

Complete the following sentences by filling in the blanks with the correct case ending and translate

1. Quīntus ad casam patr– aduenit.
2. pater fili– fort– laudat.
3. Horātia cum mātr– domum redit.
4. māter filiam fess– iuuat.
5. Trōiānī urb– fortiter dēfendunt.
6. Graecī nāu– dēfendere nōn possunt.
7. Patroclus cum omn– comit– in pugnam currit.
8. omn– Trōiānī in urb– fugiunt
9. Hector in urb– nōn fugit sed Patrocl– oppugnat.
10. Achillēs comit– mort– uindicāre (*to avenge*) cupit.
11. Hector extrā (+ acc. = *outside*) mūr– manet in perīcul– mort– .
12. Priamus in mur– urb– cum uxōr– stat, ualdē ānxius.

EXERCISE 5.4

Translate

1. comitēs Hectoris intrā mūros urbis currunt.
2. multī prīncipum fortiter pugnant.
3. Hector extrā mūrōs urbis manet sōlus.
4. Agamemnonis nāuem uidēre nōn possum.
5. ex omnibus Graeciae partibus prīncipēs conueniunt.
6. Graecōrum pars magna domum redīre cupit.
7. Hectoris arma capere cupit Achillēs.
8. Hecuba in mūrīs Trōiae stat (*is standing*) sed mortem filiī spectāre nōn potest.
9. cum rēge Graecōrum domum nāuigō.
10. fābulam Flāuī laetī audiunt puerī.

EXERCISE 5.5

Translate into Latin

1. Tell me (**dīc mihi**) all the names of the kings.
2. The angry Greeks attack the walls of the city.
3. Hector wants to burn the ships of the Greeks. He attacks (their) chiefs with (his) brave companions.
4. Don't return home, Greeks. Fight with (**cum**) the chief of the Trojans.
5. Good chiefs do not praise bad kings.
6. I want to hear (my) master's story.

THE *ILIAD*

The narrative of this chapter summarizes the whole of Homer's great poem. A recommended translation of the *Iliad* is that by Anthony Verity (Oxford World's Classics, 2011). It has an excellent introduction by Barbara Graziosi.

This bust of the reputedly blind Homer was often reproduced. The copy here is from the Louvre Museum, Paris.

Chapter 6

Graecī Trōiam capiunt

Grammar: dative case; uses of dative; complete declensions 1, 2, 3; *ego, tū, nōs, uōs; uolō, nōlō*

PATTERN SENTENCES

Note *dīc*, the irregular singular imperative of *dīcō*.

COMMENTARY

(a) Graecī Trōiam capiunt

The *Iliad* ends with the death of Hector and the return of his body to Priam; it does not include the fall of Troy. The narrative of this chapter is based on Virgil, *Aeneid* 2.

ll.17–18 *equō nē crēdite...* = *Aeneid* 2.48–9 (...*equō nē crēdite, Teucrī. /quidquid id est, timeō Danaōs et dōna ferentēs*): *nē crēdite* = *nōlīte crēdere*. *Teucrī* = Trojans; *Danaōs* = Greeks (Virgil regularly uses these names). *et* = even.

l.18 *ferentēs*: "bringing, when they bring."

l.19 *stetit*: it stood, stuck (perfect of *stō* [I stand]). Laocoon and his sons were later devoured by two sea serpents; the Trojans took this to be divine punishment for his impiety in striking the sacred horse.

l.21 *epulās*: a feast; *epulae* is plural in form but singular in meaning.

l.24 *nāuēs tacitae...petunt*: compare *Aeneid* 2.254–6: *Argīua phalanx* (the Greek host)...ī bat..tacitae per amīca silentia lūnae / lītora nōta petēns*. Note that *tacitae* agrees with *lūnae*; in verse, adjectives are often separated from the nouns they agree with. Watch the word endings.

l.28 *eīs resistunt*: "resist them"; *resistō* I stand up to, resist is another verb which takes the dative.

RV **The death of Priam:** on this vase by the Cleophrades Painter
from the first quarter of the fifth century BC, Priam, as he sits on

the altar, "holds his hands to his head in a touching gesture of despair. His head has been cut and is bleeding; the battered and gashed body of his grandson lies sprawled in his lap. A beautiful young warrior puts his hand on the old king's shoulder, not to comfort him, but to steady him before brutally delivering the fatal blow" (Susan Woodford, *An Introduction to Greek Art* [Duckworth, 1986], 72). (National Museum of Archaeology, Naples) *See page 26* in Oxford Latin Course, College Edition: Readings and Vocabulary.

R|V **The Trojan Horse:** this shows part of a relief on a funerary urn of about 670 BC. The horse is mounted on wheels. The Greek warriors are clearly visible, some of them even holding their armor out of the apertures! (Mykonos Museum) *See page 27 in* Oxford Latin Course, College Edition: Readings and Vocabulary.

(b) Aenēās Trōiānōs superstitēs ad terrās ignōtas dūcit

l.2 Aeneas was son of Venus and the Trojan prince Anchises.

R|V **Aeneas carrying his father from Troy:** Gian Lorenzo Bernini was only fifteen when he sculpted this marble group jointly with his father in 1613. It shows Aeneas as he escapes from Troy, carrying his father Anchises and leading his son Ascanius by the hand. Anchises carries an image of the goddess Vesta. Ascanius holds the sacred fire, and Aeneas wears a lion skin. This was a highly popular subject in the ancient world. (Galleria Borghese, Rome) *See page 28 in* Oxford Latin Course, College Edition: Readings and Vocabulary.

Word-building

What do the following pairs of nouns mean?

fīlius	fīlia
amīcus	amīca
dominus (= master)	domina
seruus (= slave)	serua
rēx, rēg-is	rēgīna

GRAMMAR

The Dative Case = "to" or "for"

	singular	plural
1st declension (**puell-a**)	puell-ae	puell-īs
2nd declension (**colōn-us**)	colōn-ō	colōn-īs
3rd declension (**rēx**)	rēg-ī	rēg-ibus
Note also: (**ego** = I)	mihi (to or for me)	nōbīs (to or for us)
(**tū** = you)	tibi (to or for you)	uōbīs (to or for you)

Uses

1 Indirect object, e.g.

Flāuius fābulam puerīs nārrat.
Flauius tells a story to the boys.
dīc nōbīs fābulam, Flāuī.
Tell us a story, Flavius.
Achillēs Hectoris corpus patrī reddit.
Achilles gives back Hector's body to his father.

Note that English has two ways of expressing the indirect object, e.g.

1. Mother gives dinner to her children.
2. Mother gives her children dinner.

But in Latin the indirect object is always in the dative.

2 Many verbs take the dative, e.g.

mihi crēdite, amīcī.
Believe me, friends.
tibi hoc imperō.
I order you (to do) this.

3 The dative is used with many verbs of motion, e.g.

tibi accēdō I approach you
tibi succurrō I run to help you, I help you
tibi occurrō I run to meet you, I meet you

4 The dative can mean "for," expressing the person concerned with anything, e.g.

fēmina cēnam puerīs parat. The woman is preparing dinner for her children (dative of advantage)

mihi prōpositum est terram explōrāre. It is the intention for me (i.e. it is my intention) to explore the land.

mihi nōmen est Quīntus. The name for me (i.e. my name) is Quintus.

EXERCISE 6.1

Put the following into the dative case

1. bona puella
2. filius cārus
3. rēx fortis
4. mātrēs laetae
5. omnia lītora
6. paruus puer

EXERCISE 6.2

Translate

1. dā mihi cēnam.
2. uōbis patris equum ostendō (*show*).
3. tibi omnia dīcō.
4. prīnceps arma rēgī dat.
5. rēgīna arma eī reddit.
6. nārrā nōbīs fābulam laetam.
7. fābulam uōbīs nārrō trīstem.
8. pater filiō canem dat.
9. filius canem amīcō ostendit (*show*).
10. amīcus "canis sitit (*is thirsty*)," inquit; "dēbēs aquam eī dare."

EXERCISE 6.3

Translate into Latin

1. The woman gives water to the horses.
2. The father gives his son the food.
3. The boy returns (i.e. gives back) the food to (his) father.
4. Mother is telling the girls a story.
5. The king is showing (**ostendō**) the princes the ships.
6. The farmer hands over the dog to me.

Chapter 6: Graecī Trōiam capiunt **47**

EXERCISE 6.4

Translate

1. Trōiānī Graecīs fortiter resistunt; Graecī urbem capere nōn possunt.
2. Ulixēs cōnsilium nouum prōpōnit; eōs iubet equum ligneum facere.
3. Agamemnōn prīncipibus dīcit: "Ulixēs bonum cōnsilium nōbis prōponit: mihi prōpositum est cōnsilium eius (*his*) perficere (*to carry out*)."
4. Graecī equum faciunt, sīcut (*just as*) Ulixēs eīs imperat; sīc Graecī Trōiam tandem capiunt.
5. puerī dīligenter labōrant; magister praemium (*reward*) eīs dat.
6. Quīntus domum currit mātrīque omnia nārrat.
7. Horātia ad frātrem currit et ōsculum (*a kiss*) eī dat.
8. Scintilla eīs dīcit: "festīnāte, puerī; cēnam uōbis parō."

GRAMMAR

Review of Nouns and Adjectives

You have now learned all six cases of nouns and adjectives for the first three declensions. The uses of the different cases may be summarized as follows:

nominative	**1** subject of clause; **2** complement after the verb "to be"
genitive	= "of"
dative	= "to" or "for"
accusative	**1** object of a transitive verb; **2** after some prepositions (e.g. **ad, per**, etc.)
ablative	**1** = "by," "with," or "from"; **2** used after certain prepositions, e.g. **ā/ab, ē/ex, cum**
vocative	used only in addressing or calling someone

Study the tables of nouns and adjectives in the Reference Grammar, pp. 296–299, where the full declensions are given. (Pay no attention to *gradus, cornū, rēs, alter* and *ūter*. Stop before the notes on p. 299.)

Personal Pronouns

Learn the following:

	singular	plural
nom.	**ego** I	**nōs** we
gen.	**meī** of me	**nostrī/nostrum** of us
dat.	**mihi** to/for me	**nōbīs** to/for us
acc.	**mē** me	**nōs** us
abl.	**mē** by me	**nōbīs** by us

nom.	**tū** you	**uōs** you
gen.	**tuī** of you	**uestrī/uestrum** of you
dat.	**tibi** to/for you	**uōbīs** to/for you
acc.	**tē** you	**uōs** you
abl.	**tē** by you	**uōbīs** by you

The Irregular Verbs uolō and nōlō

Learn these verbs: **uolō** I wish, I am willing, and **nōlō** I am unwilling, I refuse:

uolō	I wish	**nōlō**	I am unwilling
uīs	you wish	**nōn uīs**	you are unwilling
uult	he/she wishes	**nōn uult**	he/she is unwilling
uolumus	we wish	**nōlumus**	we are unwilling
uultis	you wish	**nōn uultis**	you are unwilling
uolunt	they wish	**nōlunt**	they are unwilling

infinitive	**uelle**	**nōlle**
imperative singular		**nōlī**
imperative plural		**nōlīte**

Note that **uolō** has no imperatives. **nōlī** and **nōlīte** are used in prohibitions, as we have seen.

EXERCISE 6.5

Pick out from the English translations below the ones that fit the following verb forms

1. tollunt
2. esse
3. canite
4. adeunt
5. uolumus
6. nōlī
7. uelle
8. quiēscimus
9. uenīte
10. nōn uīs
11. possumus
12. īte
13. nōlunt
14. posse
15. stāmus

to be, we are resting, we stand, they lift, don't/be unwilling!, sing!, you are unwilling, to wish, we can, they approach, come!, they refuse, we are willing, go!, to be able

EXERCISE 6.6

Translate into Latin

1. Horatia meets (her) mother in the road.
2. She says to (her) daughter, "Come to the fountain and help me."
3. When they are returning home, they meet Quintus.
4. Scintilla prepares supper for the children; then she tells them a story.
5. Do not trust the horse, Trojans!
6. Agamemnon's brother is called Menelaus.

VIRGIL'S *AENEID*

A recommended modern translation is the Penguin Classics *Aeneid* by David West (revised edition, 2005). West offers a brief but stimulating reading of Book 2, on which our narrative is based (pp. xiv–xvi). Substantial excerpts from the poem, as well as from the rest of Virgil's work, can be found in James Morwood, *Virgil: A Poet in Augustan Rome* (Cambridge, 2008).

A Roman mosaic of the early third century AD showing Virgil with the Muses Clio (Muse of History) or Calliope (Epic poetry) on the left, and Melpomene (Tragedy) on the right. (Bardo Museum, Tunis)

Chapter 7
Polyphēmus

> **Grammar:** 4th & 5th declensions; review of all five declensions; pronouns—*is, ille, hic, ipse*

CARTOON

The caption means "The sailors see Polyphemus; he comes down slowly from the mountain." All will become clear in the course of this chapter!

VOCABULARY

The gender of the word *homō* (= man, human being) is given as "c" (short for "common," i.e. "common to both genders"). This means that it can be either masculine or, if it refers to a female human being, feminine.

R V **Polyphemus:** this Hellenistic head of the Cyclops from the first century BC shows his single eye between the two eye sockets. (Museum of Fine Arts, Boston) *See page 30 in* Oxford Latin Course, College Edition: Readings and Vocabulary.

COMMENTARY

In the *Odyssey* of Homer, Odysseus and his companions were trapped in the cave of the one-eyed monster Polyphemus; Odysseus had blinded him and escaped. The first half of the *Aeneid* contains many echoes of Homer's *Odyssey*. Our narrative is broadly based on *Aeneid* 3.570–684.

ll.3–4 *ubi...condant*: literally, "where they may found": *condant* is in the subjunctive mood (see Chapter 19), here expressing purpose.

ll.10–11 *interdumque ātram prōrumpit* (it forces out) *ad aethera* (to the sky) *nūbem*: (*Aeneid* 3.572); note that *ātram* agrees with *nūbem*.

R̄V̄ **Mount Etna,** the famous volcano in Sicily, is here seen erupting in 1971, *See page 32 in* Oxford Latin Course, College Edition: Readings and Vocabulary.

l.20 *fūgērunt*: have fled; perfect tense of *fugiō*.

l.24 *dīxerat*: had said; pluperfect tense of *dīco*.

l.23 *summō in monte*: this means "on top of the mountain," not "on the highest mountain."

Word-building

What do the following verbs mean?

currō: incurrō, accurrō (= ad-currō), concurrō, recurrō, dēcurrō

ueniō: aduueniō, reueniō, conueniō

GRAMMAR

4th and 5th Declensions

4th declension nouns have stems in **-ū**, e.g. **gradus**, gen., **gradūs** (step).

5th declension nouns have stems in **-e**, e.g. **rēs**, gen. **rei**.

Note that most 4th declension nouns are masculine in gender; a few are feminine, e.g. **manus** (= hand), **domus** (= house, home) and a few are neuter, e.g. **cornū** (= horn).

5th declension nouns are feminine except for **diēs** (= day) which is usually masculine.

Learn the declensions of the 4th and 5th declensions from the Reference Grammar on pp. 296–7.

N.B.: **domus** has alternative 2nd declension endings in the accusative and genitive plural (**domūs** or **domōs**, **domuum** or **domōrum**); the ablative singular is **domō**; locative (place where) **domī** (= at home).

R̄V̄ **The rocks thrown by Polyphemus:** these rocks in the sea off the coast of Sicily at Acitrezza beneath Mount Etna are said to be the ones thrown by Polyphemus at Ulysses' ship. *See page 32 in* Oxford Latin Course, College Edition: Readings and Vocabulary.

EXERCISE 7.1

Fill in the blanks and translate

1. sacerdōs (*the priest*) in grad– templī stat.
2. de illā r– multa dīcunt.

3. illō di– ad Siciliam adueniunt.
4. Aenēās hastam man– tenet (*holds*).
5. Aenēās Hectorque hastās man– ten– .
6. sp– salūtis nōn habēmus.
7. Trōiānī per fluct– nāuigant ānxiī.
8. uir Graecus man– ad caelum tendit (*stretches*).
9. rē– illīs territī sunt Trōiānī. altitūdinem (*the height*) fluct– ualdē timent.
10. sacerdōs Aenēam in grad– templī uocat.

GRAMMAR

Pronouns is and ille

is he, **ea** she, **id** it; that

	singular			plural		
	m.	**f.**	**n.**	**m.**	**f.**	**n.**
nom.	is	ea	id	eī	eae	ea
gen.	eius	eius	eius	eōrum	eārum	eōrum
dat.	eī	eī	eī	eīs	eīs	eīs
acc.	eum	eam	id	eōs	eās	ea
abl.	eō	eā	eō	eīs	eīs	eīs

ille he, *illa* she, *illud* it; that

	singular			plural		
	m.	**f.**	**n.**	**m.**	**f.**	**n.**
nom.	ille	illa	illud	illī	illae	illa
gen.	illīus	illīus	illīus	illōrum	illārum	illōrum
dat.	illī	illī	illī	illīs	illīs	illīs
acc.	illum	illam	illud	illōs	illās	illa
abl.	illō	illā	illō	illīs	illīs	illīs

Note that the neuter singular nominative and accusative and the genitive and dative singular forms are irregular; the other case endings are the same as those of **bonus, -a, -um**.

ille is more emphatic than **is**, meaning "that over there."
Note the use of **ille** indicating a change of subject, e.g.
pater Quīntum uocat; ille (= Quīntus) eum nōn audit.

EXERCISE 7.2

Replace the underlined nouns with the correct forms of **is** *or* **ille** *and then translate, e.g.*
    pater filiam uocat; <u>filia</u> ad <u>patrem</u> festīnat.
    pater filiam uocat; illa ad eum festīnat.
    The father calls his daughter; she hurries to him.

1. Scintilla Horātiae fābulam nārrat; <u>Horātia Scintillam</u> laeta audit.
2. magister puerōs lūdum intrāre iubet; <u>puerī magistrō</u> pārent (*obey* + dat).
3. Quīntus amīcīs in uiā occurrit; <u>amīcī Quīntum</u> manēre iubent.
4. Flaccus Argum uocat; <u>Argus Flaccum</u> nōn audit; nam dormit.
5. Horātia puellās in forō exspectat; <u>puellae</u> ad <u>Horātiam</u> festīnant.
6. Aenēās comitēsque in lītore manent; <u>Aenēās</u> uerba laeta <u>comitibus</u> dīcit.
7. Horātia cum Scintillā in uiā ambulat. <u>Scintilla</u> fābulam <u>Horātiae</u> nārrat.

GRAMMAR

Pronouns *hic* and *ipse*

Learn the following pronouns (for their declension compare *is* and *ille*): *hic, haec, hoc* this (here)

	singular			plural		
	m.	**f.**	**n.**	**m.**	**f.**	**n.**
nom.	hic	haec	hoc	hī	hae	haec
gen.	huius	huius	huius	hōrum	hārum	hōrum
dat.	huic	huic	huic	hīs	hīs	hīs
acc.	hunc	hanc	hoc	hōs	hās	haec
abl.	hōc	hāc	hōc	hīs	hīs	hīs

ipse, ipsa, ipsum self (emphasizing, e.g. **Flaccus ipse** Flaccus himself; **Horātia ipsa** Horatia herself; **eō ipsō tempore** at that very time)

	singular			plural		
	m.	**f.**	**n.**	**m.**	**f.**	**n.**
nom.	ipse	ipsa	ipsum	ipsī	ipsae	ipsa
gen.	ipsīus	ipsīus	ipsīus	ipsōrum	ipsārum	ipsōrum
dat.	ipsī	ipsī	ipsī	ipsīs	ipsīs	ipsīs
acc.	ipsum	ipsam	ipsum	ipsōs	ipsās	ipsa
abl.	ipsō	ipsā	ipsō	ipsīs	ipsīs	ipsīs

EXERCISE 7.3

Translate
1. Aenēās ipse nōs iubet hanc terram relinquere.
2. huic magnō ducī crēdere dēbēmus.
3. hōc ipsō diē nāuēs cōnscendere dēbēmus.
4. ex hīs lītoribus ad īnsulam Siciliam nāuigāmus.
5. in īnsulā illā Polyphēmum ipsum, mōnstrum illud horrendum, Cyclōpēsque aliōs inuenīmus.
6. hōrum ē manibus uix effugimus.
7. Aenēās fortissimus (*very brave*) manet; nōs ipsī territī sumus.
8. Flāuius fābulam dē Aenēā labōribusque eius puerīs nārrat.
9. cūr haec puerīs illīs nārrās, magister?
10. ego ipse hās fābulās laetus audiō.

EXERCISE 7.4

Translate into Latin
1. After dinner Flaccus is often willing to tell stories to the children.
2. Quintus always wants to hear stories about war.
3. These stories please Flaccus himself, who tells them well.
4. Horatia does not want to hear these things; both Scintilla and she herself want to hear stories about Roman women.

5. When Flaccus and Quintus are not there, Scintilla sometimes (**nōnnumquam**) tells stories about women.
6. Horatia listens to these stories happily (happy).

HOMER AND VIRGIL

The story which lies behind our—and Virgil's—narrative is told in *Odyssey* 9. Among many excellent translations of the *Odyssey*, we recommend E. V. Rieu's in Penguin Classics (revised by Peter Jones, 1991). If you read the story in Homer, you may detect a contrast between his world and that created by Virgil. In the figure of Aeneas, Virgil is forging a different type of hero from the Homeric models. While possessed of their stature and (possibly) charisma, the prototype Roman leader is burdened by his sense of responsibility, his *pietās* (the word refers to a sense of duty towards the gods, one's family and one's country). Homer's heroes are essentially concerned with themselves. The best guide to the *Aeneid* remains W. A. Camps, *An Introduction to Virgil's* Aeneid (Oxford, 1969). Also worth a look is R. D. Williams, *The Aeneid* (second edition with a foreword by James Morwood, Bristol Classical Press, 2009).

Chapter 8
Aenēās in Āfricā

Grammar: subordinate clauses, including relatives; reflexives

---

CARTOONS
The cartoons illustrate relative clauses.

COMMENTARY
The *Aeneid* begins abruptly with Aeneas and his followers sailing from Sicily on what might have been the last lap of their journey from Troy to Italy, but they are driven by a storm to Libya, where they are hospitably received by Queen Dido, who is building the city of Carthage.

(a) Aenēās ad Libyam aduenit

[RV] **The first part of the story of Dido and Aeneas:** this beautiful miniature from a fifteenth-century manuscript of the works of Virgil shows (starting at the bottom): Aeneas (in blue) arriving at the coast of North Africa; he meets his mother Venus who in her disguise as a huntress (note the bow, arrows and dogs), tells him Dido's story; Troy being built; Dido and Aeneas at a banquet. At the top left, Aeneas' companions, who have been lost in the storm (omitted from our narrative), arrive safely and are welcomed by Dido. The words below are those of the first line of the *Aeneid: arma uirumque canō, Trōiae quī prīmus ab ōrīs* (I sing of arms and the man who [was] the first from the shores of Troy [to reach Italy]). (Edinburgh University Library) *See page 35 in* Oxford Latin Course, College Edition: Readings and Vocabulary.

ll.4–5 *uāstōs...fluctūs*: = *Aeneid* 1.86. note that *uāstōs* agrees with *fluctūs*. Remember that adjectives and nouns are likely to have different endings if they belong to different declensions.

ll.5–7 *ēripiunt....oculīs* = *Aeneid* 1, 88–9: *diem*: day, daylight.

ll.14–15 *mihi prōpositum est*: it is the intention for me = it is my intention.

ll.19–20 *"ō fortūnātī...surgunt"* = *Aeneid* 1.437. *quōrum*: gen. pl. of *quī* = of whom, whose.

l.23 *in mediā urbe*: "in the middle of the city," not "in the middle city"; cf. *"summō in monte"* (= on top of the mountain) in l.23 of the previous chapter.

l.35 *pepulit*: perfect of *pellō*: "has driven."

R|V **Aeneas looks down on the building of Carthage:** this illustration from a fourth-century AD manuscript of Virgil shows Aeneas and his companion Achates gazing in wonder from the top of a hill at the building of Carthage. The wheel—the painting is damaged—is part of a crane. (Vatican Museums, Rome) *See page 36 in* Oxford Latin Course, College Edition: Readings and Vocabulary.

l.42 *"īnfandum...dolōrem."*: *Aeneid* 2.3: *īnfandum* (inexpressible) agrees with *dolōrem*.

l.43 *sī tantus amor est tibi* = "if you have so great a desire to..."

(b) Aenēās Trōiānōrum labōrēs Dīdōnī nārrat

l.8 *accēpit*: "he received"; perfect of *accipiō*.

l.10 *seruandī*: "of saving"; this form is the genitive of the gerund, a verbal noun declining like *bellum*.

l.11 *sacra*: the sacred emblems (neuter plural); these would have included the eternal fire of Vesta, goddess of the hearth, which symbolized the continuing life of the city, and the Penates, the guardian spirits of the city. In entrusting these to Aeneas, Hector imposed on him the mission to guard the life of Troy. Almost the first words Aeneas speaks in the *Aeneid*, when he meets his mother Venus, disguised as a Carthaginian girl, on the shores of Libya are:

sum pius Aenēās, raptōs quī ex hoste penātēs/classe uehō mēcum.

(I am pious Aeneas, who rescued the Penates from the enemy and carry them with me in my fleet) *Aeneid* 1.378–9.

pius is repeatedly used by Virgil to describe Aeneas: the concept of *pietās* included the duty owed to the gods, to one's country, and to one's family.

l.13 *furor*: madness. *furor* is the opposite of *pietās*. Here it makes Aeneas forget the duty just imposed on him by Hector and rush into a hopeless battle. When he suddenly thinks of his father (line 28), he returns to a state of *pietās*, remembering his duty to his family, the gods and Troy.

R|V **Fighting around Troy:** this book from the fifth century AD shows fighting at Troy. (Bibliotheca Ambrosiana, Milan) *See page 38 in Oxford Latin Course, College Edition: Readings and Vocabulary.*

Word-building

What do the following verbs mean?

mittō: immitto, remittō, ēmittō, dīmittō
pōnō: compōnō, dēpōnō, expōnō, impōnō, prōpōnō
cadō: dēcidō, incidō
cēdō: accēdō, discēdō, prōcēdō, recēdō

GRAMMAR

Subordinate Clauses

A clause is a group of words containing a verb, e.g. "Flaccus calls Quintus."

This clause forms a complete sentence.

"When Quintus enters the field…" This group of words forms a clause, containing the verb "enters," but it is not complete. It needs another clause to complete it:

"When Quintus enters the field, <u>Flaccus calls him</u>."

This sentence consists of two clauses:

1. When Quintus enters the field (*subordinate clause*)
2. Flaccus calls him (*main clause*)

The two clauses are joined by the *conjunction* (= joining word) "when." The "when" clause, which does not form a complete sentence, is called a "subordinate" clause, which is joined to the "main" (grammatically complete) clause by the subordinating conjunction "when."

You have already met the following Latin subordinating conjunctions:

ubi when,   **quod** because,   **dum** while,   **sī** if

EXERCISE 8.1

Translate; in your translations underline the subordinating conjunctions
1. dum Horātia quiēscit, Scintilla fābulam nārrat.
2. Horātia gaudet, quod fābula eī placet.
3. sī fābulam audīre cupis, tacē et mē audī.
4. ubi Quīntus ā lūdō redit, ille quoque (*also*) fābulam audit.
5. Trōiānī lītus Libyae laetī uident quod tempestāte territī sunt.
6. dum Aenēās spectat, hominēs urbem aedificant.
7. ubi fluctūs surgunt, nautae timent.
8. Aenēās laetus est quod pictūrās Trōiae uidet.

GRAMMAR

The Relative Pronoun

Learn **quī, quae, quod** = who, which

	singular			plural		
	m.	**f.**	**n.**	**m.**	**f.**	**n.**
nom.	quī	quae	quod	quī	quae	quae
gen.	cuius	cuius	cuius	quōrum	quārum	quōrum
dat.	cui	cui	cui	quibus	quibus	quibus
acc.	quem	quam	quod	quōs	quās	quae
abl.	quō	quā	quō	quibus	quibus	quibus

Hector, quī fortis est, Achillī resistit.
Hector, who is brave, resists Achilles.
Achillēs, quem Hector timet, eum oppugnat.
Achilles, whom Hector fears, attacks him.
Flāuius est is cuius fābulam audiō.
Flavius is the man whose (literally, of whom) story I am listening to.
Aenēās accēdit ad templum quod in colle stat.
Aeneas approaches the temple that stands on a hill.

Note that the relative pronoun has the same gender and number as the word it refers to (its antecedent); its case depends on its function in the clause which it introduces.

So in the first sentence above, **quī** is masculine because its antecedent is the masculine Hector. It is nominative because it is the subject of **est** in the relative clause.

In the second sentence, **quem** is masculine because Achilles is its antecedent but it is in the accusative because it is the object of **timet**.

In the third sentence, **cuius** is masculine because it refers back to Flavius and it is in the genitive because the relative clause tells us that it is the story of him.

In the fourth sentence, **quod** is neuter because its antecedent is neuter. What case is it in?

Note

1. that in modern English the word "whom" is now used very little.
2. that the word "that" is often used instead of "who" or "which"
3. "that" in English the relative pronoun often gets left out, e.g. "I liked the last book I read." It is always present in Latin.

EXERCISE 8.2

Put the words in parentheses into Latin and then translate the whole sentence

1. Aenēās multōs hominēs uidet (who) urbem aedificant.
2. Horātia, (whom) Quīntus exspectat, prope uiam sedet.
3. puella (whom) in agrō uideō frātrem exspectat.
4. Quīntus, (whom) in uiā occurrō, ānxius est.
5. urbem (which) Dīdō aedificat, uidēre cupiō.
6. puerī (whose) tabulās Flāuius spectat ānxiī sunt.
7. Hector timet hominēs cum (whom) pugnat.
8. nolīte perīcula timēre (which) nōn magna sunt.
9. Quīntus amīcus est (to whom—*use* **ad** +acc.) scrībō.
10. terra illa ad (which) nāuigō Āfrica est.

EXERCISE 8.3

Translate

1. fēmina (quam in templī gradibus uidet) Aenēās est rēgina.
2. puella cuius manum teneō soror mea est.
3. uir cui in uiā occurrō mē benignē salūtat.
4. puerī quibus uerba laeta dīcō iam surrīdent (*smile*).
5. uerba quae uōbīs dīcō nōn sunt laeta.
6. puellae quārum tabulās spectat Flāuius ualdē timent.
7. Aenēās templum spectat cuius in gradibus stat Dīdō.

8. puellae quibuscum* ambulat Quīntus in lūdum prōcēdunt.
9. quid dīcis dē rēbus quās iam cognōscis?
10. Aenēae comitēs, quōs salūtat rēgīna, dē salūte nōn iam (*no longer*) dēspērant.

*note the position of *cum*; so also *mēcum, tēcum, nōbīscum, uōbīscum, sēcum* (see below), *quōcum* and *quibuscum*.

> If you are translating from English into Latin, you can always discover the case of the relative pronoun by phrasing the English relative clause as a full sentence. In the sentence
>   "I greet the men who I see in the street"
> You can change "who I see in the street" to "I see **them** (i.e. the men) in the street."
>   Accordingly the relative pronoun must go into the accusative.

EXERCISE 8.4

Translate
1. I want to hear the story which Flaccus is telling.
2. We are unwilling to sail to a city in which the men are enemies.
3. Gaius is the friend with whom I want to walk through the fields.
4. Horatia is a girl whom I want to meet.
5. Aeneas, who wishes to explore (**explōrāre**) the land, leaves his companions on the shore.
6. He climbs a hill and sees many men who are building a temple.
7. The queen, whom he soon sees, greets him.
8. The companion to whom he is talking is happy.
9. The Trojans, whose ships are sailing through the waves, are not happy.
10. Decimus is the boy whose tablets Flauius is looking at angrily (use adj. "angry").

GRAMMAR

Reflexive Pronouns

You have already learned the declensions of **ego**, **tū**, **nōs** and **uōs**. Review them (p. 48). Now you must learn the reflexive pronoun **sē**. It does not exist in the nominative and is both singular and plural and masculine, feminine and neuter.

nom.	—	
gen.	**suī**	of himself, herself, themselves
dat.	**sibi**	to/for himself, herself, themselves
acc.	**sē**	himself, herself, themselves
abl.	**sē**	by himself, herself, themselves

Note that the ablative of **sē** becomes **sēcum** (with himself, herself, themselves) when used with *cum*. (So also **mēcum, tēcum, nōbīscum, uōbīscum, quōcum, quibuscum**) with me, with you (sing.), with us, with you (pl.), with who(m) (sing. and pl.)).

Personal pronouns can be used reflexively, i.e. referring back to the subject of the verb, e.g.

(compare French:

ego mē lauō	I wash myself	*je me lave*
tū tē lauās	you wash youself	*tu te laves*
ille sē lauat	he washes himself	*il se laves*
nōs nōs lauāmus	we wash ourselves	*nous nous lavons*
uōs uōs lauātis	you wash yourselves	*vous vous lavez*
illī sē lauant	they wash themselves	*ils se lavent)*

Note that although Latin says **mē lauō** ("I wash myself"), in English we can simply say "I wash." So also **Scintilla sē parat** ("Scintilla prepares herself"), but we usually say "prepares," "gets ready." And **pater sē uertit** ("father turns himself"), where we usually say "turns."

Thus, in Latin such transitive verbs (i.e. verbs requiring an object) usually have the reflexive pronoun as the object where English can use the verb intransitively (i.e. without any object).

Note the following personal adjectives:

meus, mea, meum	my	**noster, nostra, nostrum**	our
tuus, tua, tuum	your	**uester, uestra, uestrum**	your
suus, sua, suum*	his/her own	**suus, sua, suum***	their own

*reflexive, e.g.

Crassus cupit suam glōriam augēre. Crassus wants to increase his (own) glory.
puerī suōs loculōs ferunt. The boys are carrying their (own) satchels.

For non-reflexive "his," e.g. the tutor is carrying his (= the boy's) satchel, **eius** (= of him) is used; **eōrum** (=of them) is used for "their," e.g.:

puerī ad lūdum festīnant; paedagōgī loculōs eōrum ferunt.

The boys are hurrying to school; the tutors are carrying their satchels.

Quīntus domum currit; amīcus lentē ambulat.

Quintus runs home; his friend walks slowly.

N.B.: Remember: "his" in English could refer either to the subject of the sentence or to someone else; but Latin uses *suus* if it refers to the subject, *eius* if it refers to someone else.

EXERCISE 8.5

Translate the following

1. Scintilla cēnam parat.
2. Horātia ad cēnam sē parat.
3. nautae nāuem ad lītus uertunt.
4. nautae sē uertunt et nōs salūtant.
5. puerī canem in uiā exercent.
6. cūr in agrō uōs exercētis?
7. pater fīlium iubet sibi succurrere.
8. fēminae fīliās iubent sēcum ad fontem uenīre.

EXERCISE 8.6

ego mē uertō = *I turn around (literally; "I turn myself").*

Translate:

you (*sing.*) turn around, he turns around, we turn around,
you (*plural*) turn around, they turn around.

EXERCISE 8.7

Translate

1. Argus malus canis est; in lutō (*mud*) sē uoluit (*rolls*) et ualdē sordidus est.
2. Scintilla "Argus," inquit, "ualde sordidus est; dēbētis eum lauāre."
3. Quīntus "ō canis sordide," inquit, "cūr nōn potes tē lauāre? ego nōn cupiō tē lauāre."
4. Scintilla "uōs parāte, puerī," inquit; "dēbētis canem uestrum statim lauāre."
5. Quīntus ad mātrem sē uertit et "ego occupātus (*busy*) sum," inquit; "Horātia ipsa suum canem lauāre dēbet."
6. Horātia "nōlī ignāuus (*lazy*) esse, Quīnte," inquit; "Argus nōn meus canis est sed tuus."
7. tandem Quīntus urnam aquae fert Horātiamque iuuat. Argum diū lauant.
8. ubi prīmum canem soluunt (*untie*), ille abit iterumque in lutō sē uoluit.

EXERCISE 8.8

In the following sentences fill the blanks with the correct pronouns and translate, e.g.

ubi — uertimus, patrem uidēmus, quī ab agrō redit. (nōs)

When we turn around, we see father, who is returning from the field.

1. Scintilla ad Horātiam — uertit; "parā — ad cēnam, Horātia," inquit.
2. Horātia, quae — lauat, "ueniō statim," inquit; "iam — parō."
3. Quīntus in agrō — exercet; arborem altam (*high*) ascendit.
4. subitō ad terram cadit; patrem iubet — succurrere.
5. puerī in agrō sedent: Flaccus "cūr in agrō ōtiōsī (*idle*) sedētis, puerī?" inquit; "cūr nōn — exercētis."
6. illī inuītī surgunt et — exercent.

Chapter 9

Īnfēlīx Dīdō

R|V **Dīdō gladium capit pectusque trānsfīgit:** the details in this reconstruction of the death of Dido reflect Virgil's description (*Aeneid* 4.645–50): "In her frenzy she climbed up the lofty pyre and unsheathed a Trojan sword, a gift she had asked for, but not for such a purpose. Here, after she saw the Trojan clothing and familiar bed, she paused a little in tearful thought and fell on the bed." *See page 39 in* Oxford Latin Course, College Edition: Readings and Vocabulary.

COMMENTARY

The Latin here is rather harder than in earlier chapters. Where possible we have kept as close as possible to Virgil's words.

l.1 *fīnem dīcendī*: an end of speaking. *dīcendī* is the genitive of the gerund. You will learn this in Chapter 27.

l.6 *sēcum = cum sē*

l.17 *rēgnī...oblītus*: forgetting your kingdom: *oblītus* is the perfect participle of *oblīuīscor* = I forget. It is one of the few verbs in Latin which takes a genitive. *rēgnī*: your (future) kingdom (in Italy). (For the perfect participle see Chapter 16.)

ll.25–7: this is a bald summary of Aeneas' only speech in *Aeneid* 4. We quote two extreme reactions. "Not all Virgil's art can make the figure of Aeneas here appear other than despicable. His conduct had been vile, and Dido's heart-broken appeal brings its vileness into strong relief." —T. E. Page. "Virgil has taken the utmost care to convey the reasons why Aeneas's reply is cold; it is because he knows he must not yield and therefore he smothers his love and his emotions. He endeavors to use logical and persuasive arguments to put his case, honestly believing that Dido will see that he has no option." —Derek Williams. What do *you* feel about him at this point?

l.29 *posterī*: my descendants. Dido's prophecy was fulfilled many centuries later when Hannibal invaded Italy in 218 BC.

RV **Aeneas' son, Dido and Aeneas out hunting:** part of the mosaic
floor of the *frigidārium* (the cooling off room in the baths) from
Low Ham in Somerset, UK (fourth century AD) which tells the
story of Dido and Aeneas. (Taunton Castle Museum, Somerset)
See page 41 in Oxford Latin Course, College Edition: Readings
and Vocabulary.

RV **Mercury, the messenger of Jupiter:** this statue of Mercury
by Giambologna (1529–1608) is Renaissance in period but
classical in feeling. Blown aloft by a cherub-faced wind, he has
wings on his hat and his ankles and he holds the caduceus,
a staff with two serpents twining round it. (Louvre, Paris) *See
page 42 in* Oxford Latin Course, College Edition: Readings and
Vocabulary.

RV **Dido and Aeneas:** another part of the Low Ham mosaic: see
above. *See page 43 in* Oxford Latin Course, College Edition:
Readings and Vocabulary.

Word-building
What do the following pairs of words mean?

ADJECTIVES	NOUNS
laetus, -a, -um	laetitia, -ae, f.
amīcus, -a, -um	amīcitia, ae, f.
trīstis, trīste	trīstitia, -ae, f.
dīligēns, dīligentis	dīligentia, -ae, f.
prūdēns, prūdentis	prūdentia, -ae, f.

COMPREHENSION EXERCISE

Read the following passage carefully and then answer the questions below

The Hero Hercules and the Monster Cacus

prope Tiberis rīpās habitant rēx Euander populusque   **rīpās** banks
eius pauper. in casīs paruīs uīuunt sed contentī omnēs   **pauper** poor
sunt et laeti; ūnum sōlum perīculum timent.   **uīuunt** live

nam prope Tiberim stat collis in quō spēlunca est
magna. hīc habitat mōnstrum ingēns, sēmihomō,
Cācus nōmine, quī flammās ex ōre ēmittit, hominēs
manibus rapit et eōs saeuē occīdit. sīc populum tōtum
diū terret. sed tandem aduenit hērōs quīdam, Herculēs
ipse, quī eōs ab illō perīculō līberat.

nam ad hunc locum Herculēs laetus adit cum taurīs
ingentibus quōs ex Hispaniā ad Graeciam dūcit.
Cācus, ubi taurōs uidet, eōs capere cōnstituit. itaque,
ubi Herculēs dormit, in spēluncam suam eōs dūcit.
postrīdiē, cum Herculēs ē somnō surgit, taurōs uidēre
nōn potest. diū trīstis quaerit. tandem mūgītum
taurōrum audit. summā īrā commōtus, ad spēluncam
accēdit saxaque dīripit. magnā uōce clāmat et "uenī
hūc, Cāce," inquit, "taurōsque mihi redde. nōn potes
mē fugere. mors tē manet." Cācus, furōre eius territus,
uix resistit. sīc facile uincit eum Herculēs et mōnstrum
illud horrendum in terrā iacet mortuum.

collis	hill
5 **spēlunca**	cave
nōmine	by name
ōre	mouth
rapit	seizes
saeuē	savagely
10 **taurīs**	bulls
itaque	and so
postrīdiē	the next day
15 **mūgītum**	the mooing, lowing
dīripit	tears open
20 **facile**	easily
horrendum	terrible
iacet	lies

(based on Virgil, *Aeneid* 8.193–267)

1. Where do Evander and his people live?
2. Describe their living conditions. How do the people feel about living there?
3. *sēmihomō* (l.5) What does this word mean?
4. In what two ways is the horrific nature of Cacus conveyed (ll.6–7)
5. In what case are the following words and why: *perīculum* (l.3); *quō* (l.4); *quī* (l.6); *manibus* (l.7); *eōs* (l.7).
6. Give an English word derived from (a) *habitant* (l.1); (b) *populus* (l.1); (c) *saeuē* (l.7).
7. Translate the third paragraph (ll.10–21).

Chapter 10
Comitia

Grammar: imperfect and perfect tenses

CARTOONS

The cartoons introduce two past tenses simultaneously: one, the imperfect tense, expresses action which is continuous, repeated or incomplete, e.g. "he was walking to school," "he walked to school every day"; and two, the perfect tense, usually expressing completed action in the past, e.g. "he saw." (But see also Chapter 11.)

The imperfect ends in *-bam, -bās, -bat, -bāmus, -bātis, -bant.*
The perfect ends in *-ī, -istī, -it, -imus, -istis, -ērunt.*

COMMENTARY

(a) Comitia

The country towns of Italy, *colōniae* or *mūnicipia*, had constitutions modeled on that of Rome. There were annual elections at which the citizens elected the chief executives (*duouirī*, or in some cases *quattuoruirī* [boards of four men]); at the end of their year of office these joined an advisory council, corresponding to the Senate at Rome. Local elections were hotly contested. Cicero remarked jestingly that it was easier to become a senator at Rome than a town councillor in Pompeii. The walls of Pompeii are thickly plastered with election posters. These show that candidates were often supported by guilds, e.g. by the bakers:

C. IŪLIUM POLYBIUM AEDĪLEM Ō[RŌ] V[ŌS] F[ACIĀTIS]. PĀNEM BO-
NUM FERT. (Dessau 6412e)

The aediles were junior officials. (The letters in brackets are omitted—abbreviations are common in inscriptions). OVF stands for ŌRŌ VŌS FACIĀTIS = I beg you to make. Another poster, presumably later, shows the same Julius Polybius standing for duouir, supported this time by the muleteers:

C. IŪLIUM POLYBIUM IIVIRUM MŪLIŌNĒS ROGANT. (Dessau 6412a)

Some candidates seem to be less serious:

M. CERRINIUM VATIAM AEDĪLEM Ō[RANT] V[ŌS] F[ACIĀTIS] SĒRIBIBĪ ŪNIVERSĪ (all the late drinkers). (Dessau 6418d)

For ease of reading we have used U, not V, for the capital u when it has been used as a vowel in these posters.

The first part of a Latin name is often abbreviated. Here C. stands for Caius and M. stands for Marcus.

R|V **Part of an election poster from Pompeii:** this election poster from a wall at Pompeii urges voters to elect Modestus, *"iuuenem probum"* (an honest young man) as *aedile*. Note OVF (see above). (Museo della Civilta Romana) *See page 46 in* Oxford Latin Course, College Edition: Readings and Vocabulary.

R|V **A Roman bar:** the bar counter in the *caupōna* on the Via dell'Abbondanza in Pompeii. The counter, which is L-shaped, contains large jars for keeping food hot. Wine jars rest against the wall addressed "to Euxinus the inkeeper, near the amphitheater, Pompeii." Behind them are three other rooms, a storeroom and a lavatory; on the right is a courtyard for eating and drinking in the open air. *See page 46 in* Oxford Latin Course, College Edition: Readings and Vocabulary.

l.1ff. *Flaccus in tabernā sedēbat...*: the names of Flaccus' friends and the tenor of their conversation are again based on Petronius, *Satyrica* 42–4. (See Chapter 2[b]).

ll.27–30 The account of the riot is suggested by Virgil, *Aeneid* 1.148–52: Virgil compares the stilling of a storm by Neptune to the quieting of a riot by a respected statesman:

"And as when a riot arises at a great meeeting of the people and the low mob goes wild at heart; now torches and stones are flying, frenzy gives them arms; then, if it happens that they see some man influential through his piety and good deeds, they fall silent and stand with ears pricked; he controls their minds by his words and soothes their hearts."

R|V **Roman coin showing a citizen voting:** this coin, dating from c. 52–50 BC, shows a Roman senator called Lucius Cassius Longinus voting. He wears a toga. *See page 47 in* Oxford Latin Course, College Edition: Readings and Vocabulary.

(b) Flāuius arithmēticam docet

On the arithmetic lesson, compare Horace, *Ars Poetica* 325–9:

Horace is contrasting the Greek genius with the Roman character narrowed and hardened by a practical and "relevant" education. He says: "The Muse has granted the Greeks genius and ability to speak in a polished style, the Greeks, greedy for nothing but praise. Roman boys...."

Rōmānī puerī longīs ratiōnibus assem
discunt in partēs centum dīducere. "dīcat
fīlius Albānī: sī dē quīncunce remōta est
uncia, quid superat? poterās dīxisse." "triēns." "eu.
rem poteris seruāre tuam."

(Roman boys learn by long calculations to divide an as (a small coin) into a hundred parts. "Let Albanus' son tell us: if a twelfth is deducted from five-twelfths, what is left? You could have answered by now." "A third." "Good, you'll be able to keep your fortune.")

He concludes after our quotation: "When once this cancer and care for cash has sunk into their minds, can we hope they can write any poems worth preserving?"

(c) Flaccus cōnstituit Quīntum Rōmam dūcere

Horace himself tells us:

If I have a good character

causa fuit pater hīs, quī macrō pauper agellō,
nōluit in Flāuī lūdum mē mittere, magnī
quō puerī magnīs ē centuriōnibus ortī,
laeuō suspēnsī loculōs tabulamque lacertō,
ībant octōnōs referentēs Īdibus aeris:
sed puerum est ausus Rōmam portāre, docendum
artēs quās doceat quīuīs eques atque senātor
sēmet prōgnātōs.
                              Horace, Satires 1.6.71–8

(My father was responsible for this, who, a poor man with a meagre little farm, refused to send me to the school of Flavius, where the big boys born of big centurions, with their satchels and tablet hanging on their left shoulder, went, each taking his eight asses on the Ides, but dared to carry me, when a boy, to Rome, to be taught the arts which any knight or senator would have his own sons taught.)

magnīs centuriōnibus: Venusia had received a colony (a settlement of veteran soldiers) in about 85 BC. The centurions were the big men of a country town.

octōnōs aeris: "eight asses each," the school fees, paid on the 15th of the month.

l.4 *mī uir*: "my husband"; *mī* is vocative of *meus* (compare *mī fīlī* = "my son").

l.9 *partēs coāctōris*: "the role of an auctioneer's agent." Horace (*Satires* 1.6.76) says that his father would not have minded if after all his education Horace had become a modestly paid auctioneer, or, like himself, an auctioneer's agent.

Word-building

Learn the following compounds of *mittō, mittere, mīsī* (the last is the perfect tense)

admittō, admittere, admīsī	I admit, commit (a crime)
āmittō, āmittere, āmīsī	I send away, lose
committō, committere, commīsī	I join together, entrust
dēmittō, dēmittere, dēmīsī	I send down
dīmittō, dīmittere, dīmīsī	I dismiss (send in different directions)
ēmittō, ēmittere, ēmīsī	I send out
immittō, immittere, immīsī	I send in, send against
permittō, permittere, permīsī	I permit
prōmittō, prōmittere, prōmīsī	I promise
remittō, remittere, remīsī	I send back

GRAMMAR

The last chapter was for review and there was no new grammatical input. There is a considerable amount in this chapter, however, and it is recommended that you take your time over it.

Tenses

Verbs in Latin alter their endings to indicate different *tenses*, i.e. the time at which an action or event takes place. So far all the stories have been told in the *present tense*; this is used when the action of the verb is happening now or happens regularly, e.g.

Flaccus in agrō labōrat. Flaccus is working in the field (now)

or Flaccus works in the field (every day).

(Latin does not always have separate tenses to indicate these different meanings.)

We now introduce two *past tenses*:

1 The Imperfect Tense

This tense is used when an action in the past is *continuous, repeated* or *incomplete*, e.g.

Flaccus in agrō diū labōrābat.

Flaccus was working in the field for a long time.

Quīntus ad lūdum cotīdiē ambulābat.

Quintus used to walk to school every day.

Horātia iānuam claudēbat, cum mater "nōlī" inquit "iānuam claudere."

Horatia was shutting the door when her mother said "Don't shut the door."

Note that English does not always indicate time so precisely, e.g.

Flaccus *worked* in the field a long time: but Latin will say *labōrābat,* since the action is continuous.

Quintus *walked* to school every day: but Latin will say *ambulābat,* since the action is repeated.

The imperfect tense is formed by adding the following endings to the present stem:

		compare personal endings
-bam	I	[**par-ō**]
-bās	you (singular)	**par-ās**
-bat	he/she	**par-at**
-bāmus	we	**par-āmus**
-bātis	you (plural)	**par-ātis**
-bant	they	**par-ant**

	1st conj.	2nd conj.	3rd conj.	4th conj.
Stem:	**parā-**	**monē-**	**reg-**	**audi-**
	parā-bam	monē-bam	reg-ē-bam	audi-ē-bam
	(*I was preparing*)	(*I was warning*)	(*I was ruling*)	(*I was hearing*)
	parā-bās	monē-bās	reg-ē-bās	audi-ē-bās
	parā-bat	monē-bat	reg-ē-bat	audi-ē-bat
	parā-bāmus	monē-bāmus	reg-ē-bāmus	audi-ē-bāmus
	parā-bātis	monē-bātis	reg-ē-bātis	audi-ē-bātis
	parā-bant	monē-bant	reg-ē-bant	audi-ē-bant

N.B.: 1 3rd and 4th conjugation verbs insert **-ē** after the stem before the imperfect person endings.

2 3rd conjugation **-iō** verbs form imperfects like **audio: capi-ē-bam** etc.

3 The imperfect of **sum** is:

eram	I was
erās	you (*sing.*) were
erat	he/she was
erāmus	we were
erātis	you (*pl.*) were
erant	they were

EXERCISE 10.1

Translate
1. litterās cotīdiē (*every day*) scrībēbāmus.
2. urbem fortiter dēfendēbant.
3. in agrīs errābam.
4. filium diū quaerēbat.
5. in casā quiēscēbās.
6. fessī erāmus.
7. ad forum ambulābant.
8. magistrum nōn audiēbātis.
9. domum fugiēbam.
10. in forō diū manēbant.

GRAMMAR

2 The Perfect Tense

The *perfect tense* is most often used to express completed past action, e.g.

Flaccus ad agrum ambulāuit. Flaccus *walked to the field.*

Flaccus ad agrum nōn ambulāuit. Flaccus *did* not *walk* to the field.

Quīntus domum celeriter ambulāuit. Quintus *has walked* home fast.

The perfect person endings are the same for every conjugation:

SINGULAR		PLURAL	
-ī	I	**-imus**	we
-istī	you (*sing.*)	**-istis**	you (*pl.*)
-it	he/she	**-ērunt**	they

These endings are attached to the perfect stem:

1st conjugation	**parāu-**
2nd conjugation	**monu-**
3rd conjugation, e.g.	**rēx-**
4th conjugation	**audīu-**

1 -a-verbs perfect stem **parāu-**		2 -e-verbs perfect stem **monu-**	
parāu-ī	I prepared	**monu-ī**	I warned
parāu-istī	you (*sing.*) prepared	**monu-istī**	you (*sing.*) warned
parāu-it	he/she prepared	**monu-it**	he/she warned
parāu-imus	we prepared	**monu-imus**	we warned
parāu-istis	you (*pl.*) prepared	**monu-istis**	you (*pl.*) warned
parāu-ērunt	they prepared	**monu-ērunt**	they warned

3 consonant verbs perfect stem, e.g. **rēx- (regs-)**		4 -i-verbs perfect stem **audīu-**	
rēx-ī	I ruled	**audīu-ī**	I heard
rēx-istī	you (*sing.*) ruled	**audīu-istī**	you (*sing.*) heard
rēx-it	he/ she ruled	**audīu-it**	he/she heard
rēx-imus	we ruled	**audīu-imus**	we heard
rēx-istis	you (*pl.*) rueld	**audīu-istis**	you (*pl.*) heard
rēx-ērunt	they ruled	**audīu-ērunt**	they heard

The perfect stem is formed in various ways:

1 Regular verbs of the 1st, 2nd and 4th conjugations form perfects as follows: The suffix *-u* is added to the verb stem, e.g.

1st **para-,**	perfect **parā-u-ī**
2nd **mone-,**	perfect **mon-u-ī**(the **e** of the stem drops out)
4th **audi-,**	perfect **audī-u-ī**

EXERCISE 10.2

Form the imperfect and perfect (1st person singular) of the following verbs

dormiō, salūtō, habeō, labōrō, exerceō, custōdiō

GRAMMAR

2 3rd conjugation verbs, the stems of which end in a consonant or in *u,* follow various patterns:

(1) The suffix *-s* is added to the verb stem, e.g.

reg-ō, reg-ere:	perfect **rēx-ī** (for **rēg-s-ī**)
dīc-ō, dīc-ere:	perfect **dīx-ī** (for **dīc-s-ī**)

(2) the verb stem is unchanged, e.g.

contend-ō, contendere:	perfect **contend-ī**
cōnstitu-ō, cōnstituere:	perfect **cōnstitu-ī**

(3) The vowel of the present stem is lengthened, e.g.

leg-ō, leg-ere:	perfect **lēg-ī**
em-ō, em-ere:	perfect **ēm-ī**

(4) The present stem is reduplicated (i.e. the first syllable is doubled), e.g.

cad-ō, cad-ere:	perfect **ce-cid-ī**
curr-ō, curr-ere:	perfect **cu-curr-ī**

(5) The suffix *-iu* or *-u* is added to the stem, e.g.

sin-ō, sin-ere:	perfect **sīuī**
pet-ō, pet-ere:	perfect **petīuī**
pōn-ō, pōn-ere:	perfect **posuī**

These rules will enable you to recognize most perfect forms in your reading. It is sensible to learn the fourth principal part (the supine) at this stage. Its use will be explained later. At present only *learn the following*, which add the suffix *-sī* to the present stem:

scrīb-ō, scrīb-ere, scrīp-sī, scrīptum	I write
dīc-ō, dīc-ere, dīx-ī, dictum	I say
dūc-ō, dūc-ere, dūx-ī, ductum	I lead
reg-ō, reg-ere, rēx-ī, rēctum	I rule
claud-ō, claud-ere, claus-ī, clausum	I close
ēuād-ō, ēuād-ere, ēuās-ī (no supine)	I escape
cēd-ō, cēd-ere, ces-sī (no supine)	I yield, go
lūd-ō, lūd-ere, lūs-ī, lūsum	I play
mitt-ō, mitt-ere, mīs-ī, missum	I send
surg-ō, surg-ere, surrēx-ī, surrēctum	I get up, rise
ger-ō, ger-ere, ges-sī, gestum	I carry, wear

N.B.: 1 When *-s* is added to the consonant in which the present stem ends, certain changes of spelling occur, e.g.

c + s = x (**dīc-si** becomes **dīxī**); **d** drops out (**claud-si** becomes **clausī**), etc.

2 The perfect of compound verbs is usually the same as that of the simple verb, e.g.

> **dūcō, dūxī; re-dūcō, re-dūxī**
> **cēdō, cessī; ac-cēdō, ac-cessī**
> **mittō, mīsī; re-mittō, re-mīsī, re-missum**

3 A few 2nd conjugation verbs also form the perfect by adding suffix *-s*; learn the following:

augeō, augēre, auxī, auctum	I increase
iubeō, iubēre, iussī, iussum	I order
maneō, manēre, mānsī, mānsum	I remain, stay
persuādeō, persuādēre, persuāsī, persuāsum + dat.	I persuade
rīdeō, rīdēre, rīsī, rīsum	I laugh

4 The perfect stem of *sum* is **fu-**:

fu-ī	I was
fu-istī	you (*sing.*) were
fu-it	he/she was
fu-imus	we were
fu-istis	you (*pl.*) were
fu-ērunt	they were

5 The perfect stem of **eō** (I go) is **-i** or **īu-**

i-ī	**īu-ī**
īstī	**īu-istī**
i-it	**īu-it**
i-imus	**īu-imus**
īstis	**īu-istis**
i-ērunt	**īu-ērunt**

EXERCISE 10.3

Put the following verb forms into (a) the imperfect (b) the perfect

1. monet
2. dormiō
3. superant
4. dēbēmus
5. clāmātis
6. custōdiunt
7. dūcō
8. mittimus
9. claudis
10. iubeō
11. manēmus
12. dīcitis
13. ēuādunt
14. amat
15. exerceō

EXERCISE 10.4

Translate
1. ad urbem ambulāuimus.
2. Quīntus nōn dormīuit.
3. mihi omnia dīxistī.
4. mīlitēs prope castra sē exercuērunt.
5. mē cūrāuistis.
6. fīlium ad agrum dūxī.
7. Flaccus puerum ad agrum mīsit.
8. eum iussit in agrō labōrāre.
9. cūr iānuam nōn clausistī?
10. puellae litterās bene scrīpsērunt.

EXERCISE 10.5

Translate the following verb forms
1. spectā
2. spectābam
3. spectat
4. spectāuī
5. spectāre
6. spectāuērunt
7. dūcēbās
8. dūcere
9. dūcunt
10. dūxistis
11. dūc
12. dūxit
13. dormīre
14. dormīte
15. dormiēbant
16. dormiō
17. dormīuistī
18. dormiēbāmus
19. monuērunt
20. monēbat
21. monēre
22. monēte
23. monuimus
24. monuit

EXERCISE 10.6

In the following sentences put each verb in parentheses into the appropriate tense (imperfect or perfect) and translate the whole sentence. For example:

Horātia Quīntusque in hortō (lūdere), cum Scintilla eōs (uocāre).
lūdēbant; uocāuit.

Horatia and Quintus were playing in the garden when Scintilla called them.

1. Scintilla Quīntum Horātiamque (uocāre); ad agrum eōs (mittere).
2. puerī ad agrum (īre); cēnam ad patrem (portāre).
3. nōn (festīnāre) sed in uiā diū (lūdere).
4. tandem ubi agrum (intrāre), Horātia patrem (uocāre).
5. ille fīliam nōn (audīre); sub arbore (dormīre); nam fessus (esse).
6. Horātia frātrem (monēre); "nōlī patrem excitāre," inquit; "fessus (esse)."
7. sed ille (ēuigilāre) puerōsque (salūtāre).
8. puerī in agrō diū (manēre); tandem Quīntus et Horātia domum (īre)

EXERCISE 10.7

Translate into Latin

1. Quintus and Horatia were going to school.
2. But on the way they stayed and played with a friend, who was exercising his dog.
3. When they approached the school, the master was standing near the door.
4. He watched them and said, "Why are you coming late?"
5. Quintus laughed and said, "We are not coming late."
6. The master was angry. He told (= ordered) them to go in at once.
7. When he dismissed the other children, he told them to stay and write their letters again.

ELECTIONS

A letter survives in which Quintus Cicero advises his brother Marcus—who is soon to feature in our story—on how to conduct his election campaign. Here is some of what he says:

> A campaign for election to a magistracy can be divided into two kinds of activity: firstly to gain the support of one's friends, secondly to win the good will of the people. The support of one's friends should be secured by kindness done and repaid, by long-standing acquaintance and by a charming and friendly nature. But the word "friend" has a wider application in an election campaign than in the rest of life. Anyone who shows any sympathy towards you, who pays attention to you, who frequents your house, should be reckoned among your "friends".... It is necessary to have friends of every kind: for the sake of appearance, make friends with men who are distinguished in rank and title. These, though they may not actively support the campaign, none the less confer some prestige upon the candidate... You should have knowledge of people's names, winning manners, persistence, generosity, reputation and confidence in your public program... You badly need to use flattery, which, though disgraceful in the rest of one's life, is essential while electioneering.... All men naturally prefer you to lie to them than to refuse them your aid.... To make a promise is not definite; it allows postponement, and affects only a few people.
>
> (Quintus Cicero, *ad Marcum* 16, 18, 41–2, 45–8)

This frieze of senators is from the lefthand side of the Altar of Peace (the Ara Pacis) which was set up in Rome on the Campus Martius on the banks of the Tiber in honor of Augustus' return from Spain and Gaul in 13 BC. It was dedicated on January 30, 9 BC.

Chapter 11

Quīntus Rōmam aduenit

Grammar: the pluperfect tense; more perfect stems and the meaning of the perfect; numerals 1–10; expressions of time and place; locative case

---

PATTERN SENTENCES

These introduce the pluperfect tense (had) and exercise the imperfect and perfect.

COMMENTARY

l.3 *mīliārium*: "milestone"; all the main roads in Italy had milestones giving the distance to Rome. Quintus and Flaccus were walking on the Via Appia, which went from Rome to Brundisium. Their whole journey from Venusia to Rome was about 240 miles, and so at this stage on the fifth day they had covered less than half at the rate of about 20 miles a day. Later in his life Horace actually made the journey from Rome to Brundisium, a distance of 374 miles (see *Satire* 5, and Chapter 26)

R|V **Roman milestone:** this milestone, set up by Augustus, is from the Via Aemilia which was constructed from Placentia to Ariminum in 187 BC. *See page 51 in* Oxford Latin Course, College Edition: Readings and Vocabulary.

l.4 *centum mīlia passuum*: a Roman mile was 1,000 paces. Note that *mīlia* is a third declension noun, hence *mīlle passūs* (a thousand paces) = one mile (*mīlle* is an adjective) but *duo mīlia passuum* (two thousand of paces) = two miles.

ll.4 & 5 *contendimus...trānsiimus*: we have walked....we have crossed: the first examples of the "perfect with have," which is always used of past action in a present context: *Roma abest...fessus sum.*

l.7 *fortis estō*: be brave: remember that *estō* is the imperative of *sum.*

l.9 *ad portās*: the Via Appia led to the Porta Appia, which was about two miles from the city center.

l.14 *Via Sacra*: the Sacred Way went through the Forum and wound up to the Capitol, which was crowned by the great temple of Jupiter Optimus Maximus.

l.17 *templum Vestae*: the first building you saw on your left as you entered the Forum was the temple of Vesta, godddess of the hearth. This housed the sacred fire, said to have been brought by Aeneas to Italy from Troy; it symbolized the life of the city and was tended by the Vestal Virgins, six girls chosen by the Pontifex Maximus (High Priest), who served a minimum of 30 years. N.B.: *ubi* = where.

[R][V] **The Temple of Vesta:** this circular building, originally with twenty Corinthian columns, was reconstituted to its present appearance in 1930. *See page 52 in* Oxford Latin Course, College Edition: Readings and Vocabulary.

l.18 *Basilica Aemilia*: a basilica was a rectangular building divided into naves by columns, like a church. There were several in Rome; the Basilica Aemilia had been completed in 50 BC. It was used as a law court. There were various permanent criminal courts, each dealing with a different type of case; each was presided over by one of the praetors with a jury of 30 or more drawn from the top two property classes (senators and knights). Barristers (*patrōnī*) for defense and prosecution pleaded their case before the jury, which gave its verdict by a majority vote. The presiding praetor then fixed the penalty. Cicero was at this time the most prominent advocate.

l.19 *rōstra*: the speakers' platform. The old rostra stood in front of the *cūria* (the senate house), adjoining the *comitia*, an open space 300 feet wide where the people met. It was replaced while Quintus was in Rome by the new rostra, begun by Julius Caesar and completed by Augustus. This was 10 feet high, 80 feet long, and 40 feet deep. From this platform senior magistrates addressed the people on any matter of current political importance and proposed laws, which had to be passed by a full meeting of the assembly.

l.20 *cūria*: the old senate house had been burnt down in 52 BC during the riot which followed the murder of Clodius, a popular revolutionary tribune of the people. In 44 BC, Julius Caesar started a new senate house, substantial remains of which still stand. While there was no senate house, the senate met at various venues, including the Theatre of Pompey, where Julius Caesar was murdered.

l.25 *lūdum Orbilī*: Orbilius is a historical figure and Horace did go to his school; see *Epistles* 2.1.69–71:

> carmina Līuī
> ...meminī quae plāgōsum mihi paruō
> Orbilium dictāre.

(the poems of Livius which I remember flogger Orbilius dictated to me when I was small).

Suetonius (*De Grammaticis* 9) says that Orbilius had been born in Beneventum and after serving in the army came to Rome to teach; here he taught *maiōre fāmā quam ēmolumentō* (with a greater reputation than salary). Livius Andronicus, at the height of his powers around 240 BC, was the first Latin poet to write poetry based on Greek models; he wrote comedies, tragedies, and a translation of the *Odyssey*.

l.29 *Subūram*: the Subura lay north of the Forum, a poor and overcrowded district with many *īnsulae*, blocks of flats often five or six stories high, jerry-built and liable to collapse.

l.33 *togam praetextam*: this was a toga with a purple border, worn only by senior magistrates and boys up to the time when they received the *toga uirīlis*, a plain white toga.

l.46 *cēnāculum*: this word oiginally meant an upstairs dining room but later an attic or garret. It was in such garrets that poor people lived. They were very inconvenient and dangerous because of the risk of fire.

RV **A Roman tenement:** this reconstruction shows a block of flats (*īnsula*, literally "island") on the Via dei Balconi at Ostia, the harbor of ancient Rome. It is characteristic of its kind. There are shops on the ground floor and rooms with windows on the first floor. At the second floor level is a projecting balcony. *See page 53 in* Oxford Latin Course, College Edition: Readings and Vocabulary.

Word-building

Learn the following compounds of *sum, esse, fuī*

absum, abesse, āfuī	I am away from, am absent
adsum, adesse, adfuī	I am present
dēsum, dēesse, dēfuī + dat.	I fail
īnsum, inesse, īnfuī + dat.	I am in
intersum, interesse, interfuī	I am among, take part in
prōsum, prōdesse, prōfuī + dat.	I benefit
supersum, superesse, superfuī	I am left over, survive

Note the tendency of compounds of **sum** to be followed by the dative.

GRAMMAR

The Pluperfect Tense

e.g. **parāu-eram** = I had prepared

The tense is used to represent a past action or event which precedes another past action or event, e.g.

nox iam <u>uēnerat</u> cum Rōmam intrāuērunt. Night <u>had come</u> already when they entered Rome.

(Both events are in the past but night had fallen before they entered Rome.)

ubi Horātia domum rediit, Scintilla ad forum iam <u>prōcesserat</u>.

When Horatia returned home, Scintilla had already gone on to the forum.

The tense is formed by adding the following endings to the perfect stem:

-eram	I had	-erāmus	we had
-erās	you (*sing.*) had	-erātis	you (*pl.*) had
-erat	he/she had	-erant	they had

(These endings are the same as those of the imperfect of **sum**)

	1st parō	2nd moneō	3rd regō	3rd -iō capiō	4th audiō	sum
Perfect stem	parāu-	monu-	rēx-	cēp-	audīu-	fu-
Pluperfect	parāu- eram	monu- eram	rēx-eram	cēp-eram	audīu- eram	fu-eram

---

EXERCISE 11.1

Give the pluperfect tense of **dīcō** *(all persons) and translate each form.*

EXERCISE 11.2

Match up the following verb forms to the translations below

ēmerant, uīcimus, prōmitte, lēgerāmus, discessit, abesse, flēbat, relīquerat, init, studuimus, iniit, frēgistī, ēgimus, clauserātis, relinquit

he/she entered, we have conquered, we did, to be absent, they had bought, he/she had left, we studied, he/she was weeping, he/she is entering, you had shut, promise!, we had read, he/she departed, you broke, he/she leaves.

EXERCISE 11.3

Translate

1. Flaccus in summō colle* stābat cum moenia Rōmae uīdit.
2. nox iam uēnerat cum Flaccus Quīntum in urbem dūxit.
3. ubi ad mediam urbem* uēnērunt, in forō diū manēbant; aedificia tam splendida numquam uīderant.
4. Flaccus tabellārium (*the postman*) quaerēbat; epistolam ad Scintillam scrīpserat.
5. Scintilla laeta erat; tandem Flaccus epistolam mīserat.
6. māter Horātiam uocāuit, quae in hortum exierat.
7. Horātia tamen extrā casam manēbat: Argus in uiam fūgerat.
8. sed tandem casam intrāuit: Argus reuēnerat.

*Note the idioms *summus collis* = the top of the hill and *media urbs* = the middle of the city.

GRAMMAR

Perfect Stems

Learn the principal parts 2a, 2b and 2c from the Reference Grammar on page 317. Again, now you must learn the fourth principal part (the supine), the use of which will be explained later.

EXERCISE 11.4

Put the following verb forms into corresponding forms of the perfect

1. dēfendimus
2. cōnstituunt
3. uertit
4. ostendō
5. incendis
6. dīcunt
7. augeō
8. sumus
9. persuādet
10. lūdunt

GRAMMAR

Numerals

Learn the following

cardinals			ordinals		
ūnus, ūna, ūnum	I	one	**prīmus, -a, -um**	first
duo, duae, duo	II	two	**secundus, -a, -um**	second
trēs, **tria**	III	three	**tertius, -a, -um**	third
quattuor	IV	four	**quārtus, -a, -um**	fourth
quīnque	V	five	**quīntus, -a, -um**	fifth
sex	VI	six	**sextus, -a, -um**	sixth
septem	VII	seven	**septimus, -a, -um**	seventh
octō	VIII	eight	**octāuus, -a, -um**	eighth
nouem	IX	nine	**nōnus, -a, -um**	ninth
decem	X	ten	**decimus, -a, -um**	tenth

The *ordinal* numbers (first, second, third, etc.) all decline like **bonus, bona, bonum**. Numerals 4 (**quattuor**) to 100 (**centum**) do not decline. For numerals 11–2,000 see Reference Grammar, pp. 301–303.

The Romans wrote their numerals I, II, III, etc. How does IX come to mean 9? They had no sign for zero; what problems would this cause in arithmetic?

	m.	f.	n.
nom.	ūnus	ūna	ūnum
gen.	ūnīus	ūnīus	ūnīus
dat.	ūnī	ūnī	ūnī
acc.	ūnum	ūnam	ūnum
abl.	ūnō	ūnā	ūnō
	m.	f.	n.
nom.	duo	duae	duo
gen.	duōrum	duārum	duōrum
dat.	duōbus	duābus	duōbus
acc.	duo/duōs	duās	duo
abl.	duōbus	duābus	duōbus

	m. f.	n.	
nom.	trēs	tria	
gen.	trium	trium	
dat.	tribus	tribus	
acc.	trēs	tria	
abl.	tribus	tribus	

ūnus declines like **ille** in gen. and dat. sing.; **trēs** declines like the plural of **omnis**.
Learn **uīgintī** = 20

30, 40, etc. are easily recognized by the termination **-gintā: trī-gintā, quadrā-gintā,** etc.

Learn **centum** = 100

200, 300, etc. are easily recognized by the termination **-centī: du-centī, -ae, -a;
tre-centī, -ae, -a**, etc.; these decline like the plural of **bonus**.

Learn **mīlle** = 1,000

duo mīlia = 2,000, **tria mīlia** = 3,000, etc.

N.B.: mīlle = 1,000

But **mīlia** is a neuter plural noun, e.g. **duo mīlia passuum** = "2,000 of paces" =
two miles.

Expressions of Time

Duration of time, saying *how long* an action or event lasts, is expressed by the *accusative*
case, e.g.

> **trēs hōrās ambulābāmus.** We were walking *for three hours*
> **sex annōs manēbāmus.** We stayed *for six years.*

Time when, saying *at what time* an action or event took place, is expressed by the
ablative case, e.g.

> **prīmā lūce domō discessērunt.** They left home *at dawn.*
> **septimō annō domum rediimus.** *In the seventh year* we returned home.

The ablative is also used to express the time *within which* something happens, e.g.

> **tribus hōrīs domum rediit.** He returned home *within three hours.*

In the following exercise we shall use **diēs** = "day"; this noun belongs to the fifth
or **-e-** declension (remember that you learnt this in Chapter 7: it's on pp. 296–7): acc.
sing. **diem,** abl. sing. **diē,** acc. plural **diēs,** abl. plural **diēbus.**

Translate

1. Quīntus paterque trēs diēs ad iter sē parābant; quārtō diē discessērunt.
2. prīmā lūce Flaccus surrēxit Quīntumque excitāuit.
3. tertiā hōrā Scintillam Horātiamque ualēre iussērunt iterque iniērunt.
4. nouem diēs in uiā Appiā contendēbant; decem diēbus urbem Rōmam adiērunt.
5. posterō diē ad forum festīnāuērunt et trēs hōrās ibi manēbant.

GRAMMAR

The Meanings of the Perfect Tense

parāuī usually means "I prepared" (*simple past tense*) but it can also mean "I have prepared." This we call the *perfect with have* or the *true perfect*.

There is nothing in the verb form to tell you which meaning is intended, but the context will usually make this clear, since the *perfect with have* occurs only in present contexts, e.g.

quīnque diēs <u>contendērunt</u> sed Rōma adhūc longē <u>abest</u>.
<u>They have walked</u> for five days but Rome <u>is</u> still far away.

<u>nōlī</u> timēre, fīlī; lupus <u>abiit</u>. <u>Don't</u> be afraid, son; the wolf <u>has gone away</u>.

Translate the following, making sure that you translate all perfect tenses appropriately, choosing between the two possible meanings

1. in uiā Appiā ambulābam; subitō lupum uīdī.
2. pater dīxit; "nōlī timēre, fīlī; lupus abiit."
3. nouem diēs contendēbāmus; decimō diē urbem intrāuimus.
4. pater "gaudē, fīlī," inquit; "iter cōnfectum est."
5. Flaccus epistolam ad Scintillam scrīpsit: "incolumēs sumus. Rōmam intrāuimus; lūdum Orbiliī spectāuimus."
6. māter ānxia erat: nam fīlius domō aberat. "ānxia sum," inquit; "trēs hōrās fīlium exspectō, sed ille domum nōn rediit."
7. tandem quīntā hōrā noctis puer rediit. māter īrāta erat.
8. "ō fīlī," inquit, "cūr tam sērō rediistī? quattuor hōrās tē exspectāuī. quīntā hōrā tandem rediistī."
9. puer respondit: "cum amīcīs duās hōrās lūdēbam. deinde domum festīnāuī."
10. ecce! tertiā hōrā noctis rediī. nōlī tē uexāre."

EXERCISE 11.7

Match up the English translations below with the following Latin verb forms

1. studuit
2. mānsistī
3. monuimus
4. trānsīre
5. dīc
6. possunt
7. erāmus
8. dēfendistī
9. dīxērunt
10. dīcēbas
11. mīsit
12. mittit
13. contendī
14. prōmīsistī
15. cōnstituērunt

we were, he/she sent, I marched, they have decided, he/she studied, to cross, he/she sends, you defended, we warned, you promised, say!, they can, they said, you have stayed, you used to say

GRAMMAR

Expressions of Place

ad urbem **festīnāuērunt.** They hurried <u>to the city.</u>
But **Rōmam** **festīnāuērunt.** They hurried <u>to Rome.</u>

ab urbe **discessērunt.** They went away <u>from the city.</u>
But **Rōmā** **discessērunt.** They went away <u>from Rome.</u>

The names of cities and towns do not have a preposition in expressions of *motion to* or *from* a place. The *accusative* case is used to express *motion towards* and the *ablative* to express *motion from*.

The same applies to **domus:**

domum rediērunt. They returned (to) home.
domō discessērunt. They left (from) home.

Note that prepositions are only omitted with the names of *towns* and the word **domus**.

Names of countries require prepositions, e.g.

ille senex ad Italiam nāuigāuit Rōmamque festīnāuit.
That old man sailed to Italy and hurried to Rome.

Quīntus ad Graeciam nāuigāuit, Flaccus Venusiam rediit.
Quintus sailed to Greeece, Flaccus returned to Venusia.

The Locative Case

You have met **dom-ī** = "at home." This is called the *locative* case, expressing *place where*; e.g. **domī manēbat; domī** tells you where he stayed.

All names of towns and cities can form a locative case.

The names of places have various forms, singular and plural, e.g.

nominative		*locative*	
Rōma	(1st decl. sing.)	**Rōmae**	at/in Rome
Athēnae	(1st decl. plural)	**Athēnīs**	at/in Athens
Corinthus	(2nd decl. sing.)	**Corinthī**	at/in Corinth
Londinium	(2nd decl. n. sing.)	**Londiniī**	at/in London
Puteolī	(2nd decl. plural)	**Puteolīs**	at Puteoli

The locative is the same in form as the genitive for place names of the 1st and 2nd declensions singular, the same as the ablative for those which are plural.

A few place names are 3rd declension and have locatives in ablative form whether singular or plural:

Carthāgō	(3rd decl. sing.)	**Carthāgine**	at Carthage
Gādēs	(3rd decl. plural)	**Gādibus**	at Cadiz

EXERCISE 11.8

In the following sentences translate the names of the towns only into the correct Latin case
1. We stayed a week in Capua.
2. We then travelled to Cumae.
3. We stayed two nights in Cumae.
4. On the next day we departed from Cumae.
5. We stayed in Antium a few days.
6. Finally we returned to Rome.

EXERCISE 11.9

Translate

1. Aenēās Trōiae nātus est (*was born*).
2. ubi Graecī Trōiānōs uīcērunt, comitēs ad Siciliam dūxit.
3. Trōiānī ad Italiam nāuigābant cum tempestās eōs ad Libyam ēgit.
4. Aenēās diū Carthāgine cum Dīdōne manēbat.
5. tandem Iuppiter eum iussit ad Italiam nāuigāre.
6. itaque Carthāgine discessit comitēsque Puteolōs dūxit.

EXERCISE 11.10

Translate into Latin

1. Flaccus and Quintus left home, but Scintilla and Horatia stayed in Venusia.
2. Father and son marched to Rome; within ten days they had reached (**peruenió ad**) the city.
3. Their journey had been long and difficult.
4. They stayed in Rome for seven years; then Flaccus decided to return home.
5. Flaccus returned to Venusia; Quintus left Italy and sailed to Athens.
6. Quintus stayed in Athens for a long time.

ROME

Rome was built on the left bank of the river Tiber about 16 miles from where it flows into the sea. A small island in the river breaks up the strong current here and the water is shallow and easy to ford. A bridge to this island, the Pons Fabricius, had been built by Horace's time (in 62 BC). This is still standing and is in fact used by traffic. Rome's control of this part of the Tiber was of great importance since anyone traveling along the western side of Italy would almost certainly cross the river at this point. Thus Rome became a key center for inland trade. Dangerous shoals in the river for a long time stopped Ostia, the port at the mouth of the Tiber, from becoming as important a harbor as the more distant Puteoli near Naples. But Rome was still able to engage in a flourishing trade abroad.

The famous seven hills of the city, especially the rocky Capitoline hill, made it comparatively safe from attack. The Roman orator and politician Cicero, who is soon to enter our story, praised the city's natural strength:

> Romulus and the other Roman kings showed great wisdom in laying out
> the course of the wall along a line of hills which are high and sheer at every
> point. The one approach, which is between the Esquiline and Quirinal
> hills, is protected by a huge rampart and ditch. The Capitoline hill is so
> well fortified by its steep walls of rock that, even in the terrible time when
> the Gauls invaded, it remained safe and undamaged. The place chosen by
> Romulus is in addition plentifully supplied with springs, and even if the
> surrounding marshes are a breeding-ground for malaria, Rome is in fact a
> healthy site. For the hills channel the breezes and give shade to the valleys.
>
> (*De Republica* 2.11)

The forum, through which Quintus and his father walk along the Sacred Way, was certainly no longer the humble marketplace which it had once been. Bankers and moneylenders had replaced the shopkeepers and it was now the busy heart of city life. Rome had almost a million inhabitants in Horace's day and it became a city of the greatest splendor. The first emperor, Augustus, boasted that he had found it brick and left it marble (Suetonius, *Augustus* 28.3). But many squalid areas remained and Horace and his father find a room in one of these, the Subura.

This poor, overcrowded district lay between the Viminal and Esquiline hills. It was such a slum that Augustus, the first emperor, had a wall more than a hundred feet high built in his forum to stop it being seen. Here there were many high-rise blocks of flats of up to four or five stories. In Horace's time a height limit of 60 feet was enforced, but even so, as the poet Juvenal wrote, these overcrowded, poorly built structures were liable to collapse:

> We live in a city largely held up by thin props, for that is how the estate
> agent supports the tottering house. And when he plasters over the gaping
> cracks on the long-neglected wall, he tells the occupants not to worry and
> to sleep soundly, though the place is about to crash down.

or to burn:

> If there is a fire panic at the bottom of the stairs, the furthest tenant will
> go up in smoke, the one who is only protected from the rain by tiles where
> the soft doves lay their eggs.
>
> (Juvenal 3.193–202)

The satirical poet no doubt exaggerates, but he is surely communicating a basic truth.

A bend in the Tiber enclosed the Campus Martius (Field of Mars), on the other side of the Capitoline hill, to the northwest. This was a huge open space used for military and athletic exercises. The theater of Pompey was nearby, the first stone theater in Rome. This was completed in 55 BC and could seat an audience of 9,000 to 10,000. Plays both comic and tragic were performed here. The huge Circus Maximus stood between the Palatine and Aventine hills. Here chariot races took place for the amusement of a vast and uncritical audience. The taste of the average Roman was for the violent, sensational and crude.

In this photograph of the Roman forum, the temple of Castor, orginally built in 484 BC, is on the right and the arch of Titus, erected in 81 AD, is right of center.

Grammar: more perfect endings; *ferō*; uses of the ablative case

---

VOCABULARY

nēmō, nūllīus, c.: remember that c. stands for common, i.e. either masculine or feminine. Note also that *nēmō* borrows its genitive and ablative from *nūllus.*

COMMENTARY

Orbilius was a *grammaticus,* his school a "grammar" school, which provided the second stage of Roman education. Grammar in the strict sense was taught, but the main part of the syllabus was the study of Greek and Roman literature. So Horace says (*Epistles* 2.2.41–2):

> Rōmae nūtrīrī mihi contigit atque docērī
> īrātus Grāīs quantum nocuisset Achillēs.

(It was my good fortune to be reared in Rome and to be taught how much the anger of Achilles harmed the Greeks).

That is to say he studied the *Iliad* at school in Rome.

In the course of studying Greek and Roman literature, students would have learned a good deal of history, geography, rhetoric and philosophy, but there was no sort of scientific education. The English grammar schools, mostly founded after the Reformation (sixteenth century), took over the system, which remained virtually unchanged until the Grammar School Act of 1840.

l.3 *partēs paedagōgī*: the sons of wealthy Romans would be accompanied to school by a *paedagōgus* (guardian), who would carry their books and watch over them. Flaccus performed this function for Quintus: see Horace, *Satires* 1.6.81–2:

ipse mihī custōs incorruptissimus omnēs
circum doctōrēs aderat.

(He himself was always there round all my teachers, a most incorruptible guardian.)

ll.11–12 Lucius Tarquinius Superbus was traditionally the last king of Rome (534–510 BC), driven out (after his son Sextus had raped Lucretia) by Brutus, an ancestor of the assassin of Julius Caesar. Hannibal, the greatest leader of the Carthaginians, came close to destroying Rome in the Second Punic War (218–201 BC). Though he spent most of the war in Italy and inflicted terrible defeats on the Romans, he was eventually conquered at the Battle of Zama in Africa. In 1985, over 2,000 years later, the Mayors of Carthage and Rome signed a peace treaty, committing the two cities to an "exchange of knowledge and the establishment of common information, cultural and artistic programs."

l.15 *librum Graecē scrīptum*: Orbilius is amazed that Quintus cannot read Greek. All educated Romans were to some extent bilingual. Wealthy Romans kept a Greek tutor at home so that children would learn Greek from an early age.

l.24 *barbarus est*: the Greeks used this word to describe any people who could not speak Greek and made a noise which sounded like "barbarbar."

l.25 *rīdēbant*: began to laugh: inceptive use of the imperfect (i.e. starting to do something).

l.33 *puer quīdam*: this boy turns out to be Marcus Cicero, the son of the famous orator and statesman. Their meeting and subsequent friendship is pure fiction. They were exact contemporaries; both were later at university at Athens at the same time; both served in the army of Brutus at Philippi in 42 BC. But there is no evidence that they ever met.

RV **A Roman boy with his teacher:** this relief is from the Louvre Museum, Paris. It is part of the frieze on p. 34 above. *See page 57 in* Oxford Latin Course, College Edition: Readings and Vocabulary.

Word-building

Learn the following compounds of **dō, dare, dedī**

addō, addere, addidī	I add
condō, condere, condidī	I found
crēdō, crēdere, crēdidī	I believe, trust
dēdō, dēdere, dēdidī	I give up, surrender
perdō, perdere, perdidī	I lose, waste
prōdō, prōdere, prōdidī	I betray
reddō, reddere, reddidī	I give back, return
trādō, trādere, trādidī	I hand over, betray

EXERCISE 12.1

Translate

1. ad agrum contendēbāmus; in uiā Gāium uīdimus.
2. Gāius arborem ascendēbat; ubi eum uocāuī, celeriter dēscendit.
3. Gāius nōbīscum contendit; ubi agrum intrāuimus, ego patrem eī ostendī.
4. pater nōs audīuit; sē uertit Gāiumque salūtāuit.
5. omnēs in agrō diū labōrābāmus.
6. tandem fessī erāmus; cōnstituimus domum redīre.

Note: the stem of **ēo** *is* **i-***; hence infinitive* **ī-re***, imperfect* **ī-bam***, perfect* **i-ī***. This verb is most commonly found in compounds.*

GRAMMAR

More Perfect Stems

Learn the principal parts from the Reference Grammar 3a on p. 317 (verbs that lengthen the vowel of the present stem).

The following verbs from the 1st, 2nd and 4th conjugations lengthen the vowel in the perfect in the same way. They must be learned as well.

1st conjugation	**iuuō, iuuāre, iūuī, iūtum**	I help
	lauō, lauāre, lāuī, lautum	I wash
2nd conjugation	**sedeō, sedēre, sēdī, sessum**	I sit
	uideō, uidēre, uīdī, uīsum	I see
	caueō, cauēre, cāuī, cautum	I beware
	faueō, fauēre, fāuī, fautum + dat.	I favor
	foueō, fouēre, fōuī, fōtum	I cherish, look after
	moueō, mouēre, mōuī, mōtum	I move
4th conjugation	**sentiō, sentīre, sēnsī, sēnsum**	I feel
	ueniō, uenīre, uēnī, uentum	I come

EXERCISE 12.2

Translate the following verb forms

1. lauāmus
2. lāuimus
3. uēnit
4. uenit
5. ēmīsistis
6. relinquunt
7. relīquērunt
8. uidēmus
9. uīdimus
10. sedēbāmus
11. sēdimus
12. sedēmus
13. uīcistī
14. lēgī
15. legō
16. cēpērunt
17. iēcistī
18. fugit
19. fūgimus
20. fēcī

GRAMMAR

ferō

Learn the verb **ferō, ferre, tulī** = I carry, bear. The present is irregular.

fer-ō	*imperatives:* **fer**	
fers		**ferte**
fert		
ferimus	*infinitive:* **ferre**	
fertis		
ferunt		

It has no perfect; it uses forms from another stem (**tul-**).

Word-building

Learn the following compounds of **ferō**, **ferre**, **tulī** I carry, bear:

afferō (=adferō), afferre, attulī	I carry to, report
auferō (=abferō), auferre, abstulī	I carry away
cōnferō, cōnferre, cōntulī	I carry together
efferō, efferre, extulī	I carry out
īnferō, īnferre, intulī	I carry into, carry against
prōferō, prōferre, prōtulī	I carry forwards, bring out
referō, referre, rettulī	I carry back, report

EXERCISE 12.3

Translate the following verb forms.

1. ascenderant
2. iaciēbat
3. tulistī
4. cēpī
5. ferre
6. fēcerātis
7. fer
8. cecidit
9. tulerat
10. fertis
11. cucurrimus
12. dederant
13. uīcī
14. stetimus
15. parāuerāmus

GRAMMAR

Uses of the Ablative Case

The ablative has a wide variety of meanings: *by, with, from, at, in, on.* We here summarize the commonest usages, which are already familiar to you:

1 from; the ablative can express *separation from* a place or thing, usually with a preposition, e.g.

ab urbe uēnit	he came from the city
ē siluā cucurrit	he ran out of the wood
dē monte dēscendit	he came down from the mountain
Rōmā discessit	he departed from Rome
domō festīnāuit	he hurried from home
forō longē aberat	he was a long way from the forum

So after some verbs and adjectives expressing *separation from*, e.g.

mē cūrā liberāuit	he freed me from care
fēminae līberae cūrā	women free from care
moenia dēfēnsōribus uacua	walls empty of defenders

2 at/in/on: the ablative can express *place where*, usually with a preposition, e.g.

in forō stābat	he was standing in the forum
sub arbore dormiēbat	she was sleeping under a tree
terrā marīque pugnābant	they fought on land and sea

3 at/on: the ablative is used to express *time when*, e.g.

prīmā lūce discessērunt	they departed at dawn
quīntō diē rediērunt	they returned on the fifth day

and *time within which*, e.g.

tribus diēbus rediit	he returned within three days

Note also:

multīs post annīs	many years after (literally: "afterwards by many years")
paucīs ante diēbus	a few days before

EXERCISE 12.4

Translate

1. ubi Quīntus Flaccusque domō discessērunt, Scintilla Horātiaque Venusiae manēbant.
2. cotīdiē prīmā hōrā diēī surgēbant diūque in agrō labōrābant; uespere domum rediērunt, ualdē fessae.
3. Scintilla rārō (*rarely*) cūrīs lībera erat sed numquam spem dēposuit.
4. paucīs post diēbus ab agrō redierat et in casā quiēscēbat cum tabellārius (*the postman*) epistolam eī trādidit.
5. Flaccus enim tandem epistolam Rōmā mīserat. Rōmam cum fīliō sine perīculō aduēnerat. haec epistola Scintillam magnā ānxietāte līberāuit.

EXERCISE 12.5

Translate into Latin

1. Quintus was hurrying to school with his father.
2. Flaccus was carrying his son's books in his hands.
3. When they reached the school, Orbilius was waiting for them outside the door on the steps.
4. He looked at them with a severe expression.
5. "Why have you arrived late, Quintus?" he said. "You must write fifty verses."

GREECE AND ROME

Why is it so important that Quintus master the Greek language? You will remember that, according to legend, when the Greeks captured and sacked the city of Troy, Aeneas and his men fled from its smouldering ruins. They established themselves in Italy after many struggles and hardships, intermarried with Italians and founded the Roman race. The Romans established their rule over the whole of Greece in 197 BC. It was a kind of revenge for the defeat which their legendary ancestors had suffered a thousand years before. But the victors were in fact not at all vindictive. The Roman general declared at the Games at Corinth the following year that all Greek states were now free and independent. The enthusiastic shouting of the liberated peoples was so loud that the birds flying overhead are said to have fallen to the ground stunned (Valerius Maximus, 4.8.5).

The Romans' attitude to the Greeks was strangely mixed in Horace's day. On the one hand, they despised the present weakness of a nation which had driven huge forces of invading Persians from their native soil five centuries before, and more recently had conquered the known world under Alexander the Great. On the other hand, they enormously admired their great art and literature. Educated Romans aimed to be bilingual, speaking both Greek and Latin, and Quintus was expected to do the same. When he later sails to Athens to complete his education in Greek philosophy, he makes a journey that many Romans had made before him.

The Parthenon: this painting of the Parthenon on the Acropolis at Athens, with Greeks in their national costume, is by Ippolito Caffi and dates from 1863. To the left are the ruins of the Erechtheum, the building of which was completed in 406 BC. (Museo d'Arte Moderna di Ca' Pesaro, Venice)

The extraordinary intellectual and creative inventiveness of the Greeks dazzled the Romans. Their discoveries in mathematics (Pythagoras), geometry (Euclid), astronomy (Ptolemy), science (Archimedes) and natural history (Aristotle), their mastery of the art of speaking (Demosthenes), their unrivalled architecture and sculpture (Pheidias, Praxiteles), their great philosophical tradition (Plato)—all seemed wonderful to the Roman nation.

It was perhaps in literature especially that the superiority of the Greeks lay. The poems of Homer; the tragic plays of Aeschylus, Sophocles and Euripides from the fifth century BC; the historical writings of "the father of history" Herodotus and of his successor Thucydides; and a whole treasury of lyric poetry—here was a great literary inheritance that gave the Romans everything to study and little to invent. So while Rome had captured Greece, Greece captivated Rome. As Horace himself put it: *Graecia capta ferum uictōrem cēpit* (captured Greece captured her wild conqueror, *Epistles* 2.1.156).

The Pont du Gard: this famous aqueduct brought water to the city of Nîmes in the South of France from the mountains 25 miles away. Where it crosses the valley of the River Gard, it is built on a triple arcade to a height of 180 feet above the river.

However, the Romans still felt superior, even while they admired. They had their feet firmly planted on the ground compared with the talented but unreliable Greeks. They rightly saw themselves as a practical and realistic race in contrast with their neighbors across the Adriatic. Their greatest building achievements were impressive but heavy feats of engineering. They brought concrete to the world. Their major achievement was not to create but to conquer and rule. In the *Aeneid*, Virgil puts in the mouth of Aeneas' father Anchises a fine statement of the world of difference that lay between the two nations:

> Others [i.e. the Greeks] will hammer out the bronze so that it breathes in softer lines, others will transform marble into living faces, will plead cases in the law courts with superior skill, will trace the movements of the planets with the rod and tell of the rising constellations. You, Roman, must bear in mind how to rule the peoples of the earth under your command (that will be your art), how to create peace and then impose civilization, how to spare those who submit and to beat down proud resisters.
>
> (*Aeneid* 6.847–53)

Chapter 13
Marcus Quīntum domum suam inuītat

Grammar: comparative and superlative adjectives and adverbs; more perfect stems

CARTOONS

Note that *maior* and *maximus* are comparative and superlative forms of *magnus* and *peior* and *pessimus* are comparative and superlative forms of *malus*.

COMMENTARY

l.6 *Tullia*: Cicero's beloved daughter died in February 45 BC at the age of thirty. Cicero was inconsolable.

l.9 *montem Palātīnum*: the Palatine hill, southwest of the Forum, was the most fashionable area of Rome.

l.11 *saluē*: imperative of *saluēō* = I am well; it only occurs in forms *saluē*, *saluēte*, used as a respectful greeting.

l.12 *scrībae*: Cicero's secretary was the freedman Tiro, who became a trusted friend of the family. After Cicero's death he collected and published Cicero's letters to his friends in 16 books; it is remarkable to reflect that he not only wrote fair copies of all the letters Cicero wrote for despatch but kept copies of them all.

R|V This imposing *ātrium* is in the House of Menander in Pompeii. This fine building belonged to a relative of the emperor Nero's wife Poppaea and was in the process of being redecorated when the city was destroyed by the eruption of Vesuvius in 79 AD. We look through the *ātrium* to the *tablīnum* (study) and then to the *peristȳlium* (inner courtyard) with its stuccoed columns. *See page 60 in* Oxford Latin Course, College Edition: Readings and Vocabulary.

l.22 *Atticum*: Titus Pomponius Atticus (109–32 BC) was Cicero's life-long friend. He was a wealthy *eques* (knight, the grade below senator), who took no part in politics and retired to Athens from 88 to 65 BC (hence his cognomen Atticus). His sister Pomponia was married to Cicero's younger brother Quintus. His multifarious business activities included banking (he looked after Cicero's financial affairs) and publishing (he published several of Cicero's books). Cicero relied greatly on his advice and sometimes wrote to him as often as twice a day, not only on politics, but on family affairs, finances and literature. Atticus collected Cicero's part of their correspondence after Cicero's death and published it in 16 books.

l.25 *cursōrī*: runner = courier, postman. Cicero would have sent his letters in Rome by his own slaves. Letters going abroad would have been carried by *tabellāriī*, freedmen or slaves employed by companies or groups of individuals for this purpose.

l.28 *uelim*: "I should like" (present subjunctive of *uolō*).

l.33 *tibi licet*: it is allowed for you = you may.

l.34 *bibliothēcam*: Cicero was very proud of his library, going to great lengths to obtain rare books and sometimes asking Atticus to have a copy made for him. Atticus, as a publisher, kept a group of copyists who wrote out the texts dictated by a secretary.

Word-building

Learn the following compounds of **pōnō, pōnere, posuī** I put, place

compōnō, compōnere, composuī	I put together, compose
dēpōnō, dēpōnere, dēposuī	I put down
dispōnō, dispōnere, disposuī	I put in different places, arrange
expōnō, expōnere, exposuī	I put out, explain
impōnō, impōnere, imposuī	I put into, put on
praepōnō, praepōnere, praeposuī	I put before, prefer
prōpōnō, prōpōnere, prōposuī	I put out, explain, propose
repōnō, repōnere, reposuī	I put back

GRAMMAR

The Comparison of Adjectives

Both English and Latin adjectives have three degrees of comparison, e.g.

	positive	*comparative*	*superlative*
English	brave	braver	bravest, very brave
Latin	**fortis**	**fortior**	**fortissimus**

The comparative is often used in comparing one thing with another, e.g.

The girl is braver than the boy.

puella fortior est quam puer. (Notice **quam** = than)

Most adjectives form the comparative by adding **-ior** and the superlative by adding **-issimus** to the stem, e.g.

long-us	**long-ior**	**long-issimus**
long	longer	longest, very long
trīst-is	**trīst-ior**	**trīst-issimus**
sad	sadder	saddest, very sad

EXERCISE 13.1

Form the comparative and superlative of the following adjectives
laetus, gravis, ingēns (stem: **ingent-**), **altus**

GRAMMAR

The comparative is a 3rd declension adjective (consonant stem: **-ior-**):

	singular		plural	
	m. & f.	**n**	**m. & f.**	**n**
nom.	fortior	fortius	fortiōrēs	fortiōra
gen.	fortiōris	fortiōris	fortiōrum	fortiōrum
dat.	fortiōrī	fortiōrī	fortiōribus	fortiōribus
acc.	fortiōrem	fortius	fortiōrēs	fortiōra
abl.	fortiōre	fortiōre	fortiōribus	fortiōribus

The superlative adjective declines like **bonus: fortissim-us, fortissim-a, fortissim-um**

A few common adjectives have irregular comparison; learn:

bonus	good	**melior**	better	**optimus**	best, very good
malus	bad	**peior**	worse	**pessimus**	worst, very bad
magnus	big	**maior**	bigger	**maximus**	biggest, very big
multus	much, many	**plūs***	more	**plūrimus**	most, very many
paruus	small	**minor**	smaller	**minimus**	smallest, very small

*****plūs** in the singular is a neuter noun, declining: **plūs, plūris, plūrī, plūs, plūre;** so **plūs uīnī** = more (of) wine. In the plural it is a 3rd declension adjective (consonant stem: **plūr-**); so **plūrēs fēminae** = more women.

The Use of **quam** = than

Marcus fortior est quam Quintus. Marcus is stronger than Quintus.

numquam iuuenem fortiōrem uīdī quam Marcum. I have never seen a young man stronger than Marcus.

When **quam** is used, the two things compared are the same case.

EXERCISE 13.2

Translate

1. numquam puellam prūdentiōrem uīdī quam Horātiam.
2. ego multīs puellīs occurrī prūdentiōribus quam Horātiae.
3. errās; Horātia multō (*much*) prūdentiōr est quam cēterae.
4. nēmō fortior fuit quam Achillēs.
5. nōn tibi crēdō; mūltōs uirōs uīdī fortiōrēs quam Achillem.
6. errās; Achillēs fortissimus erat omnium hērōum.

GRAMMAR

Ablative of Comparison

When **quam** (than) is not used, the object of comparison (i.e. the word after "than" in English) is in the ablative:

sorōre meā ingeniōsior sum.
I am more talented than my sister.

EXERCISE 13.3

*Look at Exercise 13.2 again. For numbers 1, 3 and 5, write down what the object of comparison would be if **quam** were not there*

Irregular Superlatives

Adjectives ending in **-er** in the nominative double the **r** to form the superlative, e.g.

celer, celerior, celerrimus
miser, miserior, miserrimus
pulcher, pulchrior, pulcherrimus

The following adjectives ending **-ilis** double the **l** to form the superlative

facilis, facilior, facillimus
difficilis, difficilior, difficillimus

The Comparison of Adverbs

fortiter	bravely
fortius	more bravely
fortissimē	very bravely

The accusative neuter of the comparative adjective is used as the comparative adverb:

fortior = braver; **fortius** = more bravely.

The superlative adverb is formed by changing the ending of the superlative adjective **-us** to **-ē**:

fortissimus = very brave; **fortissimē** = very bravely.

EXERCISE 13.4

Form adverbs from the following adjectives and give their comparative and superlative

lentus, longus, bonus, facilis (*adverb*: facile), miser

Irregular Comparison

ADJ	ADVERB	COMPARATIVE ADVERB	SUPERLATIVE ADVERB
multus	**multum**	**plūs**	**plūrimum**
magnus	**magnopere**	**magis**	**maximē**

Note the comparison of the following adverbs:

diū, diūtius, diūtissimē
saepe, saepius, saepissimē

Note also the use of **quam** with the superlative:

quam celerrimē = as quickly as possible; **quam maximus** = as large as possible
quam prīmum = as soon as possible

EXERCISE 13.5

Translate

1. petauristae (*acrobats*) Venusiam aduēnerant; Scintilla Horātiam iussit sē quam celerrimē parāre.
2. ubi ad forum peruēnērunt, plūrimī hominēs iam concurrēbant. Scintilla locum uacuum difficillimē quaerēbat.
3. "festīnā, Horātia," inquit, "ad templī gradūs; optimum locum uideō unde omnia melius uidēre poterimus."
4. templī gradūs ascendērunt unde petauristās clārissimē uidēre poterant.
5. petauristae optimī erant; aliī per circulōs ardentēs (*burning hoops*) saliēbant, aliī per fūnēs (*ropes*) altōs ambulābant.
6. Scintilla "nihil spectāre mālō" inquit "quam petauristās."
7. Horātia "nēmō" inquit "fortior est illō petauristā, quī per fūnem altissimum ambulāuit."
8. diūtissimē petauristās spectābant. Scintilla "numquam" inquit "melius spectāculum uīdī quam hoc."
9. Horātia "cūr nōn saepius" inquit "Venusiam ueniunt petauristae?"
10. tandem uesper aderat; discessērunt hominēs. Horātia miserrima erat quod lūdī cōnfectī erant.

EXERCISE 13.6

Translate into Latin

1. Quintus no longer enjoyed his studies.
2. He was very miserable and very often wished to leave school.
3. At last his father said, "Quintus, why aren't you enjoying your studies more?"
4. Quintus replied, "All my friends have left school. I want to leave as soon as possible."
5. Flaccus said, "My son, you are no longer a boy, but a young man now. You must leave school and become a man."

GRAMMAR

More Perfect Stems

A number of verbs have reduplicated perfects, i.e. they form their perfect by putting before the present stem either the first letter of the stem + e (e.g. **dō, de-dī**) or the first syllable of the stem (e.g. **currō, cu-currī**).

Learn the principal parts of the reduplicating verbs (4a and 4b with the N.B.) on p. 318 of the Reference Grammar.

Note that most verbs drop reduplication in compounds, e.g.

currō, currere, cucurrī	I run
incurrō, incurrere, incurrī	I run into

but

compounds of **dō** and **stō** keep reduplication, e.g.

dō, dare, dedī	I give
stō, stāre, stetī	I stand
reddō, reddere, reddidī	I give back
īnstō, īnstāre, īnstitī	I threaten, pursue

EXERCISE 13.7

Translate the following verb forms

1. dabant
2. dedī
3. dā
4. dederant
5. dare
6. crēde
7. crēdidimus
8. crēdēbam
9. crēdō
10. crēdiderat
11. currēbant
12. cucurristī
13. currite
14. currimus
15. cucurrerātis

EXERCISE 13.8

Translate the following sentences

1. Horātia per siluam ambulābat; Argus domō discesserat; Horātia eum quaerēbat.
2. Terentius ab agrō redībat, cum puellae occurrit.
3. Terentius "quid facis, Horātia?" inquit; "cūr domō discessistī?"
4. Horātia "māter" inquit "mē mīsit. nam Argus in siluam cucurrit. diū eum quaerō."

5. Terentius "nolī tē uexāre," inquit; "sine dubiō Argus iam domum rediit."
6. domum ambulābant cum Horātia lāpsāuit (*slipped*) ceciditque ad terram.
7. puella clāmāuit; Argus eam audīuit cucurritque ē siluīs.
8. puella canem laeta salūtāuit sed "Arge," inquit, "cūr domō abiistī? malus canis es. mē ualdē uexāuistī."

EXERCISE 13.9

Put the verbs in parentheses in the correct forms and translate the sentences
1. Quīntus paterque ā forō iam (discēdere) et (prōcēdere) ad Subūram.
2. uiae sordidae (esse); ubīque hominēs hūc illūc (currere).
3. Quīntus patrem (rogāre): "quō (īre)? ubi domicilium quaerere dēbēmus?"
4. pater respondit, "nolī dēsperāre, filī. ad Subūram paene (aduenīre). illīc sine dubiō domicilium inuenīre (posse)."
5. mox Quīntus īnsulam (uidēre) cuius (*of which*) porta aperta (esse).
6. Flaccus filium in īnsulam (dūcere) iānitōremque (uocāre).
7. tandem iānitōrem (inuenīre); ille (dormīre); ēbrius erat; nam multum uīnum (bibere).
8. Flaccus eum (excitāre); ille "nūllum domicilium" inquit "(habēre) uacuum."

EXERCISE 13.10

Translate into Latin
1. Flaccus led Quintus to the school of Orbilius.
2. Orbilius was sitting in the courtyard (**aula, -ae,** f.).
3. Flaccus greeted him and said, "I have brought (= led) my son to you."
4. Orbilius asked Quintus many things; Quintus could answer easily.
5. The other boys had now arrived and were playing near the door.
6. Orbilius was angry. "Why are you playing?" he said; "Why have you not entered the schoolroom (**schola, -ae,** f.)?"

CICERO

Cicero as a Young Man

Marcus Tullius Cicero (the father of Marcus) was born in 106 BC near Arpinum, a little hill town about 62 miles from Rome. His father was a wealthy member of the local nobility, but his family had never played any part in politics in Rome. Cicero proved a very bright child and his father sent him to the best teachers in Rome and then to university in Greece, where he studied law, oratory (rhetoric) and philosophy.

A series of terrible wars was tearing the Roman world apart for much of Cicero's life. When he was 17, he himself fought in one of these wars, Rome's conflict with her Italian allies. Rome emerged victorious from this, even if she was forced to treat her allies as equals, but now a bloody succession of civil wars was to begin. These were fought between her great generals in a struggle for power. Some of these generals claimed to be supporting the rule of the senate against the attacks of popular politicians. Others thought that the present system of government no longer worked and wished to reform it in the interests of the people. Cicero tried throughout his life to prop up the old system, but it was doomed to collapse.

Cicero the Attorney

This bust of a thoughtful, anxious Cicero is from the Capitoline Museum in Rome.

The young Cicero was ambitious and decided to make his way by practicing in the law courts as an attorney. He did well from the start and in 70 BC leapt to fame when the people of Sicily asked him to prosecute their ruthless Roman governor, Verres, who had plundered the island for personal gain. Apparently Verres had said when he was elected that he needed to govern Sicily for three years. One year was to cover his election expenses (he had bribed the electors), one year was to get enough money to secure acquittal when he was prosecuted for misgovernment (he intended to bribe the jury) and one year was to make some profit! (Cicero, *In Verrem* 40)

Cicero was taking a big risk since Verres was a nobleman and had many powerful friends. But he conducted the case so brilliantly that Verres fled into exile before it was even over. So Cicero was acknowledged to be the leading barrister in Rome at the age of 36.

Cicero the Consul

Cicero had already been elected quaestor in 76 BC and so was a member of the senate. But he was always looked on with suspicion by the old Roman nobility because he was born a member of the equestrian class (a knight). No one could become a consul until he was 42, since much experience was considered necessary for the post. Cicero became consul at the earliest possible age in 63 BC, but the nobility still despised him as a *nouus homo*, a self-made man who was not one of them.

While Cicero was consul, a young noble called Catiline, who had failed in his attempts to become consul himself, may have conspired to overthrow the government by force. Cicero acted decisively. He arrested and executed Catiline's chief supporters in Rome and defeated his army in Etruria. He was hailed by the people as *pater patriae* (father of the fatherland), and never tired of reminding others of this achievement.

The senators and knights had drawn closer together while they united against the conspiracy, and Cicero hoped to keep this alliance working. His political aim was to maintain the *concordia ōrdinum* (the harmony of the senatorial and equestrian classes), but this was a dream never to be fulfilled.

Three Powerful Men

The three most powerful men in the Roman world were now Gaius Julius Caesar, Marcus Licinius Crassus and Gnaeus Pompey, whom Cicero admired as a man and supported as the champion of the equestrian class. In 60 BC these three formed a political alliance which modern historians call the First Triumvirate (a ruling group of three men) and brushed the authority of the senate aside. You will be reading more about this in Chapter 15. Cicero would have nothing to do with them, but this did not worry them much; all the power was in their hands.

Caesar was consul in 59 BC and then went out to govern Gaul, where he achieved famous conquests, though a political enemy regarded him, with some reason, as a war criminal because of his mass slaughter of his opponents (Plutarch, *Cato Minor* 51.1). Meanwhile Rome was becoming a dangerous and frightening place to live. Political gangs were carrying on a reign of terror and the leader of one of them, Clodius, prepared to prosecute Cicero for executing some of Catiline's supporters illegally. Cicero panicked and fled to Greece. He was allowed back the next year and given a warm welcome by the people of Italy, but he soon realized that it was the triumvirs who had let him return and that he had to do what they told him. He was no longer independent and was deeply ashamed of the fact.

Then the triumvirate began to fall to pieces. Caesar and Pompey drifted apart and Crassus was defeated and killed at Carrhae in 53 BC by the Parthians, against whom he had set out with high hopes of conquest. Cicero himself was sent in 51 BC, very much against his will, to govern a remote province called Cilicia. Here he governed fairly but not very firmly and won a minor military victory of which he was extremely proud, although no one at Rome took it very seriously.

The busts of Caesar and Pompey are from the National Archaeological Museum, Naples, and the Archaeological Museum, Venice, respectively. Caesar is said to have combed his hair forwards to disguise his baldness. His somewhat older rival Pompey, in contrast, has a healthy head of hair.

Civil War

He returned home in 50 BC to find that civil war between Caesar and Pompey could not be long delayed. For a time he sat on the fence. Caesar took the trouble to visit him to try to win him over, but in the end he decided to join Pompey's army in Greece. Here he was given nothing to do. When Caesar defeated Pompey at the battle of Pharsalus (48 BC), Cicero was stunned and his political hopes were destroyed. He returned to Italy and was soon reconciled to Caesar, but he now lived largely in retirement. He entered upon the political scene again four years later, however, after the murder of Julius Caesar. As we shall see, this resulted in his death.

Cicero the Man

Cicero was one of the most remarkable men who ever lived. He was a brilliant orator, barrister and writer, a philosopher and a capable, if uninspired, poet. He stuck to his principles as a statesman and gave up his life for them.

He was also a great letter-writer. After his death, his letters were collected and published in 35 books. Sixteen of these are to his family and friends (some with replies from men such as Caesar and Pompey); 16 are to his closest friend Atticus, to whom he was writing when Quintus met him; and three are to his brother Quintus. Cicero's letters throw an extraordinarily vivid light on the Rome of his day.

Here is part of a letter written to his brother Quintus in February 56 BC, the year after he had returned from exile to find the political gangs at work. Clodius' gang had destroyed Cicero's house on the Palatine hill during his exile, but he received compensation by decree of the senate and quickly rebuilt it. The letter describes a meeting of the people, before whom Clodius was prosecuting the rival gang-leader Milo for using violence in politics. Pompey came forward to speak for Milo:

On 6 February [56 BC] Milo appeared in court. Pompey spoke, or rather tried to. For as soon as he got up, the gangs of Clodius raised a shout, and this went on throughout his whole speech—he was interrupted not only by an uproar but by insults and abuse. When he had finished his speech (for he was extremely brave: he said the lot and at times even amid silence), but when he had finished, up got Clodius. There was such a shout from our side (for we had decided to return the compliment) that he lost all control of his thoughts, his tongue and his expression. This went on for two hours while every insult and even obscene verses were shouted against Clodius and his sister.

Clodius, furious and pale, in the middle of all this shouting asked his supporters, "Who wants to starve the people to death?" "Pompey!" answered the gang. Then at the ninth hour, as if a signal had been given, Clodius' supporters all began to spit at ours. Tempers flared, Clodius' gang shoved to dislodge us from our place. Our side made a charge, his gang fled, Clodius was thrown from the platform, and then we fled too in case we should have trouble from the crowd. The senate was summoned to the senate house and Pompey went home.

(Cicero, *Ad Quintum Fratrem* 2.3.2)

The following year Clodius was killed in a brawl outside Rome by Milo and his supporters. In the rioting which followed Clodius' gangs burned his body in the senate house, which was burnt to the ground and had not been rebuilt when Quintus arrived in Rome.

Here is another letter which Cicero wrote to a friend when his beloved daughter Tullia died in February 45 BC:

In this lonely place, I don't talk to anyone at all. In the morning I hide myself in a thick, thorny wood and I don't come out of it until the evening. After yourself, my best friend in the world is my solitude. When I am alone, all I talk to is my books, but I keep on bursting into tears. I fight against them as much as I can, but so far it has been an unequal struggle.

(*Ad Atticum* 12.15)

Chapter 14

Caesaris triumphī

Grammar: present participle; further uses of the ablative case; more perfect stems

---

CARTOONS

The cartoons illustrate present participles and we hope that they will be easily understood.

COMMENTARY

(a) Caesaris triumphī

[R|V] **Julius Caesar:** a bronze Roman sesterce with the likeness of Julius Caesar. The inscription reads C. (= Gaius) CAESAR DICTATOR. *See page 63 in* Oxford Latin Course, College Edition: Readings and Vocabulary.

1.2 *ad balnea*: there were many elaborate public baths in Rome where men (and women) went not only to bathe but to socialize.

1.3 *ad lūdōs circēnsēs*: chariot races were held in the Circus Maximus, which is said to have held 250,000 spectators, on frequent public holidays.

1.5 *mēnse Quīntīlī*: "in the month of July": this was the fifth month in the Roman calendar since the year began on March 1. The month was later renamed Julius in honor of Julius Caesar, just as Sextilis was changed to Augustus.

ex Āfricā: after Caesar had defeated Pompey at Pharsalus (in Greece) in 48 BC, he first pursued him to Egypt and fought a campaign against the Alexandrians; he then had to fight a lightning campaign against Pharnaces, king of the Bosporus, of which he famously said "uēnī, uīdī, uīcī." After a brief return to Rome in 47 BC he sailed to Africa to deal with the diehards who were still upholding the republican cause. After defeating them at Thapsus (April 46 BC) he returned to Rome in July and in August celebrated his victories in Gaul,

Egypt, Pontus and Africa with triumphs of unprecedented splendor. Each of the triumphs was celebrated on a separate day; we run them all into one.

l.8 *in Galliā*: Caesar's campaigns in Gaul, which brought all Gaul from the Pyrenees to the Rhine under Roman control, were fought between 58 and 49 BC. They were immediately followed by the civil war, and so Caesar had never been able to celebrate a Gallic triumph.

l.30 *Vercingetorix*: he raised a revolt against Caesar in Gaul in 52 BC and held out by guerilla tactics until he was defeated in battle and besieged in Alesia; he was forced by starvation to surrender and was taken to Rome. He was held there for six years and then brought out to grace Caesar's triumph, after which he was executed by strangulation in the state prison.

l.36 *subitō axis frāctus est*: cf. Suetonius, *Dīuus Iūlius* 37. In our account we make him walk up the Capitoline hill after the accident; Dio Cassius writes that he completed the rest of the journey in another chariot (43.21.1).

RV **A Roman triumph:** this silver cup from the first part of the first century AD is from Boscoreale (overlooking Pompeii). It shows the second Roman emperor Tiberius riding in his triumphal chariot crowned by Victory. His lictors go before him. (Louvre Museum, Paris) *See page 64 in* Oxford Latin Course, College Edition: Readings and Vocabulary.

(b) Quīntus fortūnam suam cognōscit

ll.2–3 *anus dīuīna*: an old fortune-teller (note that *anus* is feminine). These characters were found near the forum; compare Horace, *Satires* 1.6.113–14:

Horace takes an evening walk:

uespertīnum...pererrō | saepe forum; adsistō dīuīnīs (I often wander round the forum in the evening; I stand by the fortune-tellers.)

l.6 *fīēs*: you will become (future of *fīō*).

cauē Germāniam: the fortune-teller foresees Publius' death in the forests of Germany. This suggests that he will die in the disaster incurred by Publius Quinctilius Varus, who was ambushed by the German chieftan Arminius in the Teutoburg forest in 9 AD; three legions were annihilated and Varus took his own life. (Perhaps Quintus' friend was this very Publius Varus, though, if so, he would have been in his sixties at the time of his death; he was consul in 13 BC.)

Word-building

What do the following pairs of words mean?

amīcus	inimīcus
cautus	incautus
certus	incertus
dignus	indignus
nōtus	ignōtus
facilis	difficilis

GRAMMAR

The Present Participle

The present participle has often occurred in the narratives.

> **in gradibus templī sedēns, Quīntus botulōs auidē dēuorāuit.**
> Sitting on the steps of the temple, Quintus gobbled up the sausages greedily.

> **Orbilius puerōs spectāuit lūdum intrantēs.**
> Orbilius watched the boys entering the school.

Participles are *verbal adjectives*; they decline like **ingēns** (except for the ablative singular which ends **-e**, not **-ī**). As *adjectives* they always agree with a noun or pronoun in case, gender and number, e.g. in the first example above **sedēns** agrees with **Quīntus,** nominative masculine singular. As verbs they can take an object, e.g. in the second example, **intrantēs** agrees with **puerōs**, the object of **spectāuit**, but it has itself an object—**lūdum**.

The present participles for the five conjugations are:

	1 parā-	2 monē-	3 reg-	3-iō capi-	4 audi-
nom.	parāns	monēns	regēns	capiēns	audiēns
gen.	parantis	monentis	regentis	capientis	audientis
	preparing	warning	ruling	taking	hearing

The present participles of all verbs are formed regularly except for **eō**, which has nominative singular **iēns** but all other cases starting **e: euntis, euntī, euntem, eunte,** etc. So also **red-eō** (I return).

EXERCISE 14.1

In the following sentences say what noun or pronoun the participle agrees with and translate the whole sentence

1. Quīntus ad lūdum festīnāns forum trānsībat.
2. subitō aliquem uīdit ad sē currentem.
3. Quīntus Marcō occurrit ad circum prōcēdentī.
4. plūrimōs hominēs spectābant ad circum conuenientēs.
5. Quīntus Marcusque circum intrantēs per turbam sē trūsērunt (*pushed*).
6. diuīna quaedam Quīntō Pūbliōque obstitit (+ dat. *stood in the way of*) prope cūriam ambulantibus.
7. Quīntus multitūdinem uīdit Caesarem salūtantem.
8. Pūblius Caesarem uīdit ē currū cadentem.
9. turba hominum prope uiam stābat magnā uōce clāmantium.
10. Quīntus patrī occurrit domum festīnantī.

N.B. Sometimes the Latin participle may be translated by a clause in English, e.g.

Horātia ad mātrem accessit in hortō quiēscentem.
Horatia approached her mother (while she was/ who was) resting in the garden.

mihi haec rogantī pater nihil respondit.
When I asked this, my father made no reply. (Literally: "To me asking this, my father replied nothing.")

EXERCISE 14.2

Translate the following sentences using clauses to translate the participles

1. Horātia ab agrō sōla rediēns iuuenī occurrit quī eam salūtāuit.
2. iuuenis Horātiae nōn nōtus erat; illa igitur festīnāuit eīque accēdentī nihil respondit.
3. eō ipsō tempore Horātia amīcum uīdit ad colōniam redeuntem.
4. ille Horātiae succurrit eamque domum ambulantem dēdūxit (*escorted*).
5. Horātia, ubi domum aduēnit, omnia mātrī nārrāuit in casā sedentī.

EXERCISE 14.3

In the following sentences put the verbs in parentheses into the correct form of the present participle and then translate the whole sentence, e.g.

Horātia mātrem spectābat cēnam (parāre).
parantem. Horatia watched her mother preparing supper.

To get the right answer, first ask yourself what the present participle means: **parāns** = preparing. Then ask, "Who was preparing supper?" Answer: **mātrem**; so the participle must agree with **mātrem**—accusative, feminine, singular.

1. Rōmānī prope uiam (stāre) Caesarem laetī salūtābant.
2. Quīntus Pūbliusque Caesarem urbem (intrāre) spectābant.
3. iuuenēs domum (redīre) diūtinae cuidam prope cūriam (manēre) occurrērunt.
4. Pūblius nōn uult plūra uerba audīre diūtinae mala (dīcere).
5. Quīntus tamen laetus est; argentum dat eī bona (prōuidēre).
6. dē mīlitibus in Germāniam (īre) ualdē ānxius eram.
7. in aulā sedēbat Orbilius ferulam in manū (gerere).
8. Orbilius Quīntum laudāuit ea quae dīxit bene (intellegere).
9. puerōs ad circum (īre) Flaccus ualēre iussit (*said goodbye to*, + acc.).
10. Quīntus domum (ambulāre) Marcō ad circum (īre) occurrit.

GRAMMAR

Further Uses of the Ablative Case

1 with/by: the ablative can express the *means* or *instrument* with or by which something is done:

mē gladiō uulnerāuit	he wounded me with a sword
pilīs lūdēbant	they were playing with balls
ad urbem pedibus ībant	they were going on foot (by feet) to the city

This use is very common in such phrases as: **equō uectus** carried by (= riding on) a horse; **gladiō armātus** armed with a sword.

2 with: the ablative can express the *manner* in which something is done, e.g.

summā celeritāte rediit	he returned with the greatest speed
magnā uōce clāmāuit	he shouted in (with) a loud voice

3 with/of: the ablative is used in describing *qualities*, e.g.

est puer magnō ingeniō	he is a boy of great talent
puella summā uirtūte	a girl of the greatest courage
uir minimā prudentiā	a man of very little prudence

> **4** Some adjectives take the ablative where English has a genitive, e.g.
>
> **iuuenis dignus est laude**   the young man is very worthy of praise
> **urna aquā plēna erat**   the pot was full of water

EXERCISE 14.4

Translate
1. prīmā lūce Horātia ā fonte domum redībat; urnam grauem manibus ferēbat.
2. Scintilla eam magnā uōce uocāuit; "redī, Horātia," inquit, "mēque celeriter iuuā."
3. Horātia urnam in terrā dēposuit summāque celeritāte ad mātrem recurrit.
4. illa ē iānuā cucurrit et "ecce, filia," inquit, "ardet (*is on fire*) casa."
5. Horātia urnam aquā plēnam tulit flammāsque celeriter exstīnxit (*put out*).
6. Scintilla filiam laudāuit; "puella es maximā uirtūte, Horātia, summāque laude digna."

EXERCISE 14.5

Put the phrases into the correct case and translate the sentences
1. (prīma lūx) Quīntus cum (pater) (domus) discessit.
2. lūdus Orbiliī (forum) nōn longē aberat. (breue tempus) ad lūdum aduēnerant.
3. amīcī, ubi Quīntum cōnspēxērunt, (magna uōx) eum uocāuērunt.
4. magister, (clāmōrēs) puerōrum commōtus, ē (lūdus) exit puerōsque (uultus seuērus) spectāuit.
5. "nōlīte, puerī," inquit "tōtam urbem (tantī clāmōrēs) excitāre; celeriter intrāte."

EXERCISE 14.6

Translate into Latin
1. One day (on a certain day) Quintus was hurrying to school.
2. He was crossing the forum when (**cum**) someone called him in a loud voice.
3. He turned round and saw Marcus, who was running at top speed toward him through the crowd.
4. "Quintus," he said, "you are a boy of great industry (**industria**) but you must not go to school today. Come with me to the races."
5. Marcus led him from the forum to the Circus Maximus, which was full of men and women.

GRAMMAR

More Perfect Stems

Learn the verbs which form perfects in **-uī** or **-īuī**. You will find these numbered 5 on p. 318 of the Reference Grammar.

EXERCISE 14.7

Match the following Latin verb forms with the translations below

1. cecidit
2. coluimus
3. mānsimus
4. lēgerat
5. prōmīsistī
6. posuerant
7. ēgērunt
8. iusserant
9. quaesīuistis
10. trādiderant
11. mōuistī
12. auxistis
13. arcessīuit
14. rediimus
15. reddidimus

you looked for, you increased, he/she fell, we stayed, they had handed over, you promised, he/she summoned, they had ordered, we cultivated, they had placed, you moved, he/she had read, we returned (= went back), they did, we gave back

THE ROMAN TRIUMPH

One of the most sensational events to be seen in ancient Rome was the triumph of a victorious general. This was not an honor which could easily be won. The *triumphātor* had to be dictator, a consul or a praetor. He must have conquered in person, and so completely that his troops could safely leave for Rome; he must have killed at least 5,000 of the enemy and added new territory to the empire.

The day of triumph was a holiday for the whole city. Flowers bedecked the buildings and statues, and every altar blazed with fire. The people, wild with excitement, poured forth to line the streets.

The *triumphātor* had spent the previous night with his troops on the Campus Martius. From here the vast triumphal procession entered the city by a special gate used only on these occasions, the *porta triumphālis.*

The city magistrates led the way, followed by trumpeters sounding the charge. After them came the plunder taken in the campaign, and pictures of the forts, cities, mountains, lakes and seas of the captured territory. Next priests walked, leading the richly adorned white oxen to the sacrifice. And then there were the captives, with the king and his family and chief nobles at their head. Behind them, musicians played and danced. It was a spectacular scene, greeted with deafening applause.

But the cheers redoubled when the *triumphātor* himself came into view, riding in a strange turret-shaped chariot drawn by four white horses. (It may have had a phallus hanging beneath it to avert the evil eye.) He was robed in gold and purple, his face was painted red, and he was crowned with a laurel wreath. He carried a laurel branch in his right hand and an ivory sceptre in his left. A public slave stood behind him on the chariot holding over his head the crown of Jupiter, an oak wreath made of gold and studded with jewels. The slave continually repeated the words "Look behind you. Remember that you are a mortal," amid the hysterical shouting. Since the *triumphātor* was the earthly representative of Capitoline Jupiter, he needed to be reminded that he was also a mere man.

The victorious soldiers came behind their general wearing olive wreaths, shouting "Iō triumphe!" (Behold the triumph!) and singing lively songs. The procession went through the Circus Maximus, round the Palatine, and then followed the Sacred Way to the forum. From there it climbed the Capitoline hill to the temple of Jupiter. Meanwhile the chief captives were being put to death in a prison next to the forum.

The oxen were sacrificed outside the temple and the *triumphātor* set his laurel wreath on the lap of the god. Afterwards there was a great banquet in his honor, and then, as evening approached, he went to his home accompanied by the music of flutes and pipes.

So ended a day in which the jubilant Romans celebrated with uncontrolled emotion the military qualities which had made their nation great.

Further Reading

In Chapter 5 of her lively book *The Roman Triumph* (Harvard, 2007), Mary Beard shows that much of the evidence for the account given above is tendentious. It is certainly misleading to suggest an unvarying pattern for a varying ritual. Even so, we hope that we have given some impression of these great occasions.

Julius Caesar's Triumphs in 46 BC

The triumphal procession of Julius Caesar described in this chapter was part of possibly the most spectacular series of triumphs in Roman history. Over the course of a month, Caesar held four triumphs in celebration of four great campaigns.

As well as staging these vast celebratory pageants, Caesar gave generous gifts to his veterans and to the people of Rome. Each of the former received a minimum of 24,000 sesterces and a grant of land; the latter were given two months' rations of grain and olive oil as well as 300 sesterces. In addition Caesar flung a vast public banquet at which 22,000 dining couches were laid out in the forum.

He put on a sensational series of public shows, a gladiatorial contest in the forum, plays in Greek and Latin in the four districts of Rome, chariot races, athletic competitions and a mock sea-battle with 4,000 oarsmen and 2,000 marines. He also staged wild beast hunts in a specially built wooden amphitheater for four days running. And the entertainment ended with a battle between two armies in the Circus Maximus, each consisting of 500 infantry, 30 cavalry and 20 elephants.

So vast a crowd flocked to see these events that large numbers of visitors had to sleep in tents placed along the streets of the city and many of them were killed in the crush.

This noble canvas from the great series of paintings by Andrea Mantegna (1413–1506 AD) called *The Triumph of Caesar* shows: bearers of coin and plate; a man carrying a large marble vase containing a candelabrum; oxen with an attendant youth; trumpeters, their instruments blazoned with tributes from the senate and the Roman people to Julius Caesar (whose deification after his assassination is foreshadowed by the word DĪVŌ (divine)). Mantegna had done a great deal of research into the Roman triumph. (Hampton Court Palace, UK)

Further Reading

The sources for this account of Caesar's triumphs are Suetonius, *Dīuus Iūlius* 37–9, Plutarch, *Julius Caesar* 55 and Dio Cassius, 43.21–4.

Chapter 15

Īdūs Martiae

Grammar: the future tense, the future perfect tense; more perfect stems

PATTERN SENTENCES

These introduce the future and future perfect tenses.

COMMENTARY

(a) Quīntus rhētoricae studet

RV **Young girl picking flowers:** perhaps a personification of the season of spring, this is from a wall painting in the Villa of Ariadne near Pompeii. (National Archaeological Museum, Naples) *See page 67 in* Oxford Latin Course, College Edition: Readings and Vocabulary.

l.1 *togam uirīlem*: boys assumed the toga of manhood in their teens; Marcus Cicero did so when he was sixteen. The rite of passage generally took place when the youth was seen as capable of penetrative sex (Suetonius, *Caligula* 24). For many the ceremony took place on March 17, the festival of Liber, the Italian god of fertility. The youth laid his boy's tunic (the straight tunic—*tunica rēcta*—so-called because it was woven on an upright loom) before the Lares and, in the case of a freedman's son such as Quintus, his leather collar with its amulet. A free citizen's son wore a golden locket (*bulla*). Instead of the purple-bordered *toga praetexta* he wore the white *toga pūra* or *toga uirīlis* of adulthood. Escorted by family and friends, he went to the *tabulārium*, the Public Records Office, on the slopes of the Capitol. Here he was registered as a full citizen and enrolled in his tribe, one of the voting groups of ancient Rome. For more information on this day, see M. Harlow and R. Laurence, *Growing Up and Growing Old in Ancient Rome* (Routledge, 2002), 67–9.

This bronze statue of an orator is an Etruscan work dating from the third or fourth century BC. The figure, known as the *Arringatore* (the Italian word for "orator"), wears a semicircular toga over a sleeveless tunic. The (purple) stripe is clearly visible. (Archaeological Museum, Florence)

l.2 *rhētoricae*: the study of rhetoric was the staple form of tertiary education, preparing young men to take part in public life. Horace nowhere mentions a rhetorical school in connection with his education; we have assumed that he attended one. Rhetoric had been developed as a teachable skill by the sophists, the traveling teachers of the Greek world, in Athens in the last quarter of the fifth century BC. They raised questions about beliefs which had been previously taken for granted—such as whether the gods had any effect on the world of men—and their weapon was argument. Thus one of the things they taught was the art of speaking.

Rhetoric, taught by the *rhētor*, involved learning how to argue a case clearly and elegantly, and it has been called the art of persuasion. The whole study was reduced to a complex system with many technical terms and rules. Students studied model speeches, composed their own on set subjects, and took part in debates, often on imaginary law cases. The practical importance of rhetoric in a world without newspapers, television or radio can scarcely be exaggerated. The public speech was the only way of communicating with one's fellow citizens in the mass and any Roman who hoped to make his mark had to strive to excel in this art.

In Horace's day, debates divided into (1) abstract, general themes such as "Should one marry?" and (2) particular themes related to a situation, for example with the students imagining themselves as the young Hannibal in Carthage wondering, "Should I cross the Alps to invade Italy?"

l.5 *poētā quōdam uetere*: the surviving fragments of early Latin poetry suggest that they were, as Quintus felt, extremely boring (their favorite genre was historical epic, like the *Bellum Pūnicum* of Naevius). Horace complains that these poems are praised simply because they are old while contemporary poems are criticized simply because they are modern (*Epistles* 2.1.69–78).

ll.5–6 *illō frīgidiōrem*: note the ablative of comparison (see p. 107). The alternative would be *frīgidiōrem quam illum*.

ll.8–9 *diffūgērunt...comae*: these are the opening lines of Horace, *Odes* 4.7, but the first line should read "*diffūgēre niuēs*." Quintus is trying to write a dactylic hexameter but *diffūgērunt* does not form an acceptable rhythm; he should have written the alternative form, *diffūgēre*. The mistake annoys Orbilius extremely (see ll.18–20).

l.18: *nē rēctī quidem*: note the use of *nē quidem* sandwiching a word.

l.31 *Hēliodōrum*: Heliodorus may stand for a historical figure who accompanied Horace on his journey to Brundisium (see Chapter 26): Horace, *Satires* 1.5.1–2: *rhētor comes Hēliodōrus, Graecōrum longē doctissimus*. Horace may have given this name to Apollodorus, the teacher chosen by Julius Caesar to teach Octavian. The name Apollodorus does not fit the rhythm Horace is using. Hence Heliodorus, which does. Helios and Apollo were both gods of the sun.

l.41 *poētīs Graecīs*: Horace came to know the Greek poets backwards, especially the Greek lyric poets on whom he modeled his *Odes*.

R|V **Statue of a young man:** the statue dates from the first century BC. Dressed in a toga, he holds a scroll as he stands beside his box of books. (Museo Pio-Clementino, Vatican, Rome) *See page 69 in* Oxford Latin Course, College Edition: Readings and Vocabulary.

(b) Īdūs Martiae

(The narrative follows the account of Suetonius, *Diuus Iulius* 81–2.)

Vocabulary: the verb *feriō* does not have a perfect tense. We supply this with the perfect of *percutiō*, which has the same meaning.

R|V This coin was issued by the assassins of Julius Caesar to celebrate the killing of the dictator. The cap of freedom in the center of the coin is a *pīleus*, a felt hat worn by freed slaves (and given a new lease on life by supporters of the French revolution in 1789). The inscription reads EID MAR (the Ides of March). The E in EID is the old Latin E. It had largely been dropped by Caesar's time. *See page 69 in* Oxford Latin Course, College Edition: Readings and Vocabulary.

ll.3–4 *Campum Martium*: the Field of Mars lay on a bend of the Tiber to the northwest of the Capitol. It had been originally a parade ground for reviewing the army (hence its name), but it had become a public park to which the youth came to take exercise and swim in the Tiber. The Via Triumphalis led from the forum past the theater of Pompey to the Campus. The theater was the first stone theater in Rome, built by Pompey in 55 BC. To the east of the theater was a rectangular portico off which opened the Curia Pompei (senate house of Pompey); it was here that Caesar was murdered at the foot of the statue of Pompey.

ll.10–11 *conuēnissent*: this form is the pluperfect subjunctive; the subjunctive is used in indirect questions (see Chapter 22).

ll.16–18 *circumstant, rogat, tenet, ferit, uulnerat*: at moments of excitement, narrators can switch to the present tense. We call this the historic present. It creates a sense of vividness. This works less well in English and it is probably sensible to translate historic presents as past tenses in prose. In translating poetry, the present can often be preserved in English to excellent effect.

l.21 *et tū, Brūte*: "you too, Brutus"; Suetonius quotes a tradition which made Caesar say (in Greek): *"kai su, teknon?"* (you too, my son?); for there was a belief that Brutus was the illegitimate son of Caesar. Caesar certainly loved him and Brutus was reluctant to join the conspiracy.

l.25 *līberāuimus*: the assassins of Julius Caesar became known as the Liberators, i.e. *patriae līberātōrēs* (cf. Cicero, *Philippics* 1.6). .

R̄V̄ **Caesar lies dead:** Jean Léon Gérome, *The Death of Caesar* (The Walters Art Museum, Baltimore). *See page 70 in* Oxford Latin Course, College Edition: Readings and Vocabulary.

Word-building

Remember that **con-** either = "together" or simply strengthens the meaning of the uncompounded verb, e.g. **iaciō** = "I throw," **coniciō** = either "I throw together" or "I hurl."

What is the meaning of the following compounded verbs?

concurrō, conclāmō, cōnficiō, commoueō, conuocō, compōnō, conueniō, cōnferō

The prefix **per-** either means "through," like the preposition, e.g.

percurrō	I run through
perrumpō	I break through

or gives the notion of completeness, e.g.

faciō	I do	**perficiō**	I carry through, complete
suādeō	I persuade	**persuādeō**	I (completely) persuade
ueniō	I come	**peruenoō**	I come all the way, reach

This prefix is attached to some adjectives, e.g.

facilis	easy	**perfacilis**	extremely easy
dūrus	hard	**perdūrus**	extremely hard

The prefix **dī-/dis-** means "in different directions," e.g.

dīmittō	I send in different directions, dismiss
dispōnō	I put in different places, arrange
diffugiō	I flee in different directions, scatter
discurrō	I run in different directions, run about

The preposition **circum** + acc. = "around"; it is found prefixed to many verbs, e.g.

circumueniō	I surround
circumuolō	I fly around
circumeō	I go around
circumdūcō	I lead around

GRAMMAR

The Future Tense

The future tense of verbs of the 1st and 2nd conjugations goes as follows:

1 para-	**2 monē-**
parā-bō (I shall prepare)	**monē-bō** (I shall warn)
parā-bis	**monē-bis**
parā-bit	**monē-bit**
parā-bimus	**monē-bimus**
parā-bitis	**monē-bitis**
parā-bunt	**monē-bunt**

The future of verbs of 3rd and 4th conjugations and mixed conjugation goes as follows:

3 reg-	**3rd -iō capi-**	**4 audi-**
reg-am (I shall rule)	**capi-am** (I shall take)	**audi-am** (I shall hear)
reg-ēs	**capi- ēs**	**audi-ēs**
reg-et	**capi-et**	**audi-et**
reg-ēmus	**capi-ēmus**	**audi-ēmus**
reg-ētis	**capi-ētis**	**audi-ētis**
reg-ent	**capi-ent**	**audi-ent**

Learn both sets of endings carefully

The future of **sum** is:	The future of **ēo** is:
erō (I shall be)	**ībō** (I shall go)
eris	**ībis**
erit	**ībit**
erimus	**ībimus**
eritis	**ībitis**
erunt	**ībunt**

EXERCISE 15.1

Translate the following verb forms
1. rogābimus
2. docēbit
3. dīcent
4. dīcunt
5. dormiam
6. eris
7. mittet
8. mittit
9. poterit
10. scrībēmus
11. pugnābunt
12. monēbitis

EXERCISE 15.2

Translate into Latin
1. We shall come
2. They will sail
3. I shall laugh
4. He/she will lead
5. I shall run
6. You (*sing.*) will come
7. They will flee
8. He/she is playing
9. He/she will play
10. We shall climb

11. We are climbing
12. You (*pl.*) will love

EXERCISE 15.3

Translate

1. Quīntus domum curret patrīque omnia nārrābit.
2. Flaccus "in magnō perīculō erimus," inquit. "Rōmā discēdēmus.
3. ego Venusiam redībō, tū in urbe manēbis."
4. Quīntus "ad Hēliodōrum festīnābō" inquit "eīque omnia expōnam."
5. Brūtus multa dē lībertāte dīcet, sed nēmō eī crēdet.

GRAMMAR

The Future Perfect Tense

By now Quintus will have left the city. **iam Quīntus urbem relīquerit.**

This tense, rare in English, is used to indicate an action completed in the future. It is commonly used in Latin in sentences such as:

cum Rōmam relīqueris, tūtus eris.
When you leave / have left (i.e. will have left) the city, you will be safe.
sī patrem meum uīderis, omnia eī nārrā.
If you see (i.e. will have seen) my father, tell him everything.

The tense is formed by adding the following endings to the perfect stem:

-erō	**-erimus**
-eris	**-eritis**
-erit	**-erint**

1. parāu-erō, etc.	I shall have prepared
2. monu-erō, etc.	I shall have warned
3. rēx-erō, etc.	I shall have ruled
3rd -iō. cēp-ēro, etc.	I shall have taken
4. audīu-erō, etc.	I shall have heard

EXERCISE 15.4

Translate

1. cum Rōmam aduēneris, tumultum magnum inueniēs.
2. cum cēnāculum nostrum intrāuerimus, perīculum effugiēmus.
3. cum mē abīre iusseris, urbem relinquam.
4. sī prūdentēs fuerimus, Venusiam sine perīculō adueniēmus.
5. sī dīligenter studueris, multa discēs.
6. cum domum redierō, omnia tibi nārrābō.
7. sī coniūrātī Caesarem occīderint, trīstissimus erō.
8. sī Venusiam accēdēs, ego tēcum ībō.

EXERCISE 15.5

Translate the following verb forms

1. redīte
2. redībō
3. redībāmus
4. redierint
5. rediērunt
6. audiunt
7. audient
8. audīuimus
9. audīuerimus
10. audientēs
11. posse
12. possunt
13. poterāmus
14. poterimus

GRAMMAR

More Perfect Stems (concluded)

Learn the verbs which add the suffix **-sc-** to the verb stem in the present, future and imperfect but drop it in the perfect on p. 318 of the Reference Grammar, e.g. **cognō-sc-ō, cognō-sc-ere, cognō-uī**   I get to know, learn

EXERCISE 15.6

Give the correct Latin form for the English verbs in parentheses and translate the sentences

1. diē quōdam Scintilla Horātiam māne (*woke*); nūndinae (*market day*) erant.
2. "ēuigilā," inquit; "tempus est ad forum (*to hurry*)."
3. Horātia mātrī (*obeyed*) et celeriter (*got up*).
4. ubi ad forum (*they arrived*), plūrimī hominēs iam (*were there*).
5. in gradibus templī (*they stood*) et rēs suās (*they put out*).
6. mox omnēs rēs (*they had sold*) domumque (*to return*) parābant.
7. per forum lentē ambulābant amīcīsque (*met*) quī ipsī rēs (*were selling*).

8. sed nihil (*they bought*); nam pauperēs (*they were*).

Translate into Latin

1. When we arrive at Rome, I will send you a letter without delay.
2. When Quintus has gone away, I shall return to Venusia.
3. If I leave Rome at once, I shall reach Venusia within ten days.
4. When I see you, you will hear everything.
5. If Antonius rouses the people, there will be civil war.

THE END OF THE REPUBLIC

A key moment in the long drawn-out death of the Roman republic occurred in 60 BC. As we saw in Chapter 13, the three most powerful men of the time, Julius Caesar, Gnaeus Pompey and Marcus Licinius Crassus, joined in an alliance known as the First Triumvirate. They made it clear that nothing would stand in their way and, when he became consul in 59 BC, Caesar made sure that nothing did. The Triumvirate was supported by the army, the *equitēs* and the people, and so the senate was unable to oppose it. Nobody paid any attention to Cicero's frantic appeals to save the republic.

Over the next decade Caesar fought his famous and brilliant campaigns in Gaul (France, Holland and Belgium), through which he established a justified reputation as one of the greatest generals in the history of the world. He ensured that his military genius gained a wide circulation by writing his own history of his campaigns in the seven books of his *Commentaries on the War in Gaul*. These show him not only as a great general but as a fine war correspondent. They are direct and plain in style but always exciting. His two raids on Britain (in 55 and 54 BC) proved of little lasting value but had all the glamour of perilous journeys into the unknown. However, the situation at Rome was less happy for him. The alliance between Pompey, Crassus and himself, all of them ruthlessly ambitious, lasted a surprisingly long time; it threatened to dissolve in 56 BC, but the three met and patched things up. Crassus, however, was killed in Parthia in 53 BC, and Pompey became more and more closely allied to the senate. Caesar and Pompey were being driven further apart, and the senate voted on January 1, 49 BC that Caesar, who was still in Gaul, should lay down his command.

Caesar's response came on January 10, when he brought his army into Italy. This was in effect a declaration of civil war since it was treason for a general to enter Italy at the head of an army. Caesar fully realized the great significance of what he was doing. He spent some time in solitary thought. Then he crossed the river Rubicon, which marked the frontier between Gaul and Italy, and exclaimed "*iacta ālea est!*" ("The die is cast!"; Suetonius, *Julius Caesar* 31–2)

Pompey and most of the senate withdrew across the Adriatic to Greece. Caesar defeated Pompey's supporters in Spain, then followed him to Greece and in 48 BC won a great victory over him at Pharsalus. Pompey fled on horseback and succeeded in escaping to Egypt, but was stabbed to death as he landed. Ptolemy, the boy king of Egypt, sent his head to Caesar, hoping to win favor with him, but the victor was revolted and distressed by this grisly gift.

The portrait of Antony is on a seal ring of red jasper dating from about 40 BC. (British Museum, London)

Other wars were to follow—including the lightning campaign in Pontus in Asia when he polished off his opponents there with the celebrated boast "uēnī, uīdī, uīcī" ("I came, I saw, I conquered"—see Chapter 14). He had a notorious love affair with Cleopatra, the irresistible Egyptian queen. He was by now the most powerful man in the Western world, and, great statesman that he was, he embarked on a series of major reforms and a vast building program. Yet many worried that he was taking so much power into his hands. He was appointed dictator, first in 49 BC and then for life in February 44 BC. Though he refused the title *rēx* (king), he put on the purple robe worn by the Tarquins, the last kings of Rome, and his supreme power struck many as intolerable. A conspiracy to assassinate him led by Marcus Brutus and Gaius Cassius succeeded in 44 BC. His mutilated body fell at the foot of the statue of his great opponent Pompey, as you have read.

It was now the task of his friend Marcus Antonius and of his great-nephew and heir Octavian to avenge his death.

The cameo of Octavian is in sardonyx, first century AD. (Carlyle Collection, British Museum, London)

Further Reading

For a more detailed account of Caesar's career and achievements, see the *Oxford Classical Dictionary* (4th edition, 2011).

> **Grammar:** passive voice; perfect passive participle & indicative; future perfect passive indicative; pluperfect passive indicative; future participle (active)

CARTOONS

The two captions under the first cartoon in effect mean the same thing. This is your first introduction to the passive.

The third cartoon contains two future participles.

COMMENTARY

(a) Caesaris fūnus

According to Suetonius (*Dīuus Iūlius* 84) Caesar's body was to be cremated in the Campus Martius; a pyre was built near the tomb of his daugher Julia. There "Antony, instead of a funeral laudation, ordered a herald to proclaim the decree of the senate by which Caesar was voted all honors human and divine and added a few words on his own account. The magistrates carried his body into the forum and placed it before the rostra. Suddenly two men, wearing swords and carrying spears, set fire to the couch with torches."

But Dio Cassius (historian, c. 164 AD–after 229–44.36–9), Plutarch (biographer, in his prime 100 AD–*Antony* 14.3–4, *Brutus* 20.2–6) and Appian (historian, second century AD–*Bella Cīuīlia* 2.143–7) write that Antony made a full funerary laudation in the forum, by which he roused the people to frenzy, and Cicero, who was in Rome at the time, concurs (*Ad Atticum* 14.10.1, *Philippics* 2.91). Antony had been Caesar's Master of the Horse, i.e. the dictator's deputy; as Caesar's chief henchman he was next in line for the assassins' daggers (Cicero wrote to Cassius in February 43 BC regretting that the assassins had not completed their work; "*uellem Īdibus Martiīs mē ad cēnam inuītāssēs; reliquiārum nihil fuisset*"; "I wish you had invited me to your dinner on the Ides of March; there would have been no leftovers"–*Ad Familiārēs* 12.4.1). If Cicero, Plutarch, Dio Cassius and Appian are right, this was the moment at which Antony decided to win over the people and make a bid for Caesar's power.

ll.18–19 *bellum cīuīle*: civil war had racked the Roman state for 50 years and would continue until the Republic was destroyed:

90–89 BC The Social War, i.e. the war in which the Italian allies (*sociī*) fought for Roman citizenship

88–87 Marius versus Sulla and the Optimates (the more conservative upper class)

83–82 Sulla versus Cinna and the Populares (the less conservative upper class)

49–45 Caesar versus Pompey and the senate

43 Antony versus Octavian and the senate (battle of Mutina)

42 Antony and Octavian versus Brutus and Cassius (battle of Philippi)

38–36 Octavian versus the sons of Pompey

32–31 Octavian versus Antony and Cleopatra

The last of these left Octavian as sole ruler of the Roman world and he became the emperor Augustus. It is said that there was not a family in Italy which did not suffer loss in lives or property or both during these wars. At the battle of Philippi alone a survivor estimated that there were over 24,000 dead (Plutarch, *Brutus* 45.1, Appian, *Bella Cīvīlia* 4.112).

l.33 *rempūblicam*: note that both parts of this word decline. What is its genitive?

Heliodorus' gloomy predictions express sentiments which occur repeatedly in the literature of these years; so Virgil *Georgics* 1.505–11:

> fās uersum atque nefās; tot bella per orbem,
> tam multae scelerum faciēs....
> saeuit tōtō Mars impius orbe.

(right and wrong are turned upside down; so many wars throughout the world, so many types of crime...wicked Mars rages throughout the world...)

l.39 *Acadēmīae*: the Academy was founded by Plato in about 385 BC as a training school for statesmen (philosopher kings); it flourished as a philosophical school until it was closed by the emperor Justinian in 529 AD. Horace says that it was there that he studied moral philosophy (ethics) and theory of knowledge, still the most important branches of philosophical training. He says of his education:

> adiēcēre bonae paulō plūs artis Athēnae.
> scīlicet ut uellem curuō dīnōscere rēctum,
> atque inter siluās Acadēmī quaerere uērum.
> *(Epistles 2.2.43–5)*

(kind Athens gave me a little more skill, so that I wanted to distinguish the straight from the crooked [i.e. right from wrong—moral philosophy] and to search for truth [i.e. to study theory of knowledge] in the groves of Academus.)

(b) Quīntus Rōmā discēdit

l.6 *Ōstia*: Ostia was 16 miles from Rome at the mouth of the Tiber. It was a substantial port with warehouses and granaries for storing imported goods; its walls at this time enclosed 170 acres. But it had no adequate harbor; large ships had to anchor offshore. And so it was used mostly by smaller ships which transferred their cargo to larger ones at the great port of Puteoli in the bay of Naples. Caesar did some work to improve the harbor and a completely new harbor was built in the time of Claudius (43 AD), which made it the largest port in the ancient world. There is a good summary of activities at Ostia in P. Jones and K. Sidwell (eds), *The World of Rome* (Cambridge, 1997), Chapter 6, first section. See also S. Keay and L. Paroli (eds), *Portus and its Hinterland* (British School at Rome, 2011).

R|V **Roman merchant ship in the harbor at Ostia:** a tomb painting from Ostia. The ship is named as the Isis Giminiāna. The captain Farnācēs stands on the *puppis* (poop, stern), holding the steering oar. The owner (?) Arascantus supervises the loading of the cargo (marked rēs, which is clearly grain. Beside him stands a winged figure, presumably Mercury, the god of profit and good luck. The painting dates from the second or third century AD. (Vatican Museums, Rome) *See page 75 in* Oxford Latin Course, College Edition: Readings and Vocabulary.

Word-building

What are (1) an *ardent* lover, (2) an *ordinal* number, (3) an *ultimate* goal, (4) a *capital* city, (5) a *vesper* hymn? From what Latin word is each English adjective derived?

R|V **Ostia:** from a marble relief of about 200 AD found at Ostia. The emblem of Rome (the wolf and the twins) is twice depicted on the sails of the merchant ship. Flames curl up from the lighthouse at the rear. In the center right stands Neptune with his trident. Note the large eye, a charm against the evil eye, also to the right. *See page 76 in* Oxford Latin Course, College Edition: Readings and Vocabulary.

GRAMMAR

Active and Passive

All the verb forms you have met until this chapter have been in the active voice. In the *active voice*, the subject *acts*, e.g.

Quintus *calls* Marcus   Scintilla *leads* Horatia

In the *passive voice*, the subject is *acted upon*, e.g.

Marcus *is called by* Quintus   Horatia *is led by* Scintilla

In these sentences Marcus/Horatia are not acting but are the recipients of the action: he is being called, she is being led.

EXERCISE 16.1

Rewrite the following sentences in passive form, e.g.
Brutus killed Caesar = Caesar was killed by Brutus.
1. Heliodorus helped me.
2. Flaccus contributed money.
3. They entered the harbor.
4. Flaccus gave the captain the fare.
5. Quintus shed many tears.

GRAMMAR

The Perfect Passive Participle

You have already met a number of perfect passive participles, e.g.

apertus, -a, -um:	having been opened, open (from **aperiō**)
parātus, -a, -um:	having been prepared, prepared (from **parō**)
commōtus, -a, -um:	having been moved, moved (from **commoueō**)
territus, -a, -um:	having been terrified, terrified (from **terreō**)
dēsertus, -a, -um:	having been deserted, deserted (from **dēserō**)

The perfect passive participle is a verbal adjective, declined like **bonus, -a, -um**. It is formed from the supine of the verb. The *supine* is the fourth of the principal parts of verbs, which appears in all vocabularies from this chapter; its uses will not be explained until later. It is most commonly formed by adding the suffix **-tum** (sometimes **-sum**) to the present verb stem. The perfect passive participle itself is formed by changing the final **-m** of the supine to **-s**, so:

supine	perfect passive participle	
parāt-um	**parāt-us, -a, -um**	having been prepared, prepared
monit-um	**monit-us, -a, -um**	having been warned, warned
rēct-um	**rēct-us, -a, -um**	having been ruled, ruled
capt-um	**capt-us, -a, -um**	having been taken, taken
audīt-um	**audīt-us, -a, -um**	having been heard, heard

Examples of verbs with supines in **-sum**:

iubeō, iubēre, iussī, iussum	**iussus, -a, -um**
uideō, uidēre, uīdī, uīsum	**uīsus, -a, -um**
mittō, mittere, mīsī, missum	**missus, -a, -um**

In the following examples notice that the participles agree with the noun to which they refer in number, gender, and case.

1. **<u>Aenēās</u>, ā Mercuriō <u>monitus</u>, nāuēs parāuit.**
   Aeneas, warned by Mercury, prepared the ships.
2. **omnēs <u>cēnam</u> ā Scintillā <u>parātam</u> ēdērunt.**
   They all ate the dinner prepared by Scintilla.
3. **centuriō <u>hostēs</u> in proeliō <u>captōs</u> ad imperātōrem dūxit.**
   The centurion led the soldiers (who had been) captured in battle to the general.
4. **cōnsul <u>militibus</u> <u>conuocātis</u> haec dīxit.**
   The consul called together the soldiers and said this (these things).
   (Literally: The consul said this to the soldiers having been called together.)
5. **Marcus <u>Quīntum</u> in uiā <u>uīsum</u> in tabernam dūxit.**
   Marcus saw Quintus in the street and led him to a tavern *or* When Marcus saw Quintus in the street, he led him to a tavern. (Literally: Marcus led Quintus having been seen in the street to a tavern.)

N.B.: 1 In the last three examples Latin and English idiom differ; English often uses a clause where Latin uses a participle. You must always grasp the sense of the Latin and express it in natural English.

2 ā/ab = "by" is always used with people (*agents*) but not with things (*instruments*), e.g.

mīles ab hostibus vulnerātus the soldier wounded by the enemy

but:

miles hastā vulnerātus the soldier wounded by a spear

EXERCISE 16.2

What do the following words mean (and say what verb each comes from)?

uocātus, territus, audītus, excitātus, scrīptus, doctus, factus, clausus, dēfēnsus, uersus

EXERCISE 16.3

Translate

1. Caesar ā coniūrātīs occīsus prope statuam Pompēī iacēbat.
2. coniūrātī ab Antōniō oppugnātī ex urbe fūgērunt.
3. Flaccus, cīuium tumultibus territus, cōnstituit Venusiam redīre.
4. Quīntus epistolam ab Hēliodōrō scrīptam laetus accēpit.
5. Quīntus ā patre monitus ad portum fēstīnāuit.
6. in portū nāuem ad nāuigātiōnem parātam inuēnit.
7. magister nāuis uiāticum ā Flaccō sibi datum in manū tenēbat.
8. Quīntum in portū relictum nōn iam uidet Flaccus.

EXERCISE 16.4

Translate the following sentences into natural English, avoiding "having been" (which is unidiomatic English), e.g.

Scintilla Horātiam salūtātam in casam dūxit.

either Scintilla greeted Horatia and led her into the house.

or When Scintilla had greeted Horatia, she led her into the house.

1. coniūrātī Caesarem occīsum in terrā iacentem relīquērunt.
2. Antōnius cīuēs in forum conuocātōs ad furōrem excitāuit.
3. Flaccus Quīntum ad portum ductum ualēre iussit.
4. Flaccus Quīntum māne excitātum ad Hēliodōrum mīsit.
5. epistolam eī datam Flaccus Quīntum ad Theomnēstum ferre iussit.

EXERCISE 16.5

Put the verbs in parentheses into the correct form of the perfect passive participle and translate the whole sentence

1. coniūrātī ad theātrum (conuocāre) Caesarem ānxiī exspectābant.
2. ille aduēnit et ab omnibus (salūtāre) tandem sēdit.
3. coniūratī eum pugiōnibus (*with daggers*) (oppugnāre) ferōciter occīdunt.
4. ultima uerba eius ā Brutō (audīre) sicārium (*the assassin*) terrent.
5. Quīntus dē spectāculō (uidēre) omnia patrī nārrāuit.
6. uerbīs eius (commouēre) Flaccus Rōmam relinquere cōnstituit.
7. Flaccus filiusque, tumultibus (terrēre), ad portum iērunt.
8. Quīntus nāuem idōneam (inuenīre) cōnscendit.

EXERCISE 16.6

Translate into Latin

1. The girls, warned by their mother, stayed at home.
2. Flaccus, terrified by his son's words, decided to return home.
3. The sailors, ordered by the captain, rowed fast.
4. Scintilla happily read the letter written by Quintus.
5. The young men bought the books praised by Heliodorus.

GRAMMAR

The Perfect Passive Indicative

The perfect passive indicative consists of the past participle passive in conjunction with the present tense of *sum* (which usually follows the participle).

parātus sum (I was prepared, have been prepared)	**monitus sum**
parātus es	**rēctus sum**
parātus est	**audītus sum**
parātī sumus	
parātī estis	
parātī sunt	

The participle declines and agrees with the subject, e.g.

Dīdō dēserta est	Dido has been deserted
Quīntus paterque	Quintus and his father have been terrified by
tumultibus territī sunt	the riots.

The perfect active has two different meanings (**dūxit** = he led, he has led), and so the perfect passive (**ductus est** = he was led, he has been led).

EXERCISE 16.7

Translate
1. ō nautae, ā deō iussī sumus ab Āfricā nāuigāre.
2. nōnne ā rēgīnā bene rēctī estis, ō cīuēs?
3. ad nāuigātiōnem parātus es, Quīnte?
4. imperia Mercurī ab Aeneā sunt audīta.
5. "imperiīs deī territus sum."

EXERCISE 16.8

Put the verbs in parentheses into the correct form of the perfect passive and then translate the sentences
1. cīuēs omnēs tumultibus (terrēre).
2. urbs ab hostibus (capere).
3. hostēs ā cīuibus (uidēre).
4. epistola Quīntō (dare).
5. Caesar ā coniūrātīs (occīdere).

GRAMMAR

The Future Perfect and Pluperfect Passive

These tenses are formed in the same way, with tenses of *sum* (the future and imperfect) used with the past participle passive.

future perfect passive	*pluperfect passive*
parātus erō (I shall have been prepared)	**parātus eram** (I had been prepared)
parātus eris	**parātus erās**
parātus erit	**parātus erāt**
parātī erimus	**parātī erāmus**
parātī eritis	**parātī erātis**
parātī erunt	**parātī erant**

The Future Participle

You have already met the future participle in the course of your reading, e.g.

mortem crūdēlissimam obitūrus
about to meet a very cruel death

It is formed by changing the supine ending **-um** to **-ūrus**:

parāt-um	**parāt-ūrus**	about to prepare
monit-um	**monit-ūrus**	about to warn
rēct-um	**rēct-ūrus**	about to rule
capt-um	**capt-ūrus**	about to take
audīt-um	**audīt-ūrus**	about to hear

It is active in meaning and declines like **bonus, -a, -um.**
N.B.: The future partciple of **sum** is **futūrus** = about to be.

EXERCISE 16.9

Translate the following verb forms

1. scrīpsit
2. scrībit
3. scrīptūrus
4. scrīptus
5. scrībet
6. amā
7. amātae sumus
8. amābis
9. amātūrus
10. amāuērunt
11. dūcimus
12. ductī sumus
13. dūc
14. ductus
15. ductūrus

EXERCISE 16.10

Translate

1. marītum suum iterum uīsūra, Scintilla laetissima erat.
2. Caesar theātrum intrāuit mortem obitūrus.
3. Quīntum Rōmam relictūrum Hēliodōrus ualēre iussit.
4. Athēnās aduentūrus, Quīntus ānxius erat.
5. quis Caesaris mortem est uindicātūrus?
6. dē fīliō meō ex urbe abitūrō ualdē ānxius sum.

7. quid iam futūrum est? tempora laeta numquam uīsūrī sumus.
8. in nāuem conscēnsūrus Quīntus uiāticum magistrō dedit.

EXERCISE 16.11

Translate into Latin
1. On the point of sailing to Athens Quintus said goodbye to Heliodorus.
2. "I am about to give you a letter in which I recommend you to Theomnestus."
3. Am I going to see my wife again? Is she going to be happy when she sees (*fut. perf.*) me?
4. O Venusia, when am I going to see you?
5. Brutus entered the theater where he would (was about to) kill Caesar.

EXERCISE 16.12

Translate
1. Aenēās, ā deō iussus, ā Dīdōne moritūrā crūdēliter abiit.
2. Quīntus, Athēnās nāuigātūrus, patrem in portū relictum trīstis spectābat.
3. Quīntus ā patre iussus Rōmam relīquit.
4. Scintilla Horātiaque Venusiae relictae erant.
5. Caesar ā coniūrātīs ferōciter occīsus est.
6. Marcus Antōnius Caesarem occīsum uindicātūrus est.
7. Flaccus, Caesaris morte commōtus, Venusiam est abitūrus.
8. epistolam ab Hēliodōrō scrīptam Quīntus Theomnēstō est lātūrus.
9. puellae a uirīs scelestīs (*wicked*) in uiā uīsae sunt.
10. sī Venusia iterum ā mē uīsa erit, laetus mortem obībō.

Chapter 17

Athēnīs

Grammar: present, future & imperfect passive

PATTERN SENTENCES

The pattern sentences contrast these tenses in their active and passive forms.

COMMENTARY

(a) Quīntus ad Graeciam nāuigat

l.1 *abeuntem*: present participle of *ab-eō* (*eō*—present participle *iēns, euntis*).

l.2 *magister*: master, i.e. captain of the ship.

l.5 *futūrōrum īnscius*: "ignorant of the future"; *futūra* (n. pl.) is the future participle of *sum* = "things about to be."

l.10 *ubīque caelum*: the verb, "was," as often, is omitted.

l.17 *Pīraeum*: Piraeus was the port of Athens; a superb natural harbor, it was the greatest port in the eastern Mediterranean, four miles from the city of Athens.

l.20 *Acropolis*: on the Acropolis were the holiest temples of Athens, dominated by the Parthenon, completed in 432 BC.

R|V Piraeus: an aerial view of the three harbors of Athens at Piraeus: (from the front) Munychia, Zea, Kantharos (the grand harbor). *See page 78 in* Oxford Latin Course, College Edition: Readings and Vocabulary.

l.21 *Parthenōna*: this is a Greek form of the accusative.

R|V The Parthenon, Athens: the great Doric temple of the goddess Athena, was built between 437 and 432 BC. It stands on the Acropolis, the citadel of Athens, whose summit is 156 meters high. For a good modern book on the temple, see Mary Beard, *The Parthenon* (Profile, 2010). *See page 79 in* Oxford Latin Course, College Edition: Readings and Vocabulary.

l.24 *salūtem plūrimam dīcit*: "gives heartiest greetings": this is the usual formula for starting letters, often abbreviated to s.d.p. (Shackleton Bailey, *Cicero: Select Letters* [Cambridge], 12).

(b) Acadēmīa

Vocabulary 17B: cōnfīdō is semi-deponent (see p. 103 in RV): its perfect tense (**cōnfīsus sum**) is passive in form but active in meaning.

l.6 *uīsne?* "are you willing to?" = "please."

ll.13–14 *utrum…an*: *utrum* followed by *an* introduces a double question, e.g. "Are you coming or staying put?" "Are you visiting her or me?" *utrum* simply shows that an alternative question is coming up: don't translate it. (But the situation is different in indirect questions: see p. 198.)

l.21 *Marcus Cicero*: Cicero sent his son Marcus to Athens in 45 BC to study at the Lyceum. The Lyceum was the other great university in Athens, founded by Aristotle in 335 BC; its head at this time was Cratippus. Marcus was not a good student and had soon dissipated the generous allowance his father gave him.

l.22 *nōnne*: remember that this introduces a question expecting the answer yes (see p. 31). "Can I really be seeing Quintus?" ("Yes, I can!")

R V **The Academy:** this mosaic panel was found at Boscoreale above Pompeii. It belongs to the late second or first century BC. The figure pointing to the globe is Plato, who is leading a discussion on astronomy. (National Archaeological Museum, Naples) *See page 80 in* Oxford Latin Course, College Edition: Readings and Vocabulary.

Comprehension Exercise

ll.7–8 *ad eum rescrībam*: the letter Marcus writes to Tiro is an adaptation of a letter he actually did write in September 44 BC (*Ad Familiārēs* 16.21). Toward the end of the original Marcus tactfully makes his purpose clear: he would like to give Tiro some money to help him purchase his farm, but he is short of cash:

> "I'm delighted you have bought a farm and hope it turns out well for you….You are a landowner now and must give up your city ways; you've become a Roman country gentleman. What a delightful picture of you I now have before my eyes; I imagine you buying what you need for the farm, talking with your farm manager, preserving the seeds from your

dessert in your pocket. But, more to the purpose, I am as sorry as you that I have failed you. But be assured, my Tiro, that I would help you, if only fortune helped me [i.e. if only I had some cash]."

l.12 *quadrāgēsimō diē*: "on the fortieth day"; the letter would probably have been sent by one of the companies of *tabellāriī*; forty days seems a very slow delivery and perhaps this is why Marcus remarks on it.

ll.25–6 *librārium...hypomnēmata*: "secretary...memoranda (i.e. lecture notes)." Many an undergraduate would be glad of a secretary to make sense of his lecture notes. It seems unlikely that Marcus would have made much use of him, but perhaps Tiro would have been impressed by this apparent evidence that Marcus was a reformed character.

(c) Marcus ā dīs seruātur

ll.5–6 *pater Athēnās uenit*: Cicero had heard bad reports of Marcus' behavior in Athens and decided to go and see for himself. He set sail from Pompeii on July 17 (44 BC) but was driven back to Italy by adverse winds. On hearing that Antony was planning a reconciliation with the Liberators (the assassins of Julius Caesar), he decided to return to Rome and attend a meeting of the Senate on September 1.

l.7 *ō mē miserum!* the accusative is used in exclamations; cf. *ō diem nigrum!* (l.14).

l.19 *nunc est bibendum*: "now (we) must drink"; literally: "now it must be drunk (by us)"; gerundive of obligation—see Chapter 27. These are the first words of Horace's ode on the death of Cleopatra (*Odes* 1.37).

Word-building

Three types of noun are formed from the supines of many verbs, e.g. from **moneō** (I warn, remind), supine **monit-um**:

1. **monit-or, monitōris**, *m.* a reminder (someone who reminds)
   (masculine 3rd declension nouns ending in **-or** in the nominative denote the person who performs the action of the verb);
2. **monit-us, monitūs**: *m.* a reminder, a warning
   (4th declension nouns ending in **-us** denote the action of the verb);
3. **monit-iō, monitiōnis**: *f.* a reminding, warning
   (3rd declension feminine nouns with nominative **-iō** also denote the action of the verb).

What do the following nouns mean?

verb	supine	nouns
currō	cursum	cursor, cursōris, *m.*
		cursus, cursūs, *m.*
audiō	audītum	audītor, audītōris, *m.*
		audītiō, audītiōnis, *f.*
inueniō	inuentum	inuentor, inuentōris, *m.*
		inuentiō, inuentiōnis, *f.*

GRAMMAR

Present, Future and Imperfect Passive

A new set of person endings must be learned for the present, future and imperfect passive; these are set out below in parallel with the person endings of the active:

	active	passive	*e.g. Present active* *1st conjugation*	*Present passive* *1st conjugation*
			I prepare, I am preparing	I am prepared, I am preparing
I	-ō /m	-r	**par-ō**	**par-or**
you	-s	-ris	**parā-s**	**parā-ris**
he/she	-t	-tur	**para-t**	**parā-tur**
we	-mus	-mur	**parā-mus**	**parā-mur**
you	-tis	-minī	**parā-tis**	**parā-minī**
they	-nt	-ntur	**para-nt**	**para-ntur**

Write out the present passive of **mone-ō** and **audi-ō** (check the forms in the Reference Grammar, p. 309).

The present passive of 3rd conjugation verbs, e.g.	*The present passive of 3rd conjugation -iō verbs, e.g.*
reg-or I am being ruled	**capi-or** I am being ruled
reg-eris	**cap-eris**
reg-itur	**cap-itur**
reg-imur	**cap-imur**
reg-iminī	**cap-iminī**
reg-untur	**capi-untur**

Future passive		
1 parā-bor I shall be prepared	**2 monē-bor** I shall be warned	**3 reg-ar** I shall be ruled
parā-beris	**monē-beris**	**reg-ēris**
parā-bitur	**monē-bitur**	**reg-ētur**
parā-bimur	**monē-bimur**	**reg-ēmur**
parā-biminī	**monē-biminī**	**reg-ēminī**
parā-buntur	**monē-buntur**	**reg-entur**

Future passive	
3 -iō capi-ar I shall be taken	**4 audi-ar** I shall be heard
capi-ēris	**audi-ēris**
capi-ētur	**audi-ētur**
capi-ēmur	**audi-ēmur**
capi-ēminī	**audi-ēminī**
capi-entur	**audi-entur**

Imperfect passive		
1 parā-bar I was being prepared	**2 monē-bar** I was being warned	**3 reg-ēbar** I was being ruled
parā-bāris	**monē-bāris**	**reg-ēbāris**
parā-bātur	**monē-bātur**	**reg-ēbātur**
parā-bāmur	**monē-bāmur**	**reg-ēbāmur**
parā-bāminī	**monē-bāminī**	**reg-ēbāminī**
parā-bantur	**monē-bantur**	**reg-ēbantur**

Imperfect passive	
3 -iō capi-ēbar I was being taken	**4 audi- ēbar** I was being heard
capi-ēbāris	**audi- ēbāris**
capi-ēbātur	**audi- ēbātur**
capi-ēbāmur	**audi- ēbāmur**
capi-ēbāminī	**audi- ēbāminī**
capi-ēbantur	**audi- ēbantur**

EXERCISE 17.1

Translate

amantur, regitur, audīminī, monēris, dūcēbāris, uidēbimur, oppugnābantur, trāditur, trādētur, mittēris, mitteris.

EXERCISE 17.2

Translate the following verb forms

1. uocābimur
2. uocātī estis
3. uocābātur
4. uocātus eram
5. uocābant
6. uocāris
7. uocāuī
8. terrēbantur
9. terrētur
10. territī sunt
11. terrēbant
12. territa erat
13. terrēmur
14. terruit
15. pōnor
16. pōnēris
17. pōneris
18. posuērunt
19. positae erant
20. posueram
21. positī sunt

EXERCISE 17.3

Translate
1. cotīdiē nūntiī peiōrēs Venusiam Rōmā afferēbantur.
2. Flaccus hīs rūmōribus magnopere commouēbātur.
3. cum amīcīs in tabernā sedēbat, quibus nūntius nouus allātus erat.
4. Flaccus "quid dīcitis?" inquit. "rēspūblica in bellum cīuīle iterum trahitur, nec iūs nec lēgēs ualēbunt."
5. Ganymēdēs "nōlī tē uexāre," inquit; "Rōmā longē absumus; nōs bellō cīuīlī nōn uexābimur."
6. Flaccus "nōlī nūgās (*nonsense*) nārrāre," inquit; "tōta Italia ēuertētur, immō (*or rather*) tōtus orbis terrārum.
7. fīlius meus Athēnīs studet; in bellum ā Brūtō trahētur."
8. amīcī eum iussērunt meliōra dīcere; "nōlī dēspērāre, Flacce," inquiunt; "pāx sine dubiō seruābitur; ducēs in concordiam (*agreement, harmony*) addūcentur."
9. Flaccus tamen eīs nōn crēdēbat. hīs rūmōribus semper uexābātur, propter quōs et prō rēpūblicā et prō fīliō suō timēbat.

EXERCISE 17.4

Change the following Latin sentences into passive forms and then translate the new sentences, e.g.
> **Flaccus Argum domum dūcēbat. = Argus ā Flaccō domum dūcēbātur.**
> Argus was being led home by Flaccus.
1. Theomnēstus multōs iuuenēs in Acadēmiā docuit.
2. Marcus multum argentum cōnsūmpserat.
3. ego patris meī mortem uindicābō.
4. Cicerō sōlus rempūblicam dēfendit.
5. mīlitēs Antōnī exercitūs coniūrātōrum facile superābunt.
6. omnēs cīuēs et Octāuiānum et Antōnium laudābunt.
7. Flaccus uxōrem Venusiamque mox uidēbit.
8. Brūtus ipse Caesarem occīdit.

EXERCISE 17.5

Translate into Latin
1. Quintus was being led to a tavern by a friend.
2. Suddenly someone called him; "By whom was I called?" he said.
3. His friend replied, "Look! You are being called by Marcus."
4. Marcus was greeted cheerfully by Quintus.

5. "If you go to (*future perfect*) Cratippus' lecture," he said, "you will be praised by your father."
6. Marcus was not delighted by these words.
7. "I shall steer clear of his lectures (his lectures will be avoided by me)," he said.
8. Quīntus was disturbed by these words. Marcus had been led into difficulties (**angustiae**).
9. If Cicero is recalled (*future perfect*) to Rome, Marcus will be very glad.
10. He had been ordered by his father to study but was unwilling to obey him.

STOIC AND EPICUREAN

What is a philosopher? The literal meaning of the word is, of course, a "lover of wisdom." Philosophers try to discover the truth about the world we live in; they suggest ways in which we can lead our lives for the best; they tell us about the nature of good and evil, and about what sort of behavior is best for us both as individuals and as members of a society. The most important question for Greek philosophers was "What is the greatest good?" Their teaching was highly valued by a number of men of action in the ancient world. Marcus Cicero's teacher Cratippus was made a Roman citizen by Julius Caesar. He was the head of the Lyceum, the philosophical school founded by the famous Greek thinker Aristotle, who was tutor to Alexander the Great.

The founder of the Academy, of which Theomnestus was head when Horace arrived in Athens, was Aristotle's teacher, Plato, the greatest of the Greek philosophers, who lived from about 429 to 347 BC. The most famous of his works is the *Republic*, which we call a "dialogue" because Plato presents his views through an imaginary discussion led by his own teacher Socrates. It sets forth the belief that the ideal state should be governed by philosophers since they know best what is good and what is bad.

The busts of Aristotle and Plato come from the Louvre Museum, Paris, and the Fitzwilliam Museum, Cambridge, respectively. That of Epicurus is a Roman copy of a Greek original of the third century BC. It was found in Rome in 1775. (British Museum, London)

As time passed, new schools of thought developed, notably the Stoic and the Epicurean, the two philosophies which dominated the Roman world in Horace's day. The Stoics preached that to be virtuous was the only good and not to be virtuous the only evil. Man must always act in accordance with reason. He should accept whatever happens to him with calm, giving way neither to intense joy nor to excessive grief. Thus he will come into harmony not only with the universal brotherhood of man but also with God. Brutus, the assassin of Julius Caesar, seemed to many to display the Stoic qualities at their noblest.

The Stoic school was founded by Zeno of Cyprus (335–263 BC) who came to Athens early in life and taught there in the Painted Porch (Stoa) from which the philosophy took its name. It had a greater effect on Roman life than any other philosophy, lasting from its introduction to Rome in the second century BC until the third century AD. It proved a humane influence in the treatment of slaves whom Stoics believed to be equal with other men because all alike are the sons of God. The Stoic emperor Marcus Aurelius Antoninus (121–180 AD) wrote, "My city and my country, so far as I am Antoninus, is Rome, but so far as I am a man, it is the world" and "Men exist for the sake of one another." (*Meditations* 6.44, 8.59)

The Stoics involved themselves in the real world of politics and war, but the followers of Epicurus (341–270 BC), who had founded the other main philosophy of the age, tried to avoid such disturbing pursuits. Epicurus' main purpose was to lead men to a happy life. This did not mean that they should always aim at the most obvious pleasures. After all, an evening of drinking is followed by a hangover. Their ideal was peace of mind. The fear of death, for example, could be overcome by the belief that the soul dies with the body and that there is no danger of survival. The great Roman poet Lucretius (first half of the first century BC) gives 28 proofs that the soul is mortal. The Epicureans recommended withdrawal from the turmoil and confusion of the active life into the study of philosophy. This is celebrated by Lucretius in the following passage:

> It is sweet, when the winds are lashing the waves on the high seas, to view
> from the land the great struggles of someone else. But nothing is sweeter
> than to dwell in the serene temples built on the teaching of the wise, from
> where you can look down on others and see them wandering this way
> and that and going astray while they seek the path of life, as they strive to
> outdo each other in their ability and their claims to noble birth, struggling
> night and day by supreme efforts to rise to the height of power and gain
> dominion over the world.
>
> (*Dē Rērum Nātūrā* 2.1–13)

Further Reading

For further reading on Stoics and Epicureans, see Bertrand Russell, *History of Western Philosophy* (Routledge, 1991) 249–71. A good summary of Lucretius' Epicurean beliefs is given in E. J. Kenney, ed., *Lucretius 3* (revised edition, Cambridge, 2011), introduction.

Chapter 18
Brūtus Athēnās aduenit

No new grammar

COMMENTARY

The sequence of events between the murder of Julius Caesar and the death of Cicero is so complex that we give below a chronological table:

44 BC

March 15: Assassination of Julius Caesar

April: C. Octavius, adopted by Caesar in his will, returns from Apollonia (in modern Albania) to Italy to claim his inheritance. From now on he is called C. Julius Caesar Octavianus.

Antony rebuffs overtures from Octavian and raises troops.

Cicero, convinced that there will be civil war, retires to the country.

July: Cicero sets out for Greece to visit Marcus but returns to Rome on hearing that Antony is prepared to compromise with Brutus and Cassius.

August: Final rupture between Antony and the conspirators. Brutus and Cassius leave Rome for the East.

September 2: Cicero attacks Antony in the Senate (1st *Philippic*). Brutus in Athens.

October: Antony raises troops in Italy; Octavian also raises troops and marches on Rome.

November 29: Antony leaves Rome. He marches to Cisalpine Gaul (= northern Italy) at the head of a large army.

December: Antony besieges Decimus Brutus (Governor of Cisalpine Gaul) in Mutina (= modern Modena) when he refuses to surrender his province.

Cicero launches fierce attacks on Antony in the senate (3rd *Philippic*) and before the people (4th *Philippic*). He thus emerges as the leader of the republican cause against Antony.

43 BC

January: Octavian is made a senator and given propraetorian *imperium*. The senate sends an embassy to Antony ordering him to leave Italy.

February 3: Senate declares a state of war.

April: Both consuls and Octavian march against Antony to relieve the siege of Mutina. Antony is defeated at Mutina and retreats into Gaul. But both consuls are killed in the battle, leaving Octavian in sole command.

July: Octavian sends an embassy to Rome demanding that the senate make him consul. When they refuse, he marches on Rome.

August 19: Octavian made consul.

October: Octavian marches north, ostensibly to deal with Antony. Antony leads his army into Cisalpine Gaul. Antony, Octavian and Lepidus* (governor of Gallia Narbonensis and Nearer Spain) meet at Bononia (= Bologna in central Italy) and form an alliance called by historians the Second Triumvirate.

November: The *Triumviri* arrive at Rome and are formally instituted to regulate affairs of state for five years. Proscriptions.

December 7: Cicero killed by Antony's soldiers.

(a) Rēspūblica in bellum cīuīle trahitur

l.26 *prōscrībuntur*: the proscriptions were notices giving lists of the names of those who were outlawed and whose property was confiscated; they were posted publicly and rewards were offered for the execution of the proscribed. Sulla had first used this weapon of tyranny in 82–81 BC; now the *triumvirs* revived it.

(b) Brūtus Athēnās aduenit

Brutus arrived at Athens in September 44 BC; his arrival caused a great stir. He attended the lectures of both Theomnestus and Cratippus, and fraternized with the students, asking some of them to dinner. When he left to join his army in Macedonia, many, including Marcus Cicero, went with him. We make Quintus join him a little later.

l.7 *dē officiīs*: "about duties"; great stress was laid by the philosophers, especially the Stoics, on the duties owed by the good man to his fellows. Cicero was writing a work on this topic at this very time (*Dē Officiīs* in three books, completed November 44 BC).

l.9 *Harmodī et Aristogītōnis*: according to popular tradition, Harmodius and Aristogeiton, two Athenian nobles, liberated Athens from the tyrant Hippias, son of Pisistratus, in 514 BC. They were honored as Liberators and their statues were set up in the Agora. In fact they killed Hippias' younger brother Hipparchus; Hippias was driven out of Ath-

---

*Lepidus, as governor of two provinces, had an army under his command and so had to be included in the pact; but he was soon shipped off to Africa, leaving Antony and Octavian in control of the rest of the empire; Octavian took Italy and the West, and Antony the East.

ens three years later. (Thucydides goes to some length to correct the false popular tradition—1.20.)

Brutus' arrival was greeted entusiastically by the Athenians, who decreed that statues of him and Cassius, as Liberators, should be set up beside those of Harmodius and Aristogeiton.

R|V **Brutus:** this coin is in the British Museum. *See page 86 in* Oxford Latin Course, College Edition: Readings and Vocabulary.

R|V **Harmodius and Aristogeiton:** the original statues of the tyrant-slayers were carried off by Xerxes, the Persian king, when he sacked Athens in 480 BC. Our illustration shows two good copies of the statues that replaced them in 477 BC. The older Aristogeiton advances more cautiously with his robe available as a protective shield, while his boyfriend, the younger Harmodius, whose right arm has been wrongly restored—it should be back over his shoulder—exposes himself to danger with the brash assurance of youth. (National Archaeological Museum, Naples) *See page 86 in* Oxford Latin Course, College Edition: Readings and Vocabulary.

l.17 *Brūtī abauum*: Lucius Junius Brutus drove out the last king of Rome, Tarquinius Superbus, in 509 BC and established the Republic.

l.24 *ālae equitum*: "a cavalry wing." The cavalry of the Roman army was at this time provided by allies (non-citizens) but commanded by citizens called *praefectī*.

Marcus Cicero proved a good officer. Brutus praised him extravagantly in a letter he wrote to Cicero in April 43 BC, "Your son Cicero impresses me by his industry, his endurance, his hard work, his greatness of spirit, so much that he seems absolutely never to forget whose son he is." (*Ad Brūtum* 2.3.6)

Cicero must have been pleased and surprised by this encomium of his son, and his reply suggests that he took it with a pinch of salt: "About my son Cicero, if he is as good as you say, I am naturally as delighted as I should be, but if you are exaggerating because you are fond of him, I am incredibly pleased that he has won your affection." (*Ad Brūtum* 2.4.6) In all fairness, Marcus was not suited to academic life and may well have proved a good soldier.

(c) Mors Cicerōnis

The account of Cicero's death is adapted from Livy fragment 120. Livy (59 BC–17 AD) wrote a history of Rome from its foundation to 9 BC in 142 books, of which only 1–10 and 21–45 survive, but we have ancient summaries of the rest, including this fragment.

R|V **The *rōstra*:** the ruins of the rostra, brought forward from the original site in front of the senate house during Caesar's restoration in 44 BC. The first structure was adorned with the rostra (beaks of ships for ramming) of the ships captured from the Volscians at the battle of Antium (338 BC). *See page 88 in* Oxford Latin Course, College Edition: Readings and Vocabulary.

R|V **Mark Antony:** this coin is from the British Museum. *See page 88 in* Oxford Latin Course, College Edition: Readings and Vocabulary.

R|V **The tomb of Cicero:** the so-called tomb of Cicero is near the spot where he was murdered in the vicinity of Caieta (modern Gaeta) in South Italy. *See page 88 in* Oxford Latin Course, College Edition: Readings and Vocabulary.

(d) Horātiae nūptiae

There are good chapters on Roman marriage in U. E. Paoli, *Rome: Its People, Life and Customs* (Bristol Classical Press, 1990), Chapter 9, and J. Carcopino, *Daily Life in Ancient Rome* (Penguin, 1991), Chapter 4, and M. Harlow and R. Laurence, *Growing Up and Growing Old in Ancient Rome* (Routledge, 2002), 58–64. A good modern book on the subject is K. K. Hersh, *The Roman Wedding: Ritual and Meaning in Antiquity* (Cambridge, 2010). It is worth remarking that the order of some of the customs was varied in practice.

l.9 *amōre eius*: of love for her: an objective genitive; i.e. it's not "her love" but "his love of her"—he loves her.

l.11 *dē dōte*: the dowry, the property the bride contributed to the union, was a vital element in ancient marriage and still is in contemporary Greece. In the event of divorce, the husband had to return the dowry to his ex-wife.

R|V **Roman marriage ceremony:** this relief from a Roman marble sarcophagus of the second century AD shows the Roman ceremony of *dextrārum iūnctiō* (the joining of right hands). In their left hands, the bride holds a rose and the bridegroom the wedding contract. Behind them stands the *prōnuba* (a married woman who assisted the bride). (British Museum, London) *See page 89 in* Oxford Latin Course, College Edition: Readings and Vocabulary.

l.23 *auspicēs*: the augurs were present to take the auspices (*auspicia*) on important occasions in public and in private life such as weddings. They consulted the will of heaven by watching the behavior of birds.

l.25 *bene uerruncet*: this is an archaic religious formula, used in blessing any undertaking: "may it turn out well."

l.31 *ades*: the singular imperative of *adsum*.

l.33 *ignem et aquam*: these represent the basic components which make human life possible.

R V **A bride preparing for her wedding:** this wall-painting is a Roman work from the time of Augustus inspired by a Greek model of the fourth or third century BC. It was found on the Esquiline hill in Rome in 1605 and then kept at the Villa Aldobrandini. Hence it is known as the "Aldobrandini Wedding." It contains telling symbolism as scantily clad women purify and prepare the bride for the wedding. (Vatican Museums, Rome) *See page 90 in* Oxford Latin Course, College Edition: Readings and Vocabulary.

COMPREHENSION EXERCISE

Read the following passage carefully and then answer the questions below

A mysterious woman offers Tarquin, the king of Rome, some holy books. Later the king is driven into exile but attempts to regain power.

anus ignōta ad Tarquinium Superbum adiit, nouem	**anus** old woman
librōs ferēns, quī, ut dīcēbat, dīuīna ōrācula er-	**Superbum** the Proud
ant. eōs uendere uoluit. Tarquinius igitur pretium	**ōrācula** prophecies
rogāuit. fēmina pretium ingēns poposcit et rēx eam	**pretium** price
dērīsit. tum illa, nihil commōta, foculum cum ignī 5	**poposcit** demanded
prope rēgem posuit, trēs librōs ex nouem incendit, et	**dērīsit** laughed at
"ō rēx," inquit, "librōs reliquōs eōdem pretiō emere	**foculum** brazier,
uīs?" Tarquinius, ubi haec audīuit, eam multō ma-	standing fire
gis dērīsit. fēmina statim trēs aliōs librōs incendit	
iterumque uultū placidō rēgī "trēs reliquōs" inquit 10	**placidō** calm
"eōdem pretiō emēs?" Tarquinius, cōnstantiā eius	**cōnstantiā** determi-
superātus, haec uerba neglegere nōluit et librōs trēs	nation
ēmit nōn minōre pretiō quam quod prō omnibus	
petītum erat. posteā haec fēmina nūllō in locō	
uidēbātur. librī in Capitōliō ā rēge positī auxilium 15	
magnum reīpūblicae praebuērunt.	**praebuērunt** gave

sed haud multō post Tarquinius propter facta sua
pessima in exilium expulsus est. mox tamen cum
cōpiīs Etruscīs in Rōmānōs contendit; nam rēgnum
suum recuperāre maximē uolēbat. equitibus fīlius
eius praefectus erat; rēx ipse peditēs dūxit. Rōmānī
in magnō perīculō erant sed ab Horātiō seruātī
sunt quī pontem trāns Tiberim aedificātum fortiter dēfendit. Etruscī igitur nōn poterant Rōmam
aedificātum peruenīre.

rēgnum kingdom

recuperāre to get
    20   back

peditēs infantry

pontem bridge

aedificātum built

Adapted from Aulus Gellius, 1.19 and *Livy,* 2.6 and 10

1. Translate ll. 1–14 (*anus...petītum erat*).
2. What happened to (a) the woman and (b) the books (ll. 14–16)?
3. Why was Tarquinius driven into exile?
4. How was the command of the invading army divided?
5. Who saved the Romans, and how?
6. Between ll. 14 and 20, find and write out a verb (a) in the imperfect passive; (b) in the perfect passive; (c) in the pluperfect passive.
7. What cases are the following nouns in, and why: *rēge* (l.15); *rēipūblicae* (l.16); *equitibus* (l.19); *Rōmam* (l.23)?

Chapter 19

Horātius Delphōs uīsit

> **Grammar:** the subjunctive mood; the present subjunctive; the jussive subjunctive; purpose clauses; sequence of tenses; indirect commands

CARTOONS

The cartoons exercise the present and imperfect subjunctive in purpose clauses, indirect commands, and the jussive usage. The first two cartoons take place in front of a wall-painting showing Delphi: hence the cracks!

COMMENTARY

(a) Horātius Delphōs uīsit

Educated Romans regularly visited the famous sites of Greece and Asia Minor. So Catullus on his return journey from serving on the staff of the governor of Bithynia visited the famous sites of Asia Minor—*ad clārās Asiae uolēmus urbēs* (let us fly to the famous cities of Asia—Catullus 46.6). Pausanias (in his prime 150 AD) wrote a guide book for tourists with detailed descriptions of the sites.

Of all the sites on mainland Greece the most famous was Delphi and we guess that Horace would have visited it while he was studying in Athens.

1.3 *antequam*: before (conjunction); cf. *ante noctem* (preposition); *Delphōs nōn anteā uīserat* (adverb). So also *post, posteā, postquam.*

Delphōs: plural in form, like many place names, e.g. *Athēnae, Mycēnae.*

1.6 *Pompēiō*: Pompeius is the friend with whom Horace served in the army of Brutus at Philippi—see *Odes* 2.7: *Ō....Pompei, meōrum prīme sodālium* (O Pompeius, first of my comrades). The ode celebrates Pompeius' return to Rome after his long exile; at Philippi Horace says he himself threw away his shield and fled, while Pompeius continued the fight for the Republic under Sextus Pompeius (probably no relation of his) until he was allowed back to Rome under an amnesty.

l.11 *subitō Delphōs prōspexērunt*: the site of Delphi is spectacular. The village is perched on the lower slopes of Mount Parnassus, 2,000 feet above the valley of the Pleistos, which leads to the Gulf of Corinth. Above it rise the two great cliffs known as the Phaedriades, "the Shining One."

The sanctuary of Apollo is an elaborate complex. On passing through the gates you entered the Sacred Way, which winds up to the temple. On either side of the Sacred Way stood votive offerings made by states or individuals in thanks to Apollo; many states built treasuries, buildings like small temples, in which to store the offerings they had made; the best preserved of these is the treasury of the Athenians, built in 490 BC to commemorate the battle of Marathon. The Sacred Way ends at the great temple of Apollo; this stands on a massive platfom and measures 179 feet by 72, austerely Doric in style. Successive temples were destroyed by fire, earthquake or plundering, but it was always rebuilt until the last was left to decay afer the dissolution of the Delphic oracle by the emperor Theodosius in 385 AD. Its present ruined state makes it impossible to know anything about the *adytum* (the inner shrine) in which the Pythia delivered Apollo's oracles.

Above the temple was the theater. Apollo was the patron god of music and poetry, and every fourth year the Pythian games were celebrated, at which there were competitions in music and drama and recitations in verse and prose. To these were added later athletic competitions; a stadium was built high above the theater and chariot races were held on the plain below.

l.16 *nē*: "lest," "in case"; *nē* here expresses fear rather than purpose.

l.21 *ā fronte*: "in front." in front of the temple doors stood the altar on which the priests made sacrifices to Apollo. We envisage a group of suppliants waiting to consult the oracle. There was always a queue of people waiting, either individuals or representatives of states sent on sacred embassies. The oracle only performed once a month for nine months of the year and so pilgrims often had to wait a long time.

When the time came, the procedure was elaborate. The suppliant first purified himself by washing in the Castalian spring. He then offered sacrifice, usually a goat and a *pelanos*, a cake made from flour and honey. If the omens were propitious, he was next admitted to the room above the *adytum*. When his turn came, he handed the priest his question written on a lead tablet.

By now the Pythia, the priestess who was Apollo's medium, had descended into the *adytum*. Plutarch, philosopher and biographer, who was a priest of Apollo at Delphi in 95 AD, says of the Pythia: "She must come from one of the most honest and respectable families of those who live nearby and must always have lived a most irreproachable life. When she descends into the place of prophecy, she does not take with her any kind of skill or talent, as she was brought up in the house of poor peasants."

She was in fact simply the vehicle through which Apollo was believed to communicate with men. Before entering the *adytum* she had purified herself by washing in the Castalian spring and by drinking from another sacred spring, Cassiotis. She entered the *adytum* accompanied by the *prophētēs*, her interpreter, dressed in a simple white robe and holding in her hand a branch of laurel, sacred to Apollo. She seated herself on the sacred tripod (a three-legged stool) and fell into a trance. When she started to speak, the *prophētēs* recorded her words. It was he who gave Apollo's response to the suppliant, either verbally or written on a tablet. In Book 6 of the *Aeneid*, Aeneas consults the oracle of Apollo in Cumae and describes how the priestess is possessed by the god. When Aeneas reached the threshold of the shrine:

> The Sibyl cried, "The god, behold, the god!" As she said this, suddenly her face and her color changed, her hair ran wild; her breast heaved, and her heart swelled with fierce ecstasy; she appeared larger, her voice was not that of a mortal, as she was possessed by the spirit of the god.... But the priestess, not yet subdued to the god, raves wildly in the cave, trying to shake the god from her heart; but he tires out her foaming mouth, subduing her fierce heart, and crushes her and shapes her to his will. (*Aeneid* 6.46–51 and 77–80)

There is much doubt about what actually happened but there is no doubt that the vast majority of the Greeks took the whole business very seriously and believed the truth of Apollo's oracles. The matters on which the oracle was consulted ranged from down-to-earth personal issues to vital national ones. One old man who wanted children received the response:

> You are late looking for your family:
> But fit a new hook to an old plow-tree.

The old man was encouraged by this piece of advice and married a young wife who later bore him two sons.

Even oracles which were apparently riddles could make perfect sense. When the Persian hordes were descending on Athens in 480 BC, the Athenian general Themistocles interpreted the oracle's promise that "the wooden wall only shall not fail" as meaning that her wooden ships would save Athens (Herodotus 7.140–44). Sure enough, she won a great naval victory at Salamis.

If the rituals were not duly observed, things could go badly wrong. Plutarch tells of a disaster which occurred in his time. The preliminary sacrifice had not been propitious but the suppliant insisted on going ahead:

> The Pythia went down into the *adytum* unwillingly, they say, and half-heartedly; and at her first response it was at once clear from the harshness of her voice that she was not responding properly and was like a laboring ship, as if she was filled with a baleful spirit. Finally she became hysterical and with a frightful shriek rushed towards the exit and there threw herself down, with the result that not only the members of the deputation, but also the *prophētēs*, Nicander, and the cult officials present fled. (Plutarch, *Moralia* 438b).

A few days later the Pythia died.

A full account of the oracle's activity can be found in H. Bowden, *Classical Athens and the Delphic Oracle: Divination and Democracy* (Cambridge, 2005).

R V **The Shining Rocks:** the two Phaedriades, which tower behind the temple, are so called because they reflect the light. They are 800–1000 feet high. See *page 93 in* Oxford Latin Course, College Edition: Readings and Vocabulary.

R V **The Castalian spring:** the ruins of the spring are of Roman or Hellenistic date. See *page 93 in* Oxford Latin Course, College Edition: Readings and Vocabulary.

1.24 *afflāta* (= *adflāta*): "breathed on, inspired."

1.29 *caerimōniam*: "sacred rite." Note how Latin likes to place the subject of the main verb before an intervening phrase or clause. In English it would be ungainly to say, "Horace, watching…" Better to translate "Watching this (so) ancient ceremony, Horace was deeply moved."

1.32 *futūrus*: "about to be": future participle of *sum*.

1.32 *uātēs Apollinis*: *uātēs* originally meant a prophet but came to mean a poet, since a poet was the mouthpiece or interpreter of the Muses. Horace uses it of himself, especially in conjunction with Apollo, e.g. *quid dēdicātum poscit Apollinem / uātēs* ("What does his prophet ask of Apollo at his temple's dedication?") *Odes* 1.31.1–2. (Horace is writing at the dedication of the new temple of Apollo on the Palatine on October 9, 28 BC).

1.33 *fōns Castalius*: in drinking from the Castalian spring Horace dedicates himself to poetry, since those who drank from it were inspired by Apollo and the Muses.

(b) Horātius ad Asiam nāuigat

1.6 *sē*: in purpose clauses and indirect commands the reflexives *sē* and *suus* normally refer to the subject of the leading verb, but in this case *sē* refers to the subject of *parāret*—"to prepare himself."

1.15 *Dēlum*: the tiny island of Delos at the center of the Cyclades was the birthplace of Apollo. According to myth, Leto, pregnant by Zeus, wandered all over Greece and the islands looking for a place where she could give birth to her child, but "no land dared to make a dwelling for Phoebus Apollo" (*Homeric Hymn to Delian Apollo*, ll.47–8, 117–8); eventually Delos allowed Leto to give birth there: "casting her arms about a palm tree, while the earth laughed for joy beneath her knees, Leto gave birth to Apollo." The island thus became a holy place where the Ionians gathered every year for a festival in honor of the god.

R|V **The stone lions of Delos:** these stone figures stand beside the Sacred Way on Delos which led from the sanctuary of Apollo to the Sacred Lake. Carved from Naxos marble at the end of the seventh century BC, they are badly weathered. Five remain in situ; one more is positioned before the Arsenal in Venice. *See page 95 in* Oxford Latin Course, College Edition: Readings and Vocabulary.

GRAMMAR

The Subjunctive Mood

Consider the different ways in which the verbs are used in the following sentences:

(a) He is helping us	statement
Is he helping us?	question
(b) Help us!	command
(c) Let us help him.	exhortation (= encouragement)
Let him help us.	3rd person command
May he help us!	wish
He may help us.	possibility

These different ways of using the verb are called *moods* (Latin *modus* = way). In Latin:

(a)   statements and questions are in the *indicative* mood;
(b)   commands are in the *imperative* mood;
(c)   exhortations, 3rd person commands, wishes, and possibilities are in the *subjunctive* mood.

You have already learned the indicative and imperative moods. You now have to learn the subjunctive.

The Present Subjunctive

The present subjunctive is translated: *I may prepare* etc.

1st	2nd	3rd	3rd -iō	4th	esse
par-em	mone-am	reg-am	capi-am	audi-am	sim
par-ēs	mone-ās	reg-ās	capi-ās	audi-ās	sīs
par-et	mone-at	reg-at	capi-at	audi-at	sit
par-ēmus	mone-āmus	reg-āmus	capi-āmus	audi-āmus	sīmus
par-ētis	mone-ātis	reg-ātis	capi-ātis	audi-ātis	sītis
par-ent	mone-ant	reg-ant	capi-ant	audi-ant	sint

Note that the subjunctive endings for 1st conjugation verbs are **-em**, **-ēs**, **-et**, etc. For all the other conjugations the endings are **-am**, **-ās**, **-at**, etc. (except for *sum* and compounds, and **uolō**, **nōlō**, and **mālō**, which are irregular).

EXERCISE 19.1

Give the present subjunctive (1st person singular) of

uocō, dormiō, dēfendō, festīnō, faciō, studeō, adsum

You must watch verb endings with great care; the change of one letter alters the meaning, e.g.

dūcimus we lead, are leading

dūcēmus we shall lead

dūcāmus let us lead

EXERCISE 19.2

Translate the following verb forms

1. dīcimus
2. dīximus
3. dīcēmus
4. dīcāmus

5. ueniat
6. uenit
7. ueniet
8. uēnit
9. iuuant
10. iūuērunt
11. iuuābunt
12. iuuent
13. habeāmus
14. habēmus
15. habuimus
16. habēbimus

GRAMMAR

The Present Subjunctive (continued)

The present subjunctive is used in main clauses to express all three of the meanings listed under (c) above; thus *parēmus* can mean:

(1) let us prepare (exhortation)
(2) may we prepare! (wish)
(3) we may prepare (possibility)

We deal with wishes and possibilities later (Chapter 28). At present we only use the first of these three meanings (exhortations and 3rd person commands). This is called the *jussive subjunctive*:

ad lūdum festīnēmus.   Let us hurry to school.
nē domī maneat.   Let him not stay at home.

Note that the negative is **nē**.

EXERCISE 19.3

Translate
1. fortiter pugnēmus.
2. nē fugiāmus.
3. statim ad castra redeant.
4. amēmus patriam; pāreāmus senātuī.
5. puerī dīligenter labōrent.

GRAMMAR

Clauses of Purpose

The subjunctive is found in many types of subordinate clause, e.g. clauses expressing *purpose*. These are introduced by **ut**, if positive, **nē** = lest, if negative:

collem ascendimus <u>ut</u> templum <u>uideāmus</u>.

We are climbing the hill <u>so that we may see</u> the temple/<u>to see</u> the temple.

festīnāmus <u>nē</u> sērō <u>adueniāmus</u>.

We are hurrying <u>lest we arrive</u> late/<u>that we may not arrive</u> late/<u>so as not to arrive</u> late.

Notice that English often uses the infinitive to express purpose; Latin always uses **ut/nē** + subjunctive.

EXERCISE 19.4

Translate the following sentences

1. festīnāmus ut tē adiuuēmus.
2. Horātius Delphōs iter facit ut Apollinis fānum (*shrine*) uideat.
3. hominēs ab omnibus partibus Graeciae Delphōs ueniunt ut deī ōrācula petant.
4. multī iuuenēs Athēnās nāuigābunt ut in Acadēmīā studeant.
5. ad theātrum conuenīte, iuuenēs, ut Theomnēstum audiātis.
6. puerī ad lūdum festīnant nē sērō adueniant.
7. puellae domum celeriter redībunt nē parentēs uexent.
8. māter fīliam reuocat nē in perīculum cadat.

GRAMMAR

The Sequence of Tenses

If the verb in the main clause is present, imperative, future or "perfect with have"*, the verb in the **ut/nē** clause will be in the *present subjunctive*; if the verb in the main clause is in a past tense, the verb in the **ut/nē** clause will be in the *imperfect subjunctive*, as in English:

We are coming so that we *may* help you. (present subjunctive)
We came so that we *might* help you. (imperfect subjunctive)

*The "perfect with have" is a shorthand expression for a perfect which tells us about a present state, e.g. *cognōuī* (I have got to know = I know), *intellēxī* (I have understood = I understand) and *uēnistis* (you have come = you are present).

The Imperfect Subjunctive

The imperfect subjunctive is formed from the present infinitive, e.g. infinitive: **parāre**; imperfect subjunctive: **parārem**. This applies to all verbs of all conjugations.

parāre		**monēre**	**regere**	**capere**	**audīre**	**esse**
parārem	*I might prepare*	monērem	regerem	caperem	audīrem	essem
parārēs		etc.	etc.	etc.	etc.	etc.
parāret						
parārēmus						
parārētis						
parārent						

EXERCISE 19.5

Translate

1. festīnābāmus ut tē adiuuārēmus.
2. Horātius Delphōs iter fēcit ut Apollinis fānum uīseret.
3. hominēs ab omnibus partibus Graeciae ueniēbant ut deī ōrācula peterent.
4. multī iuuenēs Athēnās nāuigābant ut in Acadēmiā studērent.
5. iuuenēs ad theātrum conuēnerant ut Theomnēstum audīrent.
6. puerī ad lūdum festīnābant nē sērō aduenīrent.
7. puellae domum celeriter rediērunt nē parentēs uexārent.
8. pater epistolam ad fīlium mīsit ut eum dē perīculō monēret.
9. Marcus Cicerō ad Macedoniam abierat ut cum Brūtō mīlitāret.
10. Brūtus exercitum comparāuerat ut lībertātem populī Rōmānī dēfenderet.

Notice that in purpose clauses the reflexives **sē** and **suus** refer to the subject of the main verb, e.g.

> <u>puerī</u> dīligenter labōrābant ut magister <u>sē</u> mox dīmitteret.
> The boys worked hard that the master might dismiss them soon.

> <u>puella</u> domī manēbat nē māter <u>sē</u> culpāret.
> The girl stayed at home lest her mother might blame her.

EXERCISE 19.6

Translate the following verb forms (translate the present subjunctive as may, *e.g.* **parēmus** = *we may prepare; the imperfect subjunctive as* might, *e.g.* **parārēmus** *(= we might prepare)*

1. cape
2. cēpī
3. capiāmus
4. captus est
5. caperet
6. dūcat
7. ductī sumus
8. dūcerem
9. dūxistī
10. dūcet
11. uocētis
12. uocātus eram
13. uocāmur
14. uocāret
15. uocābimur

EXERCISE 19.7

In the following sentences put the verbs in parentheses into the correct form of the subjunctive, then translate, remembering to observe the "sequence of tenses" (see above)

1. Horātius Pompēiusque iter faciunt ut Delphōs (uidēre).
2. collem ascendēbāmus ut templum Apollinis (īnspicere).
3. diū hīc manēbimus ut omnia (spectāre).
4. tandem Delphīs discessērunt ut Athēnās (redīre).
5. ubi Athēnās rediērunt, Marcus Cicerō abierat ut cum Brūtō (mīlitāre).
6. epistolam Horātiō relīquerat, in quā scrīpserat: "in Macedoniam festīnāuī ut lībertātem cum Brūtō (dēfendere)."

EXERCISE 19.8

Translate into Latin

1. Horatius hurried to the Academy to see his friends.
2. I shall make a journey to Delphi to visit the temple of Apollo.
3. Many men were waiting near the door of the temple to hear the oracle.
4. Horatius woke Pompeius at first light, lest they arrive at the temple late.

5. We have come to Delphi to learn the truth.
6. They have waited in Delphi three days to hear the oracle.
7. The girls were working hard so that the master might praise them.
8. The boys are working hard so that the master may not punish (**pūnīre**) them.

GRAMMAR

Indirect Command

Direct command:

domum redī!	**mē adiuuā!**	**nōlīte lūdere!**
Return home!	Help me!	Don't play!

Indirect command:

pater puerō imperat ut domum redeat.	The father orders the boy to return home.
senex puerum rogat ut sē adiuuet.	The old man asks the boy to help him.
magister puerīs imperāuit nē lūderent.	The master forbade the boys to play.

The construction is the same as that for clauses expressing purpose: **ut/nē** + subjunctive after verbs such as I order, I ask, I beseech, I persuade, I encourage.

English usually uses the infinitive to express indirect command but Latin always uses **ut/nē** + subjunctive except after **iubeō** (**iubēre, iussī, iussum**) (I order) and **uetō** (**uetāre, uetuī, uetitum**) (I forbid), with which the infinitive is used.

As in purpose clauses, the reflexives **sē** and **suus** refer to the subject of the main verb.

The Sequence of Tenses

The rules given for purpose clauses apply equally to indirect commands, e.g.

pater filium rogat ut sē adiuuet.	Father asks his son to help him.
pater filium rogāuit ut sē adiuuāret.	Father asked his son to help him.
pater filiō persuādēbit nē domum redeat.	Father will persuade his son not to return home.
pater filiō peruāserat nē domum redīret.	Father had persuaded his son not to return home.

Remember that if the main verb is a true perfect ("perfect with have"), the subjunctive in the **ut/nē** clause is present, e.g.

hōs iuuenēs ad lēgātum dūcō; <u>uēnērunt</u> ut cum Brūtō <u>mīlitent</u>.
I am taking these young men to the legate; they <u>have come</u> so that they <u>may serve</u> with Brutus.

puer in agrō manet; patrī <u>persuāsit</u> nē sē domum <u>remittat</u>.
The boy is staying in the field; he <u>has persuaded</u> his father <u>not to send</u> him back home.

EXERCISE 19.9

Translate
1. māter filiae imperāuit nē in uiā lūderet.
2. filia mātrem rogāuit ut sē ad forum dūceret.
3. māter filiam iussit in casā manēre et sē iuuāre.
4. puella patrī persuādet ut sē ad forum dūcat.
5. puella mātrī dīxit, "in casā nōn manēbō; patrī enim persuāsī ut mē ad forum dūcat."
6. māter uirō dīxit, "quid facis, mī uir ? tē rogāuī nē filiam ad forum dūcerēs."
7. uir eius respondit, "puella mihi persuāsit ut sē mēcum dūcam."
8. māter uirō dīxit, "puella pessimē sē gessit. tē moneō nē eī sīc indulgeās (*spoil* + dat.)."
9. pater tamen filiam nōn uetuit sēcum uenīre.

EXERCISE 19.10

*Convert the following direct commands into indirect commands after **imperāuit** and translate, e.g.*

magister "soluite nāuem, nautae," inquit.
magister nautīs imperāuit ut nāuem soluerent.
The captain ordered the sailors to cast off the ship.

1. Horātius "Delphōs mēcum uenī, Pompēī," inquit.
2. Horātius Pompēium excitāuit et "surge, Pompēī," inquit.
3. iuuenis magistrō nāuis "nōs ad Asiam dūc" inquit.
4. magister iuuenibus dīcit, "nāuem iam cōnscendite."
5. deinde nautīs dīcit, "fortiter rēmigāte."

EXERCISE 19.11

Translate into Latin

1. Horace persuaded Pompeius to go to Delphi.
2. When they came to the mountains, Pompeius asked Horace not to walk so fast.
3. Many people are asking the Sibyl (**Sibylla**, **ae**, *f.*) to help them.
4. The god Apollo told (= ordered) Horace to become a poet.
5. Pompeius persuades Horace not to go to Asia alone.
6. Horace asked the captain to sail to Delos.

P.S.
What do the following pairs of words mean?

ubi? ubīque
unde? undique
quis? quisque
uter? uterque

Chapter 20

Horātius mīlitat

Grammar: passive forms of subjunctive; pluperfect subjunctives active and passive; deponent verbs; passive infinitives & imperatives

COMMENTARY

The Harbor Street, Ephesus: the street dates from the fourth century BC. The harbor to which it led has now silted up. It was one of the few streets in the ancient world to have street lighting. According to a dubious tradition, St. Paul, whose Christian teaching sparked off a serious demonstration here (*Acts 19.22–20.1*), was imprisoned on the hill to the left. *See page 97 in* Oxford Latin Course, College Edition: Readings and Vocabulary.

l.1 *portum Ephesī*: Ephesus was at this time the most important port on the coast of Asia Minor; its surviving remains are impressive.

l.6 *mīlitent*: present subjunctive in primary sequence after "perfect with have." See p. 168.

l.11 *prūdentēs uidēminī...et strēnuī*: the passive of *uideō* is used to mean "I seem"; note that it is followed by a complement (like *sum*) in the nominative case (*strēnuī uidēminī*).

l.15 *lēgātus...eōs trīstis īnspexit*: the commander of the legion is skeptical about the military potential of university students. Such recruits were often promoted rapidly to become *tribūnī mīlitum* and Caesar found to his cost that in a crisis they sometimes compared unfavorably with long-service professional soldiers (there were six *tribūnī mīlitum* to each legion; they were the senior officers of the legion whose duties were assigned by the legionary commander, the *lēgātus legiōnis*).

l.17 *optiōnem*: the *optiō* was second in command to a centurion; the centurions, 60 to each legion, were the backbone of the army.

l.20 *Lūcīlium*: Lucilius was a historical figure (though here an anachronism); his death in 14 AD at the hands of mutineers is decribed by Tacitus (*Annals* 1.23): *centuriō Lūcīlius interficitur cui mīlitāribus facētiīs uocābulum "cedo alteram" indiderant, quia frāctā uīte in tergō mīlitis alteram clārā voce et rūrsus aliam poscēbat.* (The centurion Lucilius was killed, to whom with a soldier's wit they had given the nickname "Give us another," because, when he had broken his vine staff on the back of a soldier, in a loud voice he demanded another and then yet another.)

l.22 *cedo* is an archaic imperative. Centurions carried a vine staff as a symbol of authority and an instrument of imposing discipline.

cum...frēgerat: *cum* = "when" is normally followed by the subjunctive in past time, but if it means "whenever," as here, it is followed by the indicative (see Chapter 25).

ll.24–5 The weapons of the legionary soldier were the javelin (*tēlum* or *pīlum*) and stabbing sword (*gladius*): *opus* means a work of any kind (including, for instance a literary work) but in a military context it is often used of fortifications.

l.34 *quid facere dēbeātis*: *dēbeātis* is subjunctive because the clause is an indirect question (see Chapter 22).

l.36 *mīlitēs fīetis dignī*: "you will become soldiers worthy of...": *fīō* = "I become" takes a complement in the nominative case, like *sum* and *uideor*.

ll.47–8 *cōnstituī tē tribūnum mīlitum creāre*: Horace tells us that he was a *tribūnus mīlitum* at the battle of Philippi: *quod mihi pārēret legiō Rōmāna tribūnō* (because a Roman legion obeyed me when a tribune—*Satires* 1.6.48). He here claims that he was commanding a legion while he was a tribune; possibly he was given the command when his legionary commander was killed in battle (see Chapter 21).

GRAMMAR

Passive Forms of the Subjunctive

To form the present and imperfect subjunctives passive, change the active person endings to corresponding passive forms, thus:

Present subjunctive:

active	passive	active	passive
par-em	par-er	mone-am	mone-ar
par-ēs	par-ēris	mone-ās	mone-āris
par-et	par-ētur	mone-at	mone-ātur
par-ēmus	par-ēmur	mone-āmus	mone-āmur
par-ētis	par-ēminī	mone-ātis	mone-āminī
par-ent	par-entur	mone-ant	mone-antur

active	passive	active	passive	active	passive
reg-am	reg-ar	audi-am	audi-ar	capi-am	capi-ar
reg-ās	reg-āris	audi-ās	audi-āris	capi-ās	capi-āris
etc.	etc.	etc.	etc.	etc.	etc.

Imperfect passive subjunctives (first person singular): parār-er, monēr-e, reger-er, caper-er, audīr-er.

The Pluperfect Subjunctive

1 Active

This tense is formed by adding the following endings to the perfect stem:

-issem	parāu-issem	monu-issem	rēx-issem	audīu-issem	cēp-issem
-issēs	etc.	etc.	etc.	etc.	etc.
-isset					
-issēmus					
-issētis					
-issent					

cum ad portum Ephesī aduēnissent, ad urbem festīnāuērunt.
When they had arrived at the port of Ephesus, they hurried to the city.

Note that **cum** = "when" usually takes the subjunctive (imperfect or pluperfect) when the verb is in a past tense (for exceptions to this rule, see Chapter 25).

EXERCISE 20.1

Translate
1. Horātius, cum ad nāuem rediisset, continuō dormīuit.
2. cum ad portum aduēnissēmus, ad urbem festīnāuimus.
3. cum in forō manērēmus, multōs mīlitēs uīdimus.
4. cum mīles quīdam nōs ad Brūtī castra dūxisset, tribūnō mīlitum occurrimus nōbīs nōtō.
5. tribūnus, cum nōs uīdisset, hilariter nōs salūtāuit.

GRAMMAR

The Pluperfect Subjunctive (continued)

2 Passive

The pluperfect subjunctive passive is formed by changing the pluperfect indicative (e.g. **parātus eram**) to the corresponding subjunctive form (e.g. **parātus essem**):

parātus essem	monitus essem	rēctus essem	captus essem
parātus essēs	etc.	etc.	etc.
parātus esset			
parātī essēmus			
parātī essētis			
parātī essent			

EXERCISE 20.2

Change the following active subjunctive forms into corresponding forms of the passive
1. mittāmus
2. mitteret
3. mīsissent*
4. amētis
5. amārem
6. amāuissēs*
7. custōdiant
8. custōdīuisset*
9. custōdīret
10. cēpissēmus*

*Feel free to choose the gender of the subject here.

EXERCISE 20.3

Translate

1. Brūtus Caesarem occīdit nē populus Rōmānus ā tyrannō regerētur.
2. cum ab Antōniō oppugnātus esset, Rōmā fūgit.
3. Athēnās nāuigāuit nē ab Antōniō caperētur.
4. Athēnīs diū manēbat ut iuuenēs ad suam causam addūceret.
5. Marcō Cicerōnī persuāsit ut sēcum mīlitāret.
6. cum plūrimī iuuenēs ad causam reīpūblicae adductī essent, in Macedoniam festīnāuit.
7. cum pater Marcī Cicerōnis ab Antōniī mīlitibus occīsus esset, Horātius quoque cum Brūtō mīlitāre uolēbat.
8. Pompēiō persuāsit ut sēcum ad Asiam nāuigāret.
9. cum Ephesum aduēnissent, ad forum festīnāuērunt.
10. cum in forō sedērent, mīlitī cuīdam occurrērunt quī eōs ad Brūtī castra dūxit.

EXERCISE 20.4

Translate into Latin

1. When Flaccus had returned from the field, he greeted Scintilla who was sitting in the garden.
2. When dinner was ready, she called him into the house.
3. When they were dining, Scintilla said, "I am anxious. Quintus has not sent us a letter."
4. When Flaccus had heard this, he said, "Don't be anxious. Without doubt he will write to us soon."
5. But Flaccus also was anxious. When he had finished dinner, he went out to see his friends.
6. When he was sitting in the tavern (**taberna, -ae**, f.), a messenger arrived from Rome.
7. The messenger said, "Brutus has persuaded many young men to leave Athens and serve (**mīlitō, -āre**) in his army."
8. When the words of the messenger had been heard, Flaccus hurried home to tell Scintilla everything.
9. Scintilla wrote a letter to Quintus and begged him not to be led into the war by Brutus.
10. But Quintus was already serving in Brutus' army when he received (*use inidicative*) this letter.

GRAMMAR

Deponent Verbs

(see p. 312 in Reference Grammar)

These important verbs are passive in form but active in meaning.

So the perfect participles of deponent verbs are active in meaning, e.g. **morātus** = having delayed; **ueritus** = having feared; **profectus** = having set out; **prōgressus** = having advanced.

centuriōnem secūtī ad prīncipia aduēnimus.

Having followed the centurion we arrived at headquarters.

(English often says, e.g. "Following the centurion we arrived…" but since the action of "following" precedes "arriving," Latin uses the perfect participle.)

prīmā lūce profectī merīdiē ad urbem aduēnimus.

Having set out/setting out at first light we arrived at the city midday.

Although deponent verbs are passive in form they form a present participle like ordinary verbs, e.g. **sequēns** = following, **cōnāns** = trying, **loquēns** = talking.

The present participle is used when the action of the participle takes place at the same time as that of the main verb, e.g.

in forō manēbant cum amīcīs colloquentēs.

They stayed in the forum talking with their friends.

Horātiō in lītore morantī magister imperāuit ut festīnāret.

When Horace was delaying on the shore the captain told him to make haste.

EXERCISE 20.5

Translate

1. patrem iuuāre cōnābimur.
2. eum ad agrum secūtī sumus.
3. in uiā cum amīcīs diū colloquēbar.
4. agrum ingressus patrem uocāuī.
5. in agrō diū morābar.
6. uespere domum prōfectus sum.

GRAMMAR

The Present Infinitive Passive

You will have noted the present passive form of the infinitive in learning the principal parts of deponent verbs:

1st	**cōnor, cōnārī**	to try
2nd	**uereor, uerērī**	to fear
3rd	**sequor, sequī**	to follow
3rd **-iō**	**patior, patī**	to suffer
4th	**orior, orīrī**	to rise

From ordinary (non-deponent) verbs, these infinitives are passive in meaning:

1st	**paror, parārī**	to be prepared
2nd	**moneor, monērī**	to be warned
3rd	**regor, regī**	to be ruled
3rd **-iō**	**capior, capī**	to be taken
4th	**audior, audīrī**	to be heard

They are formed by changing final **-e** of active infinitives to **-ī** (**par-āre** active, **par-ārī** passive), except in the 3rd conjugation and 3rd **-iō** conjugation verbs: these infinitives are formed by adding simply **-ī** to the present stem, e.g. **dūc-ō** I lead, **dūc-ī** to be led; **iaci-ō** (stem **iaci-/iac-**) I throw, **iacī** to be thrown.

EXERCISE 20.6

Translate

1. sequimur
2. sequēmur
3. sequāmur
4. sequī
5. secūtī sumus
6. sequēbāris
7. sequerentur
8. sequentēs

9. mitte
10. mīsī
11. mittī
12. mittēns
13. mittantur
14. mittāmus
15. mīsērunt
16. missī erant

17. cōnābantur
18. cōnārī
19. cōnātī
20. cōnantēs
21. cōnentur
22. cōnābāris
23. cōnātī sumus
24. cōnābuntur

EXERCISE 20.7

Translate

1. domum redīre cōnāmur.
2. prūdentēs uidēminī, amīcī.
3. uolumus colloquī uōbīscum, puellae.
4. prīmā lūce profectī, merīdiē in urbem ingressī sumus.
5. Brūtum ad Asiam sequī cōnstituī.
6. perīculum ueritae fēminae in casā manēbant.
7. multī cīuēs in bellō cīuīlī mortuī sunt.
8. Flaccus ē casā ēgressus ad agrum profectus est.
9. in uiā amīcō occurrit quōcum diū loquēbātur.
10. in agrum ingressus, diū labōrābat.
11. puellam in casā morantem māter iussit ad fontem festīnāre.
12. puella statim profecta multās fēminās inuēnit prope fontem colloquentēs.
13. aquam celeriter dūxit domumque regrediēbātur cum lāpsa est.
14. mātris īram uerita, ad fontem regressa, urnam iterum complēuit (*filled*).

GRAMMAR

Passive Imperatives

	1st paror	2nd moneor	3rd regor	3rd -iō capior	4th audior
sing.	parāre	monēre	regere	capere	audīre
pl.	parāminī	monēminī	regiminī	capiminī	audīminī

You will notice that the singular of the passive imperative is the same as the present active infinitive, and the plural the same as the 2nd person plural of the passive indicative.

These forms rarely occur with ordinary verbs, since sense does not often require them; you are unlikely to find, e.g. **amāre** = be loved (though you may find, e.g. **ā mē monēminī** = be warned by me). But they are common from deponent verbs, which, of course, have an active sense, e.g.

mē sequere, Quīnte.   Follow me, Quintus.

statim proficīsciminī.   Set out at once, friends.

EXERCISE 20.8

Give the imperative, active and passive, singular and plural of
1. moneō
2. uertō

EXERCISE 20.9

Translate
1. uenīte hūc, iuuenēs, et mē iuuāre cōnāminī.
2. in urbe trēs diēs morāre, fīlī; deinde domum proficīscere.
3. mē sequiminī ad agrum, puerī; agrum ingressī colōnōs adiuuāte.
4. manē, amīce, et nōbīscum colloquere.
5. nōlīte hostēs uerērī, mīlitēs, sed fortiter prōgrediminī.
6. ā mē monēminī, amīcī; nōlīte in perīculum lābī.

EXERCISE 20.10

Translate into Latin
1. We shall follow Brutus to Asia.
2. Setting out (= having set out) at once, we sailed to Ephesus.
3. When we had arrived, we tried to find Brutus' army.
4. After entering (use **ingredior**) the camp, we met a centurion.
5. He said, "Follow me to the headquarters (**prīncipia, -ōrum**, n. pl.) of the legion."
6. We did not delay but followed him at once.
7. We met the commander coming out of the headquarters.
8. He said, "Wait in the headquarters, young men. I shall soon return."
9. He returned soon and talked with us for a long time.
10. At last he said, "You seem sensible young men. I shall take you to Brutus. Follow me."

P.S.
Explain the meaning and use of the following abbreviations

i.e. = id est	cf. = confer
e.g. = exemplī grātiā	et seq. = et sequentia
etc. = et cētera	flor. = flōruit
a.m. = ante merīdiem	p.a. = per annum

p.m. = post merīdiem	lb = lībrae
A.D. = annō Dominī	R.I.P. = requiēscat in pāce
A.M.D.G = ad maiōrem Deī glōriam	no. = numerō
ad fin. = ad fīnem	MSS = manūscrīpta
ab init. = ab initiō	N.B. = notā bene
P.S. = post scrīptum	

THE ROMAN ARMY

By the beginning of the first century BC the Roman army had become a professional body, open to any citizen who was willing to serve for payment. Soldiers would undertake to join for 16 (later for 20) years. They swore an oath of allegiance to their general, who for his part promised to give them land when they retired, and so there was a great danger that the soldiers would put loyalty to an individual before their duty to the state.

The largest unit of the army was the legion. This would number 5,500 at full strength, but normally the total would be somewhat less than that. The legion was divided into nine cohorts of 480 men and one cohort of rather more.

The army commanders were usually ex-praetors or ex-consuls. These senior magistrates held *imperium*, i.e. the right to command an army. Their tent, the *praetōrium*, would be placed in the middle of the camp. Each legion was commanded by a *lēgātus* who would be aided by six *tribūnī*, usually young men of aristocratic birth. The legate and the tribunes were the higher-ranking officers.

The backbone of the army was provided by the centurions. They were the equivalent of the sergeants in a modern army. Unlike the tribunes, they were long-term professional soldiers. There were 60 of these, with six of them commanding each of the ten cohorts. They were carefully graded in authority and every centurion's ambition was to become *prīmus pīlus*, the senior centurion of the first cohort and therefore of the whole legion. These key figures were responsible for discipline among the common soldiers. They had the right to flog their men, a right mercilessly enforced by Lucilius in our story, and they carried a rod to symbolize this. Other officers were the *optiō*, the centurion's second-in-command, and the *tesserārius*, who was responsible for the watchword.

The legionary soldier wore a linen vest and over that a woollen tunic which reached almost to his knees. On top of this he placed a sort of sweater made of leather, with plates of metal, if he could afford them, loosely fitted to it with thongs. He had a brown cloak which could be used as a blanket when necessary. He wore heavy hobnailed sandals and had his hair cut short.

This illustration from Trajan's column shows a field dressing station. On the right a dresser, holding a roll of bandage, attends an auxiliary with a wound in his thigh: in his pain the soldier grits his teeth and clutches the rock he is sitting on. To the left a medical officer examines a legionary soldier.

On the battlefield he wore a crested helmet (made of leather and later of metal) and a curving shield (*scūtum*) made of wood and covered with leather. This was four feet long and two-and-a-half feet wide, strengthened by a rim of metal and a bronze or iron boss in the middle. The shield left the right leg uncovered, and so the soldier would protect the shin with a metal greave.

He fought with a sword, two javelins and sometimes a dagger. The sword was short and wide, about two feet long, two-edged and well adapted to hand-to-hand fighting. The javelins were about seven feet in length. Made of wood with a two-foot head of iron, they would be thrown at a range of about 30 yards. The metal head was often joined to the shaft with a wooden pin which snapped on impact and made the weapon useless, to prevent the enemy picking up the javelins and throwing them back at the Romans.

Another scene from Trajan's column shows Roman soldiers setting off from camp. On tent poles over their left shoulders they are carrying a heavy load of kit, including a pack, a bottle for wine, and cooking pots.

The soldier on the march carried in his pack and on his back not only his personal gear and clothing but also tools for pitching camp and stakes for forming a palisade, cooking utensils and food for several days. His wheat ration counted as part of his pay and he had to grind it himself. His drink was more like vinegar than wine. It was a tough life but it produced a superbly disciplined and effective army.

Further Reading
A valuable and finely illustrated book for futher exploration of the Roman army is Peter Connolly, *Greece and Rome at War* (Greenhill, 1998).

Chapter 21

Grammar: ablative absolute

PATTERN SENTENCES

The passages in parentheses explain the points being made in the practice sentences.

COMMENTARY

R|V **A Roman general addressing his troops:** another scene from Trajan's column. *See page 101 in* Oxford Latin Course, College Edition: Readings and Vocabulary.

l.2 *commīlitōnēs*: "fellow soldiers."

l.6 *meminerīmus*: "let us remember"; this, as the long *ī* indicates, is the perfect subjunctive of *meminī*, a verb perfect in form but present in meaning (cf. *ōdī, ōdisse* = I hate). The subjunctive here expresses an exhortation.

l.15 *Mars anceps fuerat*: "Mars (the god of war) had been two-headed," i.e. the battle had been indecisive.

R|V **Philippi:** the forum of the town built for Octavian's sister Octavia after the defeat of Caesar's assassins in this area in 42 BC. The towers in the background are medieval. *See page 101 in* Oxford Latin Course, College Edition: Readings and Vocabulary.

l.24 *rēctā = rēctā uiā*: "straight."
l.32 *scūtō abiectō*: cf. Horace, *Odes* 2.7.9–10:

tēcum Philippōs et celerem fugam
sēnsī relictā nōn bene parmulā....

(with you [Pompeius] I experienced Philippi and swift flight, abandoning my poor little shield dishonorably)

As a tribune Horace would probably not even have carried a shield; his claim should not be taken literally; he is echoing the words of earlier Greek poets, two of whom claim to have thrown away their shields and run from battle, e.g. Archilochus (at his prime in 650 BC): "One of the Saioi enjoys my shield, which I left in a bush reluctantly, but saved myself. What do I care about that shield? Let it go; I'll get another just as good." Archilochus is defying the Homeric ethos, which made courage in battle the greatest virtue; to throw away one's shield in battle and run was the ultimate cowardice.

GRAMMAR

The Ablative Absolute

Up to this chapter you have always seen participles agreeing with the subject or object of a verb or with a noun or pronoun which forms some other part of the clause it belongs to, e.g.

cōpiae Cassiī uictae ad castra fūgērunt.
The forces of Cassius having been conquered fled to the camp.
(the participle **uictae** agrees with the subject **cōpiae**)

Horātius epistolam perlēctam Pompēiō trādidit.
Horatius handed over the letter, having been read, to Pompeius (i.e. Horatius read the
    letter and handed it over to Pompeius).
(the participle **perlēctam** agrees with the object **epistolam**)

Horātiō haec rogantī Pompēius omnia dīxit.
To Horace asking this (i.e. when Horace asked this) Pompeius told (him) everything.
(the participle **rogantī** agrees with the indirect object **Horātiō**)

But sometimes the participial phrase (i.e. the noun + participle) is independent of the structure of the rest of the sentence, e.g.

Brūtus, hīs dictīs, mīlitēs dīmīsit.
Brutus, these things having been said, dismissed the soldiers (i.e. Brutus said this and
    dismissed the soldiers/After saying this, Brutus dismissed the soldiers).

dictīs agrees with **hīs**, which is not subject or object of the main verb (**dīmīsit**) but is independent (or, as the grammarians say, "absolute"); in this case both noun and participle are in the ablative case. You will notice that English does not often use such absolute participial phrases and you will need to translate them into natural English.

Here are some more examples:

cēnā parātā Scintilla quiēscēbat.

When dinner was ready (dinner having been prepared) Scintilla rested.

Horātiō haec locūtō, Marcus Cicerō gaudēbat.

When Horatius said these things (Horatius having said these things), Marcus Cicero
was delighted.

Horātiō in Acadēmiā studente Brūtus Athēnās aduēnit.

(While) Horatius (was) studying in the Academy, Brutus arrived at Athens.

(**N.B.:** Remember that the ablative singular of the present participle ends in **-e.**)

EXERCISE 21.1

Translate the following sentences and explain the use of the cases **collēctum** *(sentence 1),*
collēctus *(sentence 2),* **collēctō** *(sentence 3)*

1. Antōnius exercitum maximum collēctum ad Graeciam dūcēbat.
2. exercitus maximus ab Antōniō collēctus ad Graeciam contendēbat.
3. Antōnius exercitū maximō collēctō ad Graeciam contendit.

EXERCISE 21.2

Translate into idiomatic English

1. Horātius, labōribus cōnfectīs, cum amīcīs colloquēbātur.
2. Horātiō cum amīcīs colloquente, centuriō accessit, quī eum ad Brūtum
   arcessīuit.
3. Brūtus, mīlitibus conuocātīs, ōrātiōnem habuit.
4. "hostibus uictīs," inquit, "lībertātem populō Rōmānō reddēmus."
5. mīlitēs dīmissī ad iter sē parāuērunt.
6. Scintillā in casā sedente, intrāuit tabellārius (*postman*).
7. Scintilla, epistolā perlēctā, Flaccum uocāuit.
8. Flaccus, clāmōribus eius audītīs, in casam ānxius rediit.
9. Flaccus Scintillam flentem cōnsōlārī cōnātus est.
10. Scintillā dēspērante, Flaccus exit ut Decimum arcesseret.

EXERCISE 21.3

*In the following sentences put the participial phrases (noun + participle) in parentheses into
the correct cases; then translate*

1. (Caesar interfectus), Flaccus Quīntō imperāuit ut Athēnās nāuigāret.
2. (longum iter cōnfectum), Quīntus tandem Athēnās aduēnit.

3. (monumenta spectāta), Quīntus ad Acadēmīam festīnāuit.
4. Quīntus (Marcus in ātriō uīsus) salūtāuit. (*Be careful!*)
5. (Marcus in tabernā bibēns), Quīntus dīligenter studēbat.
6. (Quīntus Theomnēstum audiēns), Marcus in tabernā bibēbat.
7. Marcus (epistola ā patre scrīpta) Quīntō trādidit. (*Be careful!*)
8. Quīntus (epistola perlēcta) Marcō reddidit.

EXERCISE 21.4

Translate the following verb forms

1. audītus	10. locūtus est
2. audiēbātur	11. loquēbātur
3. audīrent	12. loquī
4. audīrī	13. monēbō
5. audiēmur	14. monuimus
6. audiāmus	15. monērētur
7. loquēns	16. moneāmus
8. loquētur	17. monēminī
9. loquere	18. monitus

EXERCISE 21.5

Translate into Latin (in these sentences use the ablative absolute, e.g. Quintus, after writing a letter to his parents, went to sleep = Quintus, a letter having been written to his parents, went to sleep = **Quīntus epistōlā ad parentēs scrīptā dormīuit***)*

1. After greeting her mother Horatia entered the house.
2. Scintilla prepared dinner and called Flaccus.
3. Flaccus, seeing his daughter, smiled.
4. When dinner was finished, they talked for a long time.
5. At last Horatia left her parents and returned home.

EXERCISE 21.6

Translate into Latin (N.B.: use past participles to translate where there are parentheses; in some of these sentences the participle will agree with the subject or object of the sentence, in others an ablative absolute construction is required; be careful!)

1. (After returning* from Delphi), Horace and Pompeius sailed to Asia to find Brutus.
2. (When their journey was finished), they hurried to Brutus' camp.
3. (After delaying in Asia for a long time), Brutus led his army into Greece.

4. (When battle was joined), Brutus defeated Octavian.
5. But Cassius, (when he had been defeated by Antony), killed himself.
6. (When Brutus was dead), Horace fled with his companions.

*use *regredior*

Note that the verb **esse** has no present participle:

Cicerōne cōnsule rēspūblica in magnō perīculō erat.

(**Cicerōne cōnsule** = Cicero (being) consul = when Cicero was consul, in the consulship of Cicero)

Caesare duce Rōmānī Britanniam inuāsērunt.

(**Caesare duce** = Caesar (being) leader = when Caesar was leader, under the leadership of Caesar)

The two nouns in the ablative form an ablative absolute phrase.

EXERCISE 21.7

Translate

1. Horātiō puerō plūrimī colōnī Venusiae habitābant.
2. uentō secundō celeriter ad portum aduēnimus.
3. cōnsulibus Pompēiō Crassōque Caesar in Galliā mīlitābat.
4. Brūtō duce Horātius Pompēiusque Philippīs pugnāuērunt.
5. Caesare dictātōre Brūtus cōnstituit rempūblicam līberāre.

P.S.

What is the meaning of the following nouns, all formed from supines of verbs you know?

nārrātor, fautor, scrīptor, lēctor, prōditor?

dēditiō, commendātiō, salūtātiō, monitiō, quaestiō?

cantus, reditus, monitus, rīsus, ascēnsus?

BRUTUS AND CASSIUS

Why had Brutus, Cassius and the other conspirators killed Julius Caesar? It was easy for them to say that they had done it to give Rome back the freedom it had lost through the dictatorship of one man. The proud descendant of the Brutus who had driven out the last king of Rome soon issued coins which linked the daggers of the Ides of March with the idea of republican *lībertās* (see note on illustration on p. 127). But, as we have seen, the Roman mob, stirred up by Mark Antony, did not view the assassination in this way. Brutus and Cassius were forced to flee from the city less than a month after they had killed the dictator.

Coins of Caesar, Cassius and Brutus (British Museum, London). Caesar wears a laurel wreath: the inscription reads CAESAR.DICT PERPETUO: by February 15, 44 BC, Caesar's title was *dictātor perpetuus* (dictator for ever). The inscription on the Cassius coin reads C. CASSEI. IMP. (of C. Cassius, the general); it dates from 42 BC. The Brutus coin dates from the same year and the inscription reads L.PLAET.CEST; above BRUT; to the right IMP; one of Brutus' officers, Plaetorius Cestianus, issued this coin in honor of his general Brutus.

In fact, when the murderers of Caesar talked of freedom, they meant that they wanted to return power to the small number of families who dominated the state. Put like this, their cause does not appear so noble. In any case, the senate had shown that it was incapable of running the Roman state. Sooner or later one powerful man was going to take over. All the conspirators had achieved was to delay this.

History has not passed a generous verdict on Cassius. In Julius Caesar, Shakespeare presents him as a near villain with "a lean and hungry look" (1.2.195), drawing a hesitant Brutus into the plot against Caesar. But Cassius, in whose character Shakespeare found generosity and warmth as well as villainy, was certainly sincere in his hatred of tyranny, and he was a resolute and experienced soldier as well. Brutus, his brother-in-law, would have done better if he had taken more of Cassius' advice.

Brutus, however, is the more obviously admirable character. He was a thinker rather than a man of action, and we have seen how he took a deep interest in philosophy when he was in Athens in 44 BC. He discussed philosophical matters with Theomnestus and Cratippus so eagerly that it seemed, even at this critical stage, that he was only interested in study (Plutarch, *Brutus* 24.1) Yet he showed during this time in Athens that he could fire the young with enthusiasm for his political cause. As we have noted, he was especially pleased by young Marcus Cicero whom he praised highly.

Brutus was a man who always thought he was in the right. But he was undoubtedly sincere. He wrote a book about *uirtūs*, which means not just courage but all the qualities which make a good man. He possessed many of these himself, and he died for what he believed.

Shakespeare puts into the mouth of his enemy Mark Antony a fine tribute to his enemy Brutus:

> This was the noblest Roman of them all:
> All the conspirators save only he
> Did that they did in envy of great Caesar;
> He only, in a general honest thought
> And common good to all, made one of them.
> His life was gentle, and the elements
> So mix'd in him that Nature might stand up
> And say to all the world "This was a man!"

(5.5.67–74)

Further Reading

For the political and military history of the period, see J. Osgood, *Caesar's Legacy: Civil War and the Emergence of the Roman Empire* (Cambridge University Press, 2006). For the philosophical angle, see D. Sedley, "The ethics of Brutus and Cassius," *Journal of Roman Studies* 87, 41–53.

Chapter 22

Horātius ad Italiam redit

Grammar: semi-deponent verbs; indirect questions; the perfect subjunctive

The pattern sentences illustrate indirect questions.

VOCABULARY

num: this word either introduces a direct question expecting the answer "no," e.g.

num trīstis es? Surely you are not sad?

or introduces an indirect question = whether, e.g.

Horātius Pompēium rogāuit num sēcum Delphōs uīsere uellet. Horatius asked Pompeius whether he wanted to visit Delphi with him.

COMMENTARY

(a) Horātius Athēnās fugit

The events between the battle of Philippi and the battle of Actium are complex. We give below a chronological chart correlated with events in the life of Horace (the dates of the latter are in some cases doubtful):

42	Battles of Philippi (Oct.)	
41	L. Antonius occupies Rome*	? Horace returns to Italy
41/40	Siege of Perugia	
40	Treaty of Brundisium Antony marries Octavia	? Horace begins the *Epodes* ? Virgil introduces Horace to Maecenas

39	Treaty of Misenum** amnesty	Marcus Cicero returns to Rome Horace becomes *scrība aerārius*
38	Octavian again at war with Sextus Pompeius Maecenas' embassy to Antony (see p. 224)	Horace begins writing *Satires*
37	Treaty of Tarentum: Octavian and Antony reconciled	
36	Agrippa defeats Sextus Pompeius	
35		*Satires* 1 published
33	Antony divorces Octavia and marries Cleopatra	? Maecenas gives Horace the Sabine farm
32	Rome declares war on Cleopatra	
31	Battle of Actium	Horace, *Epodes* published
30	Antony and Cleopatra commit suicide	

*Lucius Antonius was Antony's brother; while Antony was in the East he seized Rome but was forced out by Octavian and besieged in Perugia.

**Sextus Pompeius, son of Pompey the Great, carried on the war against Octavian and Antony by sea, but in 39 BC all three made a treaty, followed by an amnesty which allowed die-hard Republicans, such as Marcus Cicero, to return to Rome. War with Pompeius was soon resumed.

Horace gives his own account of what happened to him after Philippi in *Epistles* 2.2.41–52, which provides the skeleton for the narrative of the following chapters. The passage begins with his education in Rome:

Rōmae nūtrīrī mihi contigit, atque docērī
īrātus Grāiīs quantum nocuisset Achillēs.
adiēcēre bonae paulō plūs artis Athēnae,
scīlicet ut uellem curuō dīnōscere rēctum,
atque in siluīs Acadēmī quaerere uērum.
dūra sed ēmouēre locō mē tempora grātō,
cīuīlisque rudem bellī tulit aestus in arma
Caesaris Augustī nōn respōnsūra lacertīs.
unde simul prīmum mē dīmīsēre Philippī,
dēcīsīs humilem pennīs inopemque paternī
et laris et fundī, paupertās impulit audāx
ut uersūs facerem.

(It was my good fortune to be reared at Rome, and to be taught what harm Achilles in his anger did to the Greeks [i.e. he studied Greek literature at the school of Orbilius]. Kindly Athens gave me a little more skill, so that I wished to distinguish the straight from the crooked, and to seek for truth in the woods of Academus [i.e. he studied ethics and theory of knowledge at the Academy]. But the harsh times tore me from the place I loved and the tide of civil war carried me, a novice, into arms that were to prove no match for the strength of Augustus Caesar. As soon as Philippi sent me off from war, humbled, with wings clipped, and robbed of my ancestral home and farm, poverty which knows no shame drove me to write verses.)

We do not in fact know when he returned to Italy and whether he was granted an official pardon. Octavian declared an amnesty in 39 BC (the Peace of Misenum) but Horace may have come back earlier and remained inconspicuous. This passage is the authority for the loss of his home and his father's farm.

We may safely assume that Flaccus' farm was part of the land confiscated from Venusia when Octavian was resettling his veterans. What happened to Flaccus himself and his mother, Horace never tells us, although he speaks of his father with much affection. We assume that his parents disappeared, like so many others, in the appalling upheavals of the time and died somewhere in poverty.

1.3 *prōdidissent...uertissent*: the subjunctive is used because the clauses in which these verbs occur are part of Horace's thoughts, not stated as facts; subordinate clauses in indirect speech are always in the subjunctive. Lines 4–6 (*caput suum...uēnerant*) are also part of Horace's thoughts and should strictly speaking be constructed as indirect speech, but we have here simplified since indirect statement is not introduced until Chapter 23.

R|V **tandem Athēnās procul cōnspexit:** this view of the Acropolis of Athens is from the Mouseion hill. Above the great wall of the theater of Herodes Atticus (left foreground) are the Propylaia and the small temple of Athena Nike (Victory). The Parthenon, the great temple to Athena, stands proudly atop the sanctuary, and in the right background is the steep Lykabettos hill. *See page 105 in* Oxford Latin Course, College Edition: Readings and Vocabulary.

1.19 *ī cubitum*: "go to bed"; literally "go to lie down": *cubitum* is the supine of *cubō*. The supine can be used after verbs of motion to express purpose. [The supine is a fourth declension verbal noun, used only in the accusative, as explained above, and occasionally in the ablative in phrases such as *mīrābile dictū* "wonderful to say."]

1.23 *nōn tibi licet*: "it is not allowed for you...," i.e. "you may not"; *licet* is an impersonal verb—see Chapter 28.

1.31 *dī tē seruent*: "may the gods preserve you": the subjunctive here expresses a wish.

(b) Horātius Venusiam redit

l.1 *quam prīmum*: "as soon as possible," cf, e.g. *quam celerrimē* "as quickly as possible."

l.2 *gāuīsus*: "rejoicing"; the past participles of deponent (and semi-deponent) verbs are often used of actions which do not precede that of the main verb (cf. l.6 *ille uultum eius intuitus*: "the farmer looking at Horace's face...").

ll.16–17 *adimere eīs cīuitātibus*: "to take away from those states"; *eīs cīuitātibus* is either the dative of the person concerned or the dative of disadvantage.

l.23 *agrīs prīuātī*: "deprived of their fields"; *prīuāre* is used with the ablative of separation, e.g. *tē bonīs prīuō* = I deprive you of your goods.

l.24 *agellum*: *agellus* is the diminutive form of *ager* = a little field/farm, cf. *libellus* = a little book.

R|V **A southern Italian landscape:** this is a view from Monte S. Angelo in Puglia in Southern Italy. *See page 108 in* Oxford Latin Course, College Edition: Readings and Vocabulary.

R|V **A Roman farmer:** this marble statue of a poor Roman probably dates from the first century AD, and reflects the interest of the Romans in realism in their sculpture. Thought to portray a fisherman, it has been restored in modern times. (British Museum, London) *See page 108 in* Oxford Latin Course, College Edition: Readings and Vocabulary.

ll.26–7 *tōta Italia.....colōnīs*: the old man's words echo Virgil, *Georgics* 1.505–7:

...fās uersum atque nefās: tot bella per orbem,
tam multae scelerum faciēs, nōn ūllus aratrō
dignus honōs, squālent abductīs arua colōnīs.

(Right and wrong are turned upside down: so many wars throughout the world, so many faces of wickedness, the plow is given no proper respect, the fields are overgrown now that the farmers have been expelled.)

GRAMMAR

Indirect Questions

Questions can refer to present, future, or past time, e.g.

What are you doing?
quid facis?

What are you going to do?
quid faciēs? or **quid factūrus es?**

What have you done?
quid fēcistī?

In *indirect questions* Latin uses the subjunctive, e.g.

1. Present:
   He asks what they are doing
   rogat quid faciant.
2. Future:
   He asks what they are going to do.
   rogat quid factūrī sint.
3. Past:
   He asks what they have done.
   rogat quid fēcerint.

There is no future subjunctive. To express a future in indirect questions, the future participle is used with the subjunctive of **sum**, e.g.

nesciō quid factūrus sim.
I do not know what I am going to do.

nesciēbāmus quid factūrī essēmus.
We did not know what we were going to do.

The Perfect Subjunctive

Active

The perfect subjunctive is the same in form as the future perfect indicative except in the 1st person singular, which ends **-erim**; thus:

1st	**parāu-erim, -erīs, -erit, -erīmus, -erītis, erint**
2nd	**monu-erim**, etc.
3rd	**rēx-erim**, etc.
4th	**audīu-erim**, etc.
3rd -iō	**cēp-erim**, etc.
sum	**fu-erim**, etc.
possum	**potu-erim**, etc.

Often in the 2nd person singular and plural and the 1st person plural of this subjunctive (as opposed to the future perfect) the i after the r in the ending is long: **parāu-erīs, parāuerīmus, parāuerītis**.

Passive

As you would expect, the perfect subjunctive passive replaces **sum** with its subjunctive form **sim**.

1st	**parātus sim**	**monitus sim,** etc	**rēctus sim,** etc	**audītus sim,** etc	**captus sim,** etc
2nd	**parātus sīs**				
3rd	**parātus sit**				
1st	**parātī sīmus**				
2nd	**parātī sītis**				
3rd	**parātī sint**				

Indirect Questions (continued)

Indirect questions can be introduced by any of the interrogative words you have met (e.g. **quis? cūr? quandō?** etc.) and also by **num** = whether, e.g.

Quīntus senem rogāuit <u>num</u> parentēs suōs uīdisset.
Quintus asked the old man <u>whether</u> he had seen his parents.

Double questions are introduced by **utrum...an** = whether...or, e.g.

Quīntus senem rogāuit utrum parentēs suī Venusiā discessissent an ibi mānsissent.
Quintus asked the old man whether his parents had left Venusia or had stayed there.

or not = **necne**
eum rogāuī utrum fēlix esset necne.
I asked him whether he was happy or not.

Sequence of Tenses

If the main verb is *primary* (i.e. present, future, or perfect with have), the verb in the indirect question clause will be in either the present subjunctive or the perfect subjunctive, or the future participle + present subjunctive or **sum**.

If the main verb is *secondary* (i.e. imperfect, perfect or pluperfect), the verb in the indirect question clause will be in either the imperfect subjunctive or the pluperfect subjunctive, or the future participle + the imperfect subjunctive of **sum**.

EXERCISE 22.1

Translate (in the following sentences all of the main verbs are primary)

1. Theomnēstus Quīntum rogat quid passus sit.
2. Theomnēstus Quīntum rogat quid nunc factūrus sit.
3. Theomnēstus Quīntum rogat quō īre cupiat.
4. scīre uolumus quandō nāuis discessūra sit.
5. magistrum rogā cūr nāuis nōndum discesserit.
6. nesciō quandō ad portum aduentūrī sīmus.
7. Quīntus senem rogat num parentēs suōs uīderit.
8. senex Quīntum rogat utrum colōniam initūrus sit an Rōmam iter factūrus.

EXERCISE 22.2

Translate (in the following sentences all of the main verbs are secondary)

1. Theomnēstus Quīntum rogāuit quid passus esset.
2. Theomnēstus Quīntum rogāuit quid iam factūrus esset.
3. Theomnēstus Quīntum rogāuit quid facere cuperet.
4. scīre uolēbāmus quandō nāuis discessūra esset.
5. magistrum rogāuī cūr nāuis nōndum discessisset.
6. nesciēbam quandō ad portum aduentūrī essēmus.
7. Quīntus senem rogāuit num parentēs suōs uīdisset.
8. senex Quīntum rogāuit utrum in colōniā mānsūrus esset an iter Rōmam factūrus.

EXERCISE 22.3

Translate

1. Quīntus, cum Venusiam aduēnisset, nesciēbat quid accidisset.
2. senex, cuī prope uiam occurrit, eum rogāuit cūr Venusiam rediisset.
3. "nōnne scīs" inquit "quot mala colōniae nostrae acciderint?"
4. Quīntus senem rogāuit num parentēs suī Venusiae adhūc manērent.
5. senex respondit, "Venusiā discessērunt. nesciō utrum Rōmam ierint an rūrī maneant."
6. Quīntus omnēs quibus occurrit rogāuit num parentēs suōs uīdissent.
7. omnēs respondērunt, "nēmō scit quō īuerint."

EXERCISE 22.4

In the following sentences put the verbs in parentheses into the correct form of the subjunctive and translate

1. Quīntus, dum iter Rōmam facit, ueterī amīcō occurrit quem rogāuit num parentēs suōs (uidēre).
2. ille "nesciō" inquit "ubi parentēs tuī (esse)."
3. Quīntus eum rogāuit quandō parentēs suī Venusiā (discēdere) et quō (īre).
4. ille respondit, "parentēs tuī Capuam contendēbant, sed nesciō utrum Capuae adhūc (manēre) an Rōmam (proficīscī)."
5. Quīntum rogāuit quid factūrus (esse).

EXERCISE 22.5

Translate into Latin

1. We don't know where the farmer has gone.
2. I shall ask the boys whether they have seen him.
3. "Boys, do you know where the farmer is?"
4. "We asked him whether he was going to return home or stay in the field; but he made no answer (= answered nothing)."
5. Soon we saw the farmer entering the field. We asked him why he had not waited for us.
6. He said, "I did not know when you wanted to meet me. I went home to have dinner, because I was tired."

P.S.

Miscellanea: Latin Phrases in Common Use Today

1. In a mathematical problem, what are the *data*?
2. What is a *post mortem* examination?
3. What is meant by saying a law case is still *sub iūdice*?
4. What are *obiter dicta*? (*obiter* = in passing)
5. What is meant by saying someone is acting *in locō parentis*?
6. What would be meant by saying that something is mine *dē iūre*, yours *dē factō*?
7. What would be meant by saying that a law case is adjourning *sine diē*?
8. What is meant by saying that a proposal was passed *nem. con.* (= *nēmine contrādīcente*)?
9. What is an artist's *magnum opus*?
10. What is the meaning of the stage direction *exeunt omnēs*?

THE CONFISCATIONS

Antony had won the battle of Philippi without much help from Octavian. The latter, according to hostile accounts, had been ill and, warned by his doctor's dream, he was carried out of his camp only a short time before the enemy over- ran it (Velleius Paterculus 2.70.1). He may even have taken ref- uge unheroically in a marsh (Pliny, *Natural History* 7.148). So Antony had the glory of a great victory, and went off to the East to re-establish order and to raise money.

Meanwhile Octavian took on the highly unpopular task of going back to Italy to confiscate land on which to settle the 50,000 veterans of the Philippi campaign. He caused bitter an- ger. Large areas were taken from inhabitants of around 40 cities, leading to violent protests and riots. The deposed landowners flocked to Rome to plead their cause and gained the support of the people (Appian, *Civil Wars* 5.12). While the proscriptions had affected the upper classes, the confiscations uprooted vast numbers of ordinary people. Their huge scale is reflected by the remarkable fact that the three greatest poets of the era all hailed from areas affected. Horace's family lost their farm, probably in

This bust of Octavian, which makes much of his youthful good looks, is from Arles in France. The combed-forward hair is characteristic.

the confiscations. Virgil's family owned property in the region of Mantua and he vividly conveys the chaos and misery caused by the confiscations in two of his *Eclogues* (1 & 9). The unpredictability of fortune is shown in the first of these, in which a fictitious pastoral character named Tityrus is allowed to continue his old life by a young god in Rome (ll.6, 42), presumably referring to Octavian who was 21 at the time of the confis- cations. Thirdly, Propertius' family holdings were in Umbria, an area which suffered not only from the confiscations but their appalling consequences when the Umbrian city of Perugia was starved into submission by Octavian and then destroyed.

For a full account of the confiscations, see Josiah Osgood, *Caesar's Legacy* (Cam- bridge, 2006), Chapter 3.

Chapter 23

Horātius Rōmam redit

Grammar: indirect statement; all infinitives active and passive

CARTOONS

The note that follows the cartoons on p. 110 of RV should help with eliciting the way indirect statement works.

COMMENTARY

l.14 *deus Apollō uīsus est eī astāre*: Horace's vision of Apollo is fictional. Horace's own explanation of why he took to writing poetry is more down to earth (*Epistles* 2.2.51–2:

> ...paupertās impulit audāx
> ut uersūs facerem.
> (shameless poverty drove me to write poetry)

But he did claim that his inspiration came from Apollo (*Odes* 4.6.29–30):

> spīritum Phoebus mihi, Phoebus artem
> carminis nōmenque dedit poētae.
> (Phoebus Apollo gave me inspiration, Apollo gave me the art of song and the name of poet.)

RV **deus Apollō:** this expressive statue shows Apollo in movement with his lyre. A Roman copy of a Greek bronze, possibly by Praxiteles, the great sculptor of the fourth century BC, it balances an energetic sense of movement with a fine delicacy. (Museo Pio-Clementino, Vatican, Rome) *See page 111 in* Oxford Latin Course, College Edition: Readings and Vocabulary.

l.15 *scītō*: know! an archaic imperative form (compare *estō* be!).

l.23 *Marcum Cicerōnem*: Marcus Cicero joined Sextus Pompeius after Philippi but returned to Italy and was pardoned under the amnesty of 39 BC. His subsequent career is not fully known, but he became consul in 30 BC and proconsul of Asia in 29–28 BC.

l.24 *quid agis?* "how are you?"

l.31 *quō...comparāret*: "by which he might earn." The subjunctive indicates purpose.

l.32 *quaestor aerāriī*: there were two *quaestōrēs aerāriī* who were in charge of the treasury.

l.33 *scrība aerāriī*: "secretary of the treasury"; Suetonius (*Vīta Horātiī*) writes: *bellō Philippēnsī excitus ā Marcō Brūtō imperātōre tribūnus mīlitum meruit; uictīsque partibus ueniā impetrātā scrīptum quaestōrium comparāuit* ("involved in the campaign of Philippi by Marcus Brutus the general he served as a military tribune; and when his side was defeated he was granted pardon and secured a clerkship to the quaestor").

The *scrībae quaestōriī* were important officials, usually of equestrian rank, who assisted the *quaestōrēs* in the management of finances and in keeping the public records. In making Marcus Cicero present him with the job, we are again resorting to fiction.

ll.34–35 *secundā hōrā*: the first hour was dawn, throughout the year.

GRAMMAR

Indirect Statement

You have seen that the construction used for indirect statements is the *accusative and infinitive*. (This construction is occasionally used in English, e.g. I believe him to be wise = I believe that he is wise = *crēdō eum prūdentem esse*.)

In indirect statements, infinitives of all tenses are used, active and passive; these must now be learned:

Infinitive	*active*	*passive*
present	parāre	parārī
	monēre	monērī
	regere	regī
	capere	capī
	audīre	audīrī
	esse	
perfect	parāu-isse	parātus esse
	monu-isse	monitus esse
	rēx-isse	rēctus esse
	cēp-isse	captus esse
	audīu-isse	audītus esse
	fu-isse	

	active	*passive*
future	parāt-ūrus esse	
	monit-ūrus esse	
	rēct-ūrus esse	
	capt-ūrus esse	
	audīt-ūrus esse	
	futūrus esse/fore	

(The future passive infinitive is rare and is at present omitted.)

Note the future infinitive of **sum: futūrus esse** and the alternative form **fore**.

Deponent verbs have an infinitive active in meaning, though the present and perfect are passive in form, e.g.

present	cōnārī	sequī
future	cōnātūrus esse	secūtūrus esse
perfect	cōnātus esse	secūtus esse

EXERCISE 23.1

Give all infinitives, active and passive (except future passive) of (a) **dō** *(b)* **mittō**

Indirect Statement (continued)

The accusative and infinitive construction is introduced by verbs such as **dīcō** (I say), **negō** (I deny, say not), **putō** (I think), **sciō** (I know), **nesciō** (I do not know), **cognōscō** (I get to know, learn), **crēdō** (I believe), **prōmittō** (I promise), **spērō** (I hope) and a few other verbs such as **gaudeō** (I rejoice that).

The reflexives **sē** and **suus** refer back to the subject of the verb which introduces the indirect statement:

<u>Marcus</u> dīcit <u>sē</u> Quīntum adiūtūrum esse.

Marcus says that <u>he</u> will help Quintus.

puerī dīcunt sē ā magistrō dīmissōs esse.

<u>The boys</u> say that <u>they</u> have been dismissed by the master.

Notice that in the case of the infinitives formed from participles (perfect passive, e.g. **parātus esse,** and future active, e.g. **parātūrus esse**), the participle agrees with the *accusative* (subject) of the infinitive, e.g.

magister dīcit <u>puerōs</u> domum <u>dīmissōs</u> esse.
The master says that the boys have been sent home.
fēmina spērat <u>puellās</u> <u>sē</u> <u>adiūtūrās</u> esse.
The woman hopes that the girls will help her.
puellae dīcunt <u>sē</u> fēminam <u>adiūtūrās</u> esse.
The girls say that they will help the woman.

N.B.: Latin does not use **dīcō** before a negative statement. Instead of **dīcō...nōn**, it uses **negō** (= I say that...not). Do not translate **negō** with "deny" when it is used in this way. (When **negō** means "deny," it is in the sense of "refuse to give.")

puellae negant sē fēminam adiūtūrās esse.
The girls say they will not help the woman.

EXERCISE 23.2

Translate

1. Quīntus cognōscit parentēs suōs Venusiā discessisse.
2. spērat sē eōs in uiā inuentūrum esse.
3. omnēs negant sē eōs uīdisse.
4. Quīntus tamen sē eōs iterum uīsūrum esse crēdit.
5. Apollō prōmittit sē Quīntum cūrātūrum esse.
6. Quīntus tandem scit sē parentēs numquam posteā uīsūrum esse.
7. Marcus dīcit Octauiānum ueniam sibi dedisse.
8. Quīntus gaudet sē scrībam aerāriī factum esse.

Indirect Statement (continued)

If the verb introducing the indirect statement is past, English makes the verb in the indirect speech past. But in Latin the tense of the infinitive is that used in the original words, e.g.

Scintilla <u>said</u> that Flaccus <u>was working</u> in the field (indirect speech)
Scintilla said, "Flaccus <u>is working</u> in the field." (direct speech)
Scintilla dīxit Flaccum in agrō <u>labōrāre</u>. (indirect speech)

Scintilla said that he had worked for a long time. (indirect speech)
Scintilla said, "He <u>has worked</u> for a long time." (direct speech)
Scintilla dīxit eum diū <u>labōrāuisse</u>. (indirect speech)

> Scintilla said that he would return home soon. (indirect speech)
> Scintilla said, "He <u>will return</u> home soon." (direct speech)
> **Scintilla dīxit eum mox domum <u>reditūrum esse</u>.** (indirect speech)

Note that verbs of *hoping*, *promising* and *threatening* are likely to be followed by a future infinitive.

EXERCISE 23.3

Translate
1. Quīntus cognōuit parentēs suōs Venusiā discessisse.
2. spērāuit sē eōs in uiā inuentūrum esse.
3. omnēs negāuērunt sē eōs uīdisse.
4. Quīntus tamen sē eōs iterum uīsūrum esse crēdidit.
5. eī quibus Quīntus in uiā occurrit negāuērunt sē parentēs eius uīdisse.
6. Apollō prōmīsit Horātium carmina optima scrīptūrum esse.
7. Quīntus, cui Marcus in forō occurrerat, gaudēbat sē amīcum suum ueterem uīdisse.
8. Quīntus Marcō dīxit sē nescīre quid factūrus esset sed spērāre sē satis argentī mox habitūrum esse.
9. Marcus respondit sē laetissimē amīcum adiūtūrum esse.
10. dixit sē Quīntum scrībam aerāriī creātūrum esse.

EXERCISE 23.4

Turn the following sentences into indirect statements after **dīxit** *(or* **negāuit***), e.g.*

puellae laetae sunt = dīxit puellās laetās esse
puellae nōn laetae sunt = negāuit puellās laetās esse

1. magister īrātus est.
2. Quīntus in Italiam rediit.
3. Quīntus parentēs quaesīuit.
4. colōnī ab agrīs expulsī sunt.
5. Quīntus parentēs Venusiae nōn inueniet.

EXERCISE 23.5

Translate into Latin (remember that the reflexives **sē** *and* **suus** *refer back to the subject of the main clause; and that the tense of the infinitive will be the same as that of the direct words)*
1. Marcus said that he would help Quintus.
2. He said that he had been made quaestor of the treasury.

3. He hoped that Quintus would help him.
4. Quintus rejoiced that Marcus trusted him.
5. Quintus knew that the duties would not be difficult.
6. He hoped that he would write many poems (**carmina**).
7. Quintus told Marcus that he had become a friend of the principal secretary (**scrība prīncipālis**).
8. He said that he was enjoying his work.
9. Quintus was content and said that he had never been so happy (= denied that he had ever been so happy).

P.S.

Adjectives formed from verbs ending in **-ilis, -bilis** denote passive qualities, e.g.

admīrā-bilis, -e (admīror)	admirable (= to be admired)
crēd-ibilis, -e (crēdō)	believable, credible
doc-ilis, -e (doceō)	teachable
fac-ilis, -e (faciō)	doable, easy
flē-bilis, -e (fleō)	lamentable, lamented
horr-ibilis, -e (horreō)	horrible
memorā-bilis, -e (memorō)	memorable
mīrā-bilis, -e (mīror)	wonderful
terr-ibilis, -e (terreō)	terrible

LATIN POETRY

Since you will be reading some of Horace's poetry in the next chapter, it may be of help if we now explain how Latin poetry had developed up to his time.

The Romans were slow starters as far as literature was concerned. For the first five hundred years of their history they produced nothing which we would recognize as poetry. Only a few hymns, charms and spells survive. Here is a specimen, a lullaby:

lalla, lalla, lalla.
ī, aut dormī aut lactā.
(Lullaby, lullaby, lullaby.
Come, either sleep or drink your milk.)

This fresco is from Pompeii and is now in the Museo Nazionale, Naples. The man (traditionally but incorrectly identified as Paquius Proculus since the house in which it was found had an election poster for Proculus painted on its front) carries a papyrus scroll. His wife holds a stylus to her lips and has in her left hand a two-leaved wooden tablet spread with wax. Her fingers and luminous eyes are painted with great delicacy. Her hair is dressed in a fashion popular about the middle of the first century AD.

It is not unattractive but hardly ranks as poetry.

It was not until it came under the influence of the Greek writers that Roman literature got off the ground. At Orbilius' school Quintus would have had to struggle through the poems of Livius Andronicus (c. 284–204 BC). A Greek war-captive and slave, he founded the Latin literary tradition by translating Homer's *Odyssey* and Greek tragedies and comedies into Latin. These two forms of literature, epic (long narrative poems on elevated themes) and drama, were developed by a succession of Roman writers over the next two hundred years.

Tragedies and comedies were performed at the festivals which occurred at intervals throughout the year. Rome, where there were five major drama festivals taking up 14 days in all, produced at least one really great dramatist, namely Plautus (c. 254–184 BC). Twenty comedies by him, all of them with Greek settings, survive. They are still performed today and remain very funny, containing a large element of knock-about farce and a splendid gallery of characters. Ennius was another writer for whom the Romans, including Virgil, had great respect. He lived from about 239 to 169 BC and has been called "the father of Roman poetry." As well as tragedies and comedies, he wrote an epic—in hexameters, the same meter as Homer had used—on the history of Rome.

To begin with, the Roman tradition was limited to forms of poetry intended for public performance. Roman poetry was not considered a vehicle for the expression of personal feelings, which is what most of us expect of it now. Catullus (c. 84–54 BC) was the first great writer in Latin to use poetry to express his thoughts and emotions on every subject which occurred to him, from the trivial and obscene to the profound. He is the first love poet in Roman literature. He too found his inspiration in Greek models when he broke with the old Roman tradition of epic and drama. He was influenced by the early Greek lyric poets of the seventh century BC and even more by the highly sophisticated Greek poets who founded a new tradition in Alexandria four hundred years later. Neither he nor the other great Roman poets imitated Greek models slavishly. He and the circle of young poets he wrote for, the *poētae nouī* as Cicero contemptuously called them, were highly original. They found in the Greek poets they looked back to an inspiration which freed them from the old Roman tradition, and enabled them to produce an intensely personal type of poetry.

We have mentioned epic, drama and lyric. Another important genre is didactic poetry, i.e. poetry which aims to teach its readers something. The earliest surviving didactic poem is by a Greek called Hesiod who lived around the same time as Homer and wrote *Works and Days*, a poem about farming. Virgil says that this was the model for his *Georgics*, the poem on farming which he talks about when he appears in our next chapter. The first great Roman didactic poem was written by a contemporary of Catullus called Lucretius (c. 98–c. 55 BC) who created an amazing poem in six books called *The Nature of the Universe* (*Dē Rērum Nātūrā*) in which he gives a scientific exposition of Epicurus' philosophy (see p. 153). Lucretius intended the pleasure given by poetry to help to "sell" his useful philosophical message (l.925–950 = 4.1–25). Horace gives his approval when he says that "the poet who has mixed the useful with the pleasurable wins every vote, by delighting and advising the reader at one and the same moment" (*Art of Poetry* 343–4). But such a comment is an inadequate response to the tremendous excitement of Lucretius' poetry. He overwhelms by the sheer force of his poetic inspiration.

Further Reading

Revised or new essays on all of the poets mentioned above can be found in the *Oxford Classical Dictionary* (4th edition, 2011).

Chapter 24
Horātius carmina scrībit

Grammar: result clauses

The pattern sentences should present no problems.

(a) Horātius carmina scrībit

COMMENTARY

l.1 *satis argentī*: "enough of money" = "enough money."

beātus ille...: the whole poem is 70 lines long; we omit lines 17–22 and 29–66, which continue the catalog of the joys of country life. This catalog is a literary commonplace; Virgil (*Georgics* 2.467–71) also lists cool valleys, lowing cattle and soft sleep under a tree amongst the joys of country life. But if Horace is ironical, since we eventually learn that Alfius never intends to exchange moneymaking for retirement to country life, he is also ambivalent, since Horace himself was at heart a countryman and longed for the tranquillity of the country (stuck in Rome, he writes *"ō rūs, quandō ego tē aspiciam?" Satires* 2.6.60). The description of country life is lovingly made and carries conviction.

The *Epodes*, which were composed between 41 and 31 BC and published in about 30 BC, comprise 17 poems, mostly in iambic meters and inspired by the Greek poet Archilochus (at his prime 650 BC).

For the meter, see Metrical Appendix, p. 291–5 below. It is extremely simple—iambic trimeters alternating with iambic dimeters. If you read it aloud with correct pronunciation, you will easily feel the rhythm.

The language of the poem is simple, apart from the vocabulary, but watch the word endings carefully—in verse, adjectives are often separated from the nouns they agree with, e.g. line 11, *pressa* agrees with *mella*, *pūrīs* with *amphorīs*.

RV **A pastoral scene:** this fresco centers around a statue of Priapus, god of gardens and fertility. Goats and cows graze contentedly amid a landscape which contains a number of sanctuaries. (National Archaeological Museum, Naples) See *page 114 in* Oxford Latin Course, College Edition: Readings and Vocabulary.

(b) Vergilius amīcitiam Horātī petit

We do not know when Virgil (the standard English spelling of his name) met Horace, but we assume it was soon after Horace's earliest poems were circulating. Virgil then introduced Horace to Maecenas:

> nūlla etenim mihi tē fors obtulit: optimus ōlim
> Vergilius, post hunc Varius, dīxēre quid essem.
>> (Horace, *Satires* 1.6.54–5)

(For it was no chance that brought me in your way; good Virgil, and after him Varius, told you what I was.) (Varius Rufus was a friend of both Virgil and Maecenas; after Virgil's death he helped prepare the unfinished *Aeneid* for publication.)

The rest of the story of Horace's relations with Maecenas is told in subsequent chapters.

ll.12–13 *poēma compōnere cōnor dē rēbus rūsticīs*: Virgil composed the *Georgics* between 37 and 29 BC. Ostensibly a didactic poem on agriculture, modeled on the *Works and Days* of Hesiod (at his prime 700 BC), it ranges far beyond this narrower theme, having a strong moral message on the virtues necessary to save the Roman world from destruction.

l.16 *ille nēgāuit sē carmen eī recitātūrum esse*: Virgil was a perfectionist; it took him seven years to write the *Georgics* at an average rate of less than one line a day. In his Life of Virgil, Aelius Donatus informs us that because the *Aeneid* was unfinished, in his last days he asked repeatedly for the manuscript to be burnt, but Augustus countermanded these instructions and told Virgil's literary executors to publish it.

RV **Virgil:** this portrait of Virgil is from the Codex Romanus, the fifth- or sixth-century edition of Virgil's works in the Vatican Library in Rome, which is one of the two earliest Virgil manuscripts. Note the box which contains the scrolls of his poetry and the lectern from which he recites it. See *page 116 in* Oxford Latin Course, College Edition: Readings and Vocabulary.

RV **A pastoral landscape:** this work by the great French seventeenth-century painter Claude Lorraine captures the spirit of Virgil's Georgics, the poem he speaks of in this chapter. (Barber Institute of Fine Arts, Birmingham) See *page 116 in* Oxford Latin Course, College Edition: Readings and Vocabulary.

GRAMMAR

Result Clauses

Hōrātius tot bona carmina scrīpserat ut omnēs eum salutāre uellent.
Horace had written so many good poems that everybody wanted to greet him.

Hōrātius adeō timēbat ut Athēnīs manēre nōn posset.
Horace was so afraid that he could not stay in Athens.

Clauses expressing consequences are introduced by **ut** + subjunctive, negative **nōn**. The main clause usually contains one of the words meaning "so," e.g.
tam (with adjectives and adverbs):

<u>tam</u> fessus erat <u>ut</u> diū dormīret.
He was <u>so</u> tired <u>that</u> he slept a long time.

tantus = so great:
<u>tanta</u> erat tempestās <u>ut</u> omnēs timērent.
The storm was <u>so great that</u> all were afraid.

tot = so many:
tot spectātōrēs aderant ut locum uacuum inuenīre nōn possēmus.
There were <u>so many</u> spectators present <u>that</u> we could not find an empty place.

totiēns = so often:
Marcus dē tē <u>totiens</u> mihi dīxit <u>ut</u> carmina tua audīre cupiam.
Marcus has spoken to me of you <u>so often that</u> I want to hear your poems.

ita = in such a way:
Hōrātius carmen ita recitāuit <u>ut</u> Vergilius eum laudāret.
Horace recited the poem <u>in such a way that</u> Virgil praised him.

N.B.: In result clauses the reflexive refers to the subject of the *ut* clause; hence in this sentence **eum**, not **sē**.

adeō = to such an extent, so much:
tua carmina Vergilium <u>adeō</u> dēlectant <u>ut</u> tē cognōscere cupiat.
Your poems please Virgil <u>so much that</u> he wants to get to know you.

EXERCISE 24.1

Translate

1. Horātius tam ingeniōsus erat ut Vergilius carmina eius magnopere admīrārētur.
2. cum eō conuenīre adeō cupiēbat ut ad tabernam adierit in quā Horātius bibere solēbat.
3. Horātius carmen suum nouum ita recitat ut audītōrēs omnēs dēlectentur.
4. Horātius tot optima carmina compōnit ut fāmam eius omnēs celebrātūrī sint.
5. Vergilius dē carmine suō adeō dubitābat ut id recitāre nōn posset.
6. Marcus Cicerō ad tabernam totiēns adībat ut nōn saepe sōbrius esset.
7. carmina Vergilī tantopere amat Horātius ut omnia in mentem reuocāre possit.
8. tantā celeritāte cucurrit Horātius ut ab hostibus nōn captus sit.

Result Clauses (continued)

In result clauses the normal rules of sequence are not necessarily obeyed: the tenses of the subjunctive can be varied according to the sense, e.g.

tam dīligenter herī labōrābat ut hodiē fessus sit.
He worked so hard yesterday that he is tired today.

Siciliam ita uastāuit ut restituī nūllō modō possit. (Cicero, *In Verrem* 1.4)
He so plundered Sicily that it can in no way be restored.
(The plundering took place in the past but the consequence is still present.)

The perfect subjunctive is used to stress the actuality of the event:

tot uulnera accēpit ut mortuus sit.
He sustained so many wounds that he died.

EXERCISE 24.2

Translate into Latin

1. Horace worked so hard in the treasury that he earned enough money (**satis argentī**) for himself.
2. He got up so early that he finished his work before midday.
3. He wrote so many good poems that nobody (**ut nēmō**) was willing to criticize him.
4. Virgil likes him so much that they often talk together in the pub.
5. Horace wanted to hear Virgil's poems so much that he was always trying to persuade him to recite them.

6. You write in such a way that everybody admires you.

7. Your poems are so boring (**frigidus**) that I am about to (go to) sleep (subj. of **sum** + fut. part.).

P.S.

Inscriptions on tombstones throw a great deal of light on the life of ordinary Roman citizens. Once you have mastered the abbreviations used, you will find them easy to read.

1. *Felicius Simplex, centurion of the Sixth Legion, made the following memorial for his little daughter:*

D.M. SIMPLICIAE FLORENTINAE ANIMAE INNOCENTISSI-
MAE QUAE VIXIT MENSES DECEM FELICIUS SIMPLEX LEGIO-
NIS VI CENTURIO PATER FECIT

(inscribed on a stone coffin found in York, UK – RIB 690)

D.M. = *dīs mānibus* (sacred) to the deified spirits of the dead (this formula often starts funerary inscriptions, followed by the name of the dead person in the dative, or sometimes the genitive case)

2. *Panathenais made the following inscription for her daughter who died tragically just before her marriage:*

D.M. s(acrum). Callistē uīxīt annīs xvi mēnsēs iii hōras vi et sēmissem: nūptūra īdibus Octōbris, moritur iiii īdūs Octōbrēs: Panathēnāis māter pia cārae fīliae fēcit.

(from Mauretania in North Africa, Dessau 8529a)

sēmissem half
īdibus Octōbris on October 15
iiii = *ante diem quārtum* the fourth day before the Ides (October 12)

3. *The following illustrates how barren and desolate the pagan beliefs about life and death were:*

D.M. sacrum. Aurēliae Vercellae coniugī dulcissimae, quae uīxit plūs minus annīs XVII. "nōn fuī, fuī, nōn sum, nōn dēsīderō." Anthimus marītus eius.

(Dessau 8162)

plūs minus more or less, approximately
Anthimus... supply "made this monument"

4. *The following is a funerary inscription for a Christian girl, the daughter of a veteran of the Roman army*:

Aurēliae Mariae puellae, uirginī innocentissimae, sānctē pergentī ad iūstōs et ēlēctōs in pāce. quae uīxit annōs XVII, mēnsēs V, diēs XVIIII, spōnsāta Aurēliō Damātī diēbus XXV. Aurēlius Iānisirēus ueterānus et Sextīlia parentēs īnfēlīcissimae fīliae. dulcissimae ac amantissimae contrā uōtum, quī dum uīuent, habent magnum dolōrem. Martyrēs sānctī, in mente habēte Mariam.

(from Aquileia in North Italy, *CIL* 5.1636)

sānctē pergentī   going in holiness

spōnsāta betrothed

contrā uōtum supply *hōc fēcērunt* made this monument contrary to their prayers, i.e. they had prayed that she should live

BOOKS

When we talk about a book in the Roman world, we generally mean a papyrus roll. The papyrus reed is rare today but used to grow in abundance on the banks of the Nile.

How would you convert it into the ancient equivalent of paper? Cut the pith on the papyrus stem into strips and put them side by side horizontally. Wet the layer you have formed with water and add a little glue. Place another set of strips on top of this at right angles to it. Press the two layers together. Allow to dry.

You now have a sheet on which you can write. Next join several of these together, smoothing down the joints carefully, and you have a continuous strip of papyrus. Smooth down the whole surface with pumice; otherwise the ink will blot. All you need to turn it into a book is a pair of cylindrical wooden rollers, preferably with ornamental knobs on them, which you fix to each end left and right.

Now it can be written on. You, your secretary or one of your slaves must pick up a pen (either a pointed reed or a sharpened goose quill such as was used until the nineteenth century) and dip it in ink, a black substance made of soot and glue and then diluted. You write from left to right in columns about 35 letters wide. You write in capital letters with no word division and little punctuation. Your first task, if you are reading a book, is *ēmendāre* (to correct errors) and *distinguere* (to separate words and punctuate). The papyrus can be as long or as short as you like, but in Horace's day the average length of a book of papyrus was 700 to 900 lines. Presumably this was considered a reasonable size for a scroll.

Now at last you can read your book. You pick up the rollers one in each hand. As you read, you roll it up with your left hand and unroll it with your right. (It is called a *uolūmen* from *uoluō* = "I turn, roll.") If you are a considerate person, when you have finished the book you will reroll it, since the next reader cannot start on it until the beginning faces outwards again.

You now have the problem of storing the book. You either lay it on a shelf or put it in a cylindrical box, first having made sure that a strip of parchment giving the title is stuck to it. This will either hang down from the shelf or stick out from the box, depending on your method of storage. It is extremely likely to come off. There will be serious difficulty in consulting documents. You can't simply flick through a book as you can today. And you may soon run out of space. Livy's *History of Rome*, for instance, was written in 142 books. There are further dangers in your library. Your books may become damp and rot, or insects may get at them and eat them.

If you wish to reuse a papyrus scroll, a damp sponge will wipe away the ink. The emperor Caligula is said to have forced bad poets to lick out their work with their tongues!

This manuscript, which dates from 20 BC, is the oldest Roman book in existence. It is the work of the poet Gallus.
The four most legible lines read:

FATA MIHI CAESAR TUM ERUNT MEA DULCIA QUOM TU
   MAXIMA ROMANAE PARS ERIT HISTORIAE
POSTQUE TUUM REDITUM MULTORUM TEMPLA DEORUM
   FIXA LEGAM SPOLIEIS DEIUITIORA TUEIS.

My fate, Caesar, will only be sweet to me
   when you are the most important part of Roman history
and when after your return I read how the temples of many gods
   have been made richer by your spoils fixed up in them.

The Caesar referred to is, of course, Octavian. The archaic spellings: *quom* = *cum*; *spolieīs* = *spolīīs*; *deiuitiōra* = *dīultiōra*; *tueīs* = *tuīs*.

You will see that, despite what we say in our essay, there are gaps between the words. It seems that this was a luxury production.

Schoolchildren and adults who wanted to jot down short notes would write not on papyrus but on wax tablets. These consisted of two or more wooden-framed rectangles with waxed inner sections. The frames were tied to each other with leather thongs. You wrote on the wax with a thin pointed stick (a *stilus*). Later you could rub out the writing using the round or flat head of the *stilus*. Lovers found these tablets a highly convenient method of communication. They could write on them fast and delete the messages pretty easily.

There was no real distinction between the roles of publisher and bookseller in the Roman world. Many scribes would be employed as copyists in the large number of bookshops at Rome. If they were dealing with a bestseller, the text would be dictated to a group of scribes and the book would be mass-produced. Cicero's friend Atticus was a famous publisher, running a factory with many slaves who were well trained in all aspects of book production, including making last-minute changes at the author's request.

This enchanting fresco portrait of a young girl with a golden hair-net and a stylus was discovered at Pompeii. Although it is popularly known as a portrait of Sappho, the poetess from Lesbos, it may be that the girl it portrays had no particularly literary associations and that holding the stylus against the cheek was a popular pose: compare the illustration on p. 208. (National Archaeological Museum, Naples)

Wealthy Romans such as Cicero, an enthusiastic collector of rare books, had excellent private libraries. Petronius' *nouveau riche* freedman Trimalchio in his novel *Satyrica* claimed to have two libraries, one in Latin and one in Greek. And in Horace's day the first public libraries opened in Rome: Asinius Pollio set up the first of them in 39 BC. In the fourth century AD there were 29 public libraries in the city. Libraries were available even in the baths for the pleasure of the bathers.

Further Reading

For further information, see P. V. Jones and K. Sidwell, eds., *The World of Rome* (Cambridge, 1997), 262–8, and U. E. Paoli, *Rome: Its People, Life and Customs* (Bristol Classical Press, 1990), 174–90.

Chapter 25

Horātius Maecēnātī commendātur

Grammar: summary of uses of *ut*, *cum* and *dum*

COMMENTARY

RV **A luxurious Roman villa:** the painted walls of the luxury villa at Oplontis (see note on illustration on p. 250–1 of this book) on the bay of Naples are rich in their color and characteristic of Roman wall painting in their *trompe l'oeil* effect. *See page 118 in Oxford Latin Course, College Edition: Readings and Vocabulary.*

l.2 *ēlātus*: "excited" (literally "carried away," perfect participle passive of *efferō*).

Maecēnās: Caius Cilnius Maecenas was of noble birth (*rēgibus Etrūscīs ortus* – sprung from Etruscan kings: cf. Horace, *Odes* 3.29.1), but he chose not to enter politics and remained an *eques*. However, he became a close friend and trusted counselor of Augustus; he accompanied him on the Philippi campaign, undertook a mission to Antony in 38 BC (see Chapter 26), and was left in charge of Rome and Italy when Octavian departed for the Actium campaign (or after Actium if Maecenas and Horace were present at the battle). He assumed a mask of luxurious indolence but was in fact a skilful diplomat and competent administrator. Perhaps his greatest service to Augustus was as a patron of literature; he gathered round him a circle of poets, above all Virgil and Horace, whom he encouraged to write in support of the regime.

Although Maecenas and Horace were related as patron and client, there is no doubt about the affection they felt for each other; this emerges clearly both from Horace's frequent references to Maecenas in the *Odes* and *Satires*, and from Maecenas' last request to Augustus in his will: *Horātī Flaccī ut meī memor estō* ("Remember Horatius Flaccus as you do myself").

Maecenas was an extremely wealthy man. He had a splendid house high on the Esquiline hill. His tastes were wildly extravagant. He delighted in silks, gems and perfumes—and good food: he tried to introduce the flesh of young donkeys onto Roman menus! He loved the theater and the ballet, wrote bad verses and introduced heated swimming baths to Rome.

His civilizing influence was remarkable. The story goes that Octavian was once sitting on the *tribunal* (public platform) sentencing numbers of people to death. Maecenas was present but could not get near to him because of the crowd. So he wrote on his tablets, "Get up, you executioner" and threw them into Octavian's lap. Octavian immediately left the judgment seat (Dio Cassius, 55.7).

l.6 *honōrēs*: "offices" (a common meaning of *honos*)

l.8 *Mūsas colēbat*: "he cultivated the Muses," i.e. he encouraged all forms of artistic endeavor. Although they are most often mentioned in connection with poetry, there were nine canonic Muses, each with a particular function—Clio the Muse of history, Terpsichore the Muse of lyric poetry and dance, etc.—though their names, spheres and names fluctuated.

l.14 *uelim*: "I should like"; potential subjunctive, see Chapter 28.

[R][V] **Maecenas:** this bust of Horace's patron is in the Museo Nuovo nel Palazzo dei Conservatori, Rome. *See page 119 in* Oxford Latin Course, College Edition: Readings and Vocabulary.

l.24–6 *negōtiīs...reuocātūrum*: these sentences are part of what Virgil said and so are in the accusative and infinitive construction of indirect statement. Though there are semicolons in our text before the last two infinitive clauses, the contruction remains dependent on *dicēbat* in l.23. Since the subject of the infinitives (*Maecēnātem*) does not change, it is omitted. *esse* can easily be understood with *reuocātūrum*.

[R][V] **The auditorium of Maecenas:** the so-called auditorium of Maecenas dates from the reign of Augustus and was certainly in the former's gardens. The exact purpose of the building is uncertain, but the apse has tiered seats in a semi-circle. It may be that Virgil and Horace read their poems here. In the niches are traces of red landscape paintings, but they can scarcely be seen in this photograph. *See page 119 in* Oxford Latin Course, College Edition: Readings and Vocabulary.

l.35 *prīncipī*: "the emperor"; this was the title by which Augustus preferred to be called; it has a civilian ring about it (leading citizen); he was trying to disguise the military basis of his power.

l.36 *patris tamen numquam eum paenitēbat*: "he was never ashamed of his father"; (*mē paenitet* is an impersonal verb "it repents me of..."—see Chapter 28). *tamen* cannot be translated by "but" or "however" here; "still," "nevertheless" or "even so" are the recommended translations when the word appears at this stage of the sentence.

GRAMMAR

Summary of the Uses of *ut*

ut + the indicative means either "as" or "when," e.g.

Horātius est uir ingeniōsus, ut dīcunt.	Horace is a clever man, as they say
magister īrātus est, ut uidētur.	The master is angry, as it seems.
ego ita erō ut mē esse oportet.	I shall be such as I should be.
haec rēs sīc est ut nārrō.	This situation is such as I say.
ut uēnī cōram tē, pauca locūtus sum.	When I came into your presence, I said little.
ut domum rediimus, laetī cēnāuimus.	When we returned home, we dined happily.

ut + the subjunctive is used:

(a) In purpose clauses (see Chapter 19)
(b) In indirect commands (see Chapter 19)
(c) In result clauses (see Chapter 24)

Other uses of **ut** will be met when you read Latin texts.

The Uses of *cum*

1. the conjunction **cum** most commonly means "when."
    In *past* time it is normally followed by the imperfect or pluperfect sub-junctive, e.g.
    cum domum reuēnissent, cēnāuērunt.
    When they had returned home, they dined.
    cum cēnārent, amīcus quīdam casam intrāuit.
    When they were dining, a friend entered the house.
    But:
    (a) As you have seen, if the **cum** clause follows the main clause, the indicative is used, e.g.
    cēnābant cum amīcus quīdam casam intrāuit.
    They were dining when a friend entered the house.
    sōl iam occiderat cum domum reuēnērunt.
    The sun had already set when they returned home.

(b) If **cum** means "whenever," the pluperfect indicative is used, e.g.

cum Horātius ad fundum redierat, semper gaudēbat.

Whenever Horace returned to his farm, he always rejoiced.

2. When **cum** meaning "when" is used to refer to *present* or *future* time it is always followed by the indicative, e.g.

cum Athēnās aduēnerō, ad tē scrībam.

When I arrive at Athens, I shall write to you.

cum fessī sumus, in hortō quiēscimus.

When we are tired, we rest in the garden.

3. **cum** can also mean "since"; with this meaning it is always followed by the subjunctive, e.g.

cum fessī sīmus, in hortō quiēscimus.

Since we are tired, we are resting in the garden.

cum fessī essēmus, domum nōn festīnāuimus.

Since we were tired, we did not hurry home.

4. **cum** followed by the subjunctive occasionally means "although"; this meaning is usually made clear by the insertion of **tamen** at the beginning of the main clause (**tamen** will then be translated "still," "even so"), e.g.

cum fessī sīmus, tamen dīligenter labōrāmus.

Although we are tired, we are nevertheless working hard.

EXERCISE 25.1

Translate

1. Horātius in hortō sedēbat carmen meditāns cum subitō aduēnit Vergilius.
2. cum audīuisset id quod amīcus eī dīxit, Horātius laetissimus fuit.
3. ualdē gaudēbat cum Maecēnās eum uidēre cuperet.
4. cum per urbem ad aedēs Maecēnātis ambulārent, Vergilius multa dē patrōnō suō dīxit.
5. Vergilius "Quīnte," inquit, "cum Maecēnātem uīderis, nōlī uerēcundus esse."
6. sed cum uultū benignō Maecēnās eum salutāuisset, tamen uerēcundum Horātius sē praebuit.
7. Maecēnās "cum tua carmina legō," inquit, "fēlīx sum. sed cum ualdē occupātus sim, nōn mox tē reuocābō."
8. cum Maecēnās post tempus tam breue eōs dīmīsisset, Horātius dolēbat cum tantō uirō nōn placuisset.
9. sol occidēbat cum amīcī domum Horātī rediērunt.
10. cum dē Maecēnāte cōgitāuerat, Horātius maximē dolēbat.

The Uses of *dum*

1. **dum** most commonly means "while"; with this meaning it is usually followed by the present indicative, even in past time, e.g.

   dum in forō manēmus, amīcum uīdimus ad nōs currentem.
   While we were waiting in the forum, we saw a friend running towards us.

   But if the action of the **dum** clause goes on throughout the action of the main clause, the imperfect indicative is used, e.g.

   dum in forō manēbāmus, cum amīcīs colloquēbāmur.
   While (= all the time that) we were waiting in the forum, we talked with friends.

2. **dum** can also mean "until"; like other temporal conjunctions, it usually takes the indicative, e.g.

   in forō manēbāmus dum sōl occidit.
   We waited in the forum until the sun set.

   hostēs secūtī sumus dum in castra fūgērunt.
   We followed the enemy until they fled into their camp.

   But if the **dum** clause expresses purpose as well as time, it takes the subjunctive, e.g.

   in forō manēmus dum pater ueniat.
   We are waiting in the forum for our father to come (until our father may come).

   Horātius Rōmae morābātur dum Maecēnās ad urbem redīret.
   Horace delayed in Rome until Maecenas should return to the city.

EXERCISE 25.2

Translate

1. dum in hortō sedeō carmen scrībēns, Mūsa mē uisitāuit.
2. dum pluēbat (*it was raining*), domī manēbam.
3. in hortō laetus sēdī dum uēnit nox.
4. domī manēbam dum Maecēnās mē reuocāret.
5. dum carmina mea Vergiliō recitō, ille saepe plausit.
6. dum apud Maecēnātem aderat, Horātius sē uerēcundum praebēbat.
7. Maecēnās in aedibus ānxius morātur dum Octāuiānus eum uīsat.
8. rūre manēbō dum amīcus meus aduēnerit.

P.S.

1. *The funerary inscription of a successful freedman:*

P. Decimius P(ūbliī) l(ībertus) Erōs Merula, medicus, clīnicus, chīrurgus, oculārius; VIuir. hic prō lībertāte dedit HS $\overline{L}$. hic prō sēuirātū in rem p(ūblicam) dedit HS $\overline{II}$. hic in statuās pōnendās in aedem Herculis dedit HS $\overline{XXX}$, hic prīdiē quam mortuus est relīquit patrimōnium...

(from Assisi)
(*CIL* 7812)

clīnicus physician
chīrurgus surgeon
VIuir the *sēuirī* were priests of the cult of Augustus, the highest office a freedman could attain
HS $\overline{L}$ 50,000 sesterces
HS $\overline{II}$ 2,000 sesterces
in statuās pōnendās for setting up statues
aedem temple
HS $\overline{XXX}$ 30,000 sesterces
patrimōnium a fortune/estate (figure missing)

2. *A surgeon's victim:*

D.M. Euhelpistī līb(ertī): uīxit annīs XXVII mēns(ibus) IIII diēb(us) XI: flōrentēs annōs mors subita ēripuit. anima innocentissma, quem medicī secārunt et occīdērunt. P. Aelius Aug. līb(ertus) Pecūliāris alumnō suō.

(*CIL* 9441)

anima a soul (*quem* refers to *anima*, masculine, because the soul is that of a
  man)
secārunt cut
alumnō suō for his foster child (supply "made the monument")

Chapter 26
Horātius iter Brundisium facit

> **Grammar:** conditional clauses

CARTOONS
Note the observations at the top of p. 123 of RV.

COMMENTARY
This chapter is based on Horace, *Satires* 1.5. For a stimulating discussion of the start of this poem, see L. Morgan, *Musa Pedestris: Metre and Meaning in Roman Verse* (Oxford, 2010), pp. 337–45.

In 38 BC Octavian was again involved in war with Sextus Pompeius and suffered two defeats by sea. That autumn he sent Maecenas on an embassy to Antony to ask for his help. Maecenas succeeded in effecting a reconciliation between Octavian and Antony, who met at Tarentum in spring 37 BC; the powers of the Triumvirate were extended for another five years and Antony gave Octavian 120 ships. With his enlarged fleet Octavian succeeded in finally defeating and eliminating Pompeius (Battle of Naulochus, September 36 BC). The senate voted that a golden statue of Octavian should be set up on a column with the inscription, "He established peace, long disturbed by discord, by land and sea" (Appian, *Civil Wars* 5.130). After Naulochus Octavian forced Lepidus to leave the Triumvirate. Now it was just him and Antony.

l.2 *Vergilius aderit*: Maecenas took with him a considerable train besides Horace and Virgil; apart from diplomats who went with him to Athens, Varius Rufus, a leading poet, Plotius Tucca, who, like Varius, was to be one of Virgil's literary executors, and the *rhētor* Heliodorus accompanied him to Brundisium. He must have planned to enliven a tedious journey by the company of like-minded friends.

ll.15–16 *per canālem*: the canal ran from Forum Appi to Anxur through the Pomptine marshes, a distance of about 40 miles. It enabled travelers to proceed at night to save time and to avoid a tiresome journey by foot or mule through the mosquito-infested marshes.

l.17 *pedibus*: "on foot."

ll.19–20 *dum...traheret*: *dum* = while is normally followed by the present indicative but here is subordinate to the purpose clause (*ut...possent*) and so is sub-oblique, i.e. part of the thought in their minds, and is in the subjunctive, following sequence. (Commentary on the text resumes with continuous line numbering after the poem.)

ēgressum magnā: the lines of the poem are numbered separately and notes to the poems are in the RV.

l.24 (RV p. 126) *Ānxur*: "to Anxur" (Anxur is neuter); the town lay on the top of a high hill with white limestone cliffs.

l.32 *Brundisium aduēnērunt*: the whole journey from Rome to Brundisium was 366 miles and it took them 15 days. Brundisium with its magnificent natural harbor was the port commonly used for crossing to Greece.

[R][V] **The Appian Way:** This, the first of the great Roman roads, was planned by the blind Appius Claudius in 312 BC. It is still used by traffic, though quite close to the section illustrated it is now rudely bisected by the modern peripheral road around the city. See *page 126 in* Oxford Latin Course, College Edition: Readings and Vocabulary.

l.43 *uxōrem suam Octāuiam*: Antony had married Octavia, Octavian's sister, in 40 BC; it was a dynastic marriage, to cement the alliance between the two leaders.

l.44 *Cleopātram*: Cleopatra, the last monarch of Egypt descended from Alexander the Great's general Ptolemy, became the mistress of Julius Caesar when he reached Egypt after defeating Pompey in 48 BC; she had a son by him; she followed him to Rome but returned to Egypt after his death.

Antony, who after Philippi controlled the eastern half of the Roman Empire, summoned her to Tarsus in 41 BC. She became his mistress and bore him twins, a boy and a girl. In 33 BC Antony returned to Egypt, divorced Octavia and married Cleopatra. This finally determined that he and Octavian would fight it out for supremacy.

l.49 *in diēs*: "day by day."

GRAMMAR

Conditional Clauses

These are clauses introduced by **sī** = "if" or **nisi** = "unless/if...not," which state a condition on which the truth of the main clause depends, e.g.

1. Simple fact (open) conditions

sī hoc dīcis, errās.	If you say this, you are wrong.
sī hoc fēcistī, stultus erās.	If you did this, you were foolish.

In these sentences the truth of the main clause is left open, e.g. in the second example the speaker does not say that "you were foolish" as a fact, but simply says "*If* you did this, you were foolish." You have already met many sentences of this type; they present no difficulty: both English and Latin use the indicative.

2. Contrary to fact conditional clauses

sī pater noster adesset, nōs adiuuāret.	If our father were here, he would be helping us (but he is not here).
sī hoc fēcissēs, stultus fuissēs.	If you had done this, you would have been foolish (but you didn't).

The form of the sentence suggests that the main clause is untrue. In this case Latin uses the subjunctive in both the conditional and the main clauses; English uses the conditional tense "would/should" in the main clause.

The imperfect subjunctive is used to refer to present time, the pluperfect subjunctive to past time, e.g.

sī prūdēns essēs, hoc nōn facerēs.	If you were wise, you would not be doing this (but you are doing it).
sī festīnāuissent, tempore aduēnissent.	If they had hurried, they would have arrived in time (but they didn't hurry).
nisi imprūdēns fuissēs, iam incolumis essēs.	Unless you had been imprudent, you would now be safe.

(**fuissēs** refers to past time, **essēs** to present)

3. Future conditional clauses
    These are of two sorts:

*   Future more vivid, with the indicative (you have often met these), e.g.

    sī domum reuēneris, omnia tibi nārrābō.
    If you come back home, I will tell you everything.

Notice that Latin uses the future or, more often, the future perfect, in the **sī** clause (English appears to use the present).

*   Future less vivid, when the condition is represented as improbable, e.g.

    sī domum reueniās, omnia tibi nārrem.
    If you were to return home, I should tell you everything.
    or If you returned home...

In these the present subjective is used in both the **sī** clause and the main clause.

EXERCISE 26.1

Translate (NB: all the following sentences are "contrary to fact" or "future less vivid" conditional clauses, using the subjunctive; be sure you get the time reference [present, past, future] right)

1. sī fortiter pugnāuissētis, hostēs uīcissētis.
2. sī pater noster uīueret, cōnsilium nōbīs daret.
3. nisi Horātius ē campō fūgisset, ab hostibus captus esset.
4. sī Horātius prūdēns esset, in Brūtī exercitū nōn mīlitāret.
5. sī statim proficīscāmur, domum ante noctem aduenīāmus.
6. sī puerī bonī fuissent, magister fābulam eīs nārrāuisset.
7. magister "puerī," inquit, "sī dīligenter labōrētis, fābulam uōbīs nārrem."
8. māter fīliae "sī mē adiuuēs," inquit, "pater tē laudet."
9. puella "māter," inquit, "sī ōtiōsa essem, libenter tē adiuuārem."
10. puella, nisi occupāta esset, mātrem libenter adiūuisset.

EXERCISE 26.2

Translate (NB: some of the following sentences are "simple fact" or "future more vivid" conditionals with the indicative, others "contrary to fact" or "future less vivid" with the subjunctive; be careful)

1. nisi Pompēius cum Sextō Pompēiō mīlitāuisset, iamdūdum (*long ago*) in Italiam rediisset.
2. sī Pompēius tandem redierit, omnēs gaudēbimus.
3. sī Octāuiānum ueniam rogāuissēs, ille tibi ignōuisset.
4. sī Octāuiānus mihi ignōscat, Rōmae maneam.
5. sī mēcum cēnābis, reditum tuum celebrābimus.
6. sī plūs uīnī biberitis, plānē ēbriī eritis.
7. nisi Pompēī reditum celebrārēmus, tantum uīnī nōn biberēmus.
8. sī Horātius alterum carmen recitābit, ego domum abībō.
9. nisi puellae tam pulchrae adessent, iamdūdum abiissem.
10. barbarus es, sī hōc carmine nōn dēlectātus es.

EXERCISE 26.3

Translate into Latin; before translating say what sort of conditional you are writing—"simple fact," "contrary to fact," "future more vivid" or "future less vivid"

1. If you come home soon I shall tell you everything.
2. If you were to set out at once, you would arrive here in two days.
3. If you had not delayed in Rome, I would have met you in Capua.
4. If you waited for me in Capua, you were very foolish.
5. If you were here now, you would be sitting with me under a tree drinking wine.

EXERCISE 26.4

Translate into Latin

1. If I see you, I shall be happy.
2. If I were to see you, I would be happy.
3. Unless I see you, I am sad.
4. If I saw you, I was happy.
5. If I had seen you, I would have been happy.
6. If I was seeing you now, I would be happy.
7. If I had seen you, I would be happy now.

P.S.
Note the following

quīcumque, quaecumque, quodcumque	whoever, whatever
quōcumque	(to) wherever, whithersoever
ubicumque	wherever
quācumque	by whatever way

TRAVEL

Horace and Heliodorus set off along the queen of roads (*rēgīna uiārum*), the Appian Way. Originally this went from Rome to Capua (132 Roman miles) but 50 or so years later it was extended to Brundisium (a further 234 miles). You can still walk down its first ten miles, passing by many family tombs as you go.

In Horace's day, a network of major roads led to all parts of Italy. It would soon grow to cover the vast expanse of the empire. Roman legions—and Roman civilization—could move fast. The process of road-building was as follows. First of all the engineers established a course for a section of the road. (In some places each of the sections was a mile long.) The Romans' roads are famous for their straightness, especially in Britain and France. They took sightings from one high place to another or, in wooded or flat country, they lit fires, the smoke from which served as a guide to the surveyors.

Once they had marked out the course, they could build the road. The type of surfacing depended on need, feasibility, time and place, and we here describe the construction of just one kind, the paved roads which in the collective imagination are the Roman roads *par excellence.* The builders, usually supplied by the army, dug a trench about a meter deep. Having beaten the earth flat, they crammed large stones together at the bottom. They set a layer of pebbles, sometimes binding them with cement, on top of these; above the pebbles they laid sand. The upper layer could now be set on these firm foundations. If the road was not paved with stone, this might consist of gravel or small flints. Much would depend on what material was locally available.

The surfacing was given a fairly steep camber to assist drainage, and the water would usually run off into ditches dug at both sides. An embankment *(agger)* would be made where necessary, for example if a road had to be raised above a marsh. Roman roads were built to last—and last they did.

There were four ways of travelling by road. You walked. Or you rode a horse or mule. Or you went in a wheeled vehicle. The commonest of these, the four-wheeled *raeda,* was not particularly quick. On his journey to Brundisium, Horace covered only 24 miles on the day when he took one. The *cisium,* a light two-wheeled vehicle drawn by two horses, was not so comfortable but went much faster. If you changed horses, you could try to beat the record of 200 miles in 24 hours.

The fourth and most comfortable means of transport was the litter *(lectīca),* a portable couch with curtains carried by up to eight slaves. This was used mostly for short journeys in town. It was slung on straps which passed over the bearers' shoulders. The straps were easily detachable in case you wanted to beat an incompetent bearer. *Lectīcae* were so comfortable that they could be used as ambulances.

There were hotels on the main routes. Horace had no difficulty in finding a smallish one *(modicum hospitium)* in Aricia. But the grasping hotel keepers whom he tells us he found in Forum Appi were typical of their kind. With any luck a friend of yours would live on or near the road and you could stay the night with him.

This donkey-drawn vehicle is a tomb painting from Southern Italy. (National Archaeological Museum, Paestum)

This relief of a *raeda* comes from Klagenfurt in Austria. It is from a sarcophagus and dates from the imperial period.

Land travel had its problems, but most Romans preferred it to a sea voyage. For one thing, in most ships it was only safe to sail on the Mediterranean between March and November, and Seneca complains vigorously about being seasick. If they did wish to go by sea, passengers would go to a harbor and ask if any ship was sailing to their destination or nearby. They would have to be prepared to travel on deck since the smaller ships had cabin space only for the captain and his mate. Even if they had to wait for suitable winds before they set sail, once they were on the move they could travel extremely fast, up to 100 to 120 miles a day. It may have been this factor that caused Octavian to travel by sea whenever he could.

The speed of travel did not change much between Roman times and the nineteenth century when the steam engine was invented. You could travel by land no faster than a horse, and the roads in the Roman Empire were better than those in Britain until Victorian times. It took Horace just under two weeks of admittedly rather leisurely travel to get from Rome to Brundisium, a distance of some 366 miles. (Roman miles were a bit shorter than ours.) Now you can do this comfortably in a day. It took Cicero a day and two nights to sail from Corfu in Greece to Brundisium. The hydrofoil now takes three hours. Longer distances were formidable. It took Cicero the better part of three months to get from Rome to his province of Cilicia (southern Turkey). This journey today might take only two or three days by boat and car, or just a few hours by plane.

Further Reading

R. A. Staccioli, *The Roads of the Romans* ("L'Erma" di Bretschneider, 2003); U. E. Paoli, *Rome: Its People, Life and Customs* (Bristol Classical Press, 1990), 228–31.

Chapter 27
Maecēnās poētās fouet

Grammar: gerunds and gerundives

COMMENTARY

Maecenas formed a circle of poets around him who were encouraged to support the new regime; they included Virgil, Horace and Propertius (though the last seems to have been far more detached than the others).

l.4 *recitātiōnēs*: ancient poetry was always written to be read aloud; sound was of paramount importance (though, contrary to a much-cherished belief, literate Romans of Horace's day were perfectly capable of silent reading). Public recitation was the way in which new poetry was published and it became extremely popular in the time of Augustus. Authors would hire lecture halls, and friends and the general public would flock to hear them. By the time of the Younger Pliny (born AD 61) there were so many recitations that he asserted that attendance had become a tiresome duty: "This year has brought a great crop of poets; in the whole of April there's been scarcely a day when someone didn't give a recitation" (*Letters* 1.13).

> *mīrābar quidnam*: for a discussion of this poem, see S. J. Heyworth and J. H. W. Morwood (eds.), *Propertius 3* (Oxford, 2011), pp. 196–204.—Notes on the text of the poem appear in RV.

l.13 (RV p. 130) *Stōicōrum praecepta*: in Horace's time the two most popular philosophies were those of the Stoics and the Epicureans. The Stoics held to an austere philosophy; they maintained that the true end of man was to pursue virtue; they laid great stress on duty. The Epicureans said that the only good for man was pleasure, not in a gross sense, but absence of pain, achieved by plain living and the pursuit of virtue. The doctrines of Epicurus had been expounded in Lucretius' great poem, *Dē Rērum Nātūrā* (c. 99–55 BC). (See pp. 152–3 above.)

Horace himself was an eclectic in philosophy; he writes (*Epistles* 1.1.14–15):

nūllīus addictus iūrāre in uerba magistrī,
quō mē cumque rapit tempestās, dēferor hospes.

(I am not bound to swear to any master's words but wherever the storm [of life] carries me, I put in [to port] and make myself at home [*hospes* = as a guest].)

But on the whole an Epicurean ethic predominates in his poetry; cf. ll.14–15 (RV p. 130) "ad doctrīnam Epicūri inclīnābātur."

Albī, nostrōrum sermōnum candide iūdex: for a discussion of this poem, see Horace, *Epistles, Book I*, ed. R. Mayer (Cambridge, 1994), pp. 133–6.

RV **Bronze bar marked with a pig:** When the bronze was melted, it ran off into a channel called a sow, the lateral branches of which were called pigs. Hence the stamp of the pig on this bar. (British Museum, London) *See page 131 in* Oxford Latin Course, College Edition: Readings and Vocabulary.

l.18 *Epicūrī dē grege porcum*: *grex* is used of both a flock of animals and a group or school of people. As Epicurus said that the greatest good for man was pleasure, he was often accused, wrongly, of preaching self-indulgence and excess. Horace is, of course, laughing at himself; he was growing fat with good living—compare Suetonius, *Vita Horatii: habitū corporis fuit breuis atque obēsus* (in physique he was short and fat). But in fact he advocated moderation in all things, the golden mean (*aurea mediocritās—Odes* 2.10.5). For this key Horatian concept, see D. West, Horace, *Odes II: Vatis Amici* (Oxford, 1998), p. 69.

l.23 *carmina amātōria*: *Odes* 1–3 include 17 poems in which love themes are treated. In most of these he does not seem to be wholly serious. He says of his own poetry in refusing to write of Agrippa's military exploits (*Odes* 1.6. 17–20):

nōs conuīuia, nōs proelia uirginum
sectīs in iuuenēs unguibus ācrium
cantāmus uacuī, sīue quid ūrimur,
　　nōn praeter solitum leuēs.

(I sing of dinner parties, I sing of battles waged by girls fiercely attacking boys with sharpened finger nails, heart-whole, or if I do burn at all with passion, light [in tone] as usual.)

He is saying that the themes of his lyric poetry are traditional—sympotic (celebratory of the dinner party) and erotic. His erotic poems are usually about others; he watches the battles of love with amused detachment. When he does write about his own loves, he often laughs at himself.

---

uīxī puellīs...: for an interesting discussion of this poem, see David West, *Horace, Odes III, Dulce Periculum* (Oxford, 2002), 214–18. Meter: Alcaics (see Metrical Appendix, p. 291–5).

GRAMMAR

Gerunds

ars scrībendī = the art of writing

The gerund is an active verbal noun, declined like **bellum:**

1st	2nd	3rd	3rd -iō	4th
para-	mone-	reg-	capi-	audi-
parandum	monendum	regendum	capiendum	audiendum
preparing	*warning*	*ruling*	*taking*	*hearing*

- It is common in the accusative after **ad**, expressing purpose, e.g.

  uēnī ad uōbīs succurrendum.   I have come to help you.

- It is used in the genitive with **causā** = *by reason of, for the sake of*, as another way of expressing purpose, e.g.

  uēnī uōbīs succurrendī causā.   I have come to help you.

  (Notice that **causā** follows the word it governs.)

- It is is found in the dative with verbs and phrases requiring a dative, e.g.

  nōn satis ōtiī habēbō carmina scrībendō.   I shall not have enough leisure for composing poems.

- It is common in the ablative expressing cause or means, e.g.

  celeriter currendō domum ante noctem aduēnī.   By running fast, I arrived home before night.

N.B.: 1. the gerund of **eō** is **eundum**.

2. In English the present participle (a verbal adjective) and the gerund (a verbal noun) have the same form, e.g. "writing." In Latin the verbal adjective and the verbal noun are clearly distinguished, e.g.

Maecēnās in tablīnō sedēbat epistolam scrībēns.
Maecenas was sitting in the study writing a letter.
(**scrībēns** is a verbal adjective describing Maecenas)

Maecēnās nōn satis ōtiī habēbat ad epistolās scrībendum.
Maecenas did not have enough leisure for writing letters.
(**scrībendum** is a verbal noun governed by **ad**)

EXERCISE 27.1

Translate

1. Horātius artem dīcendī Rōmae didicit.
2. deinde Athēnās uēnit philosophiae stūdendī causā.
3. dīligenter stūdendō multa ibi didicit.
4. Athēnīs discessit ad mīlitandum cum Brūtō.
5. fortissimum sē praebuit in hostibus resistendō.
6. Brūtō mortuō, ad Italiam rediit parentēs quaerendī causā.
7. scrība aerāriī ā Marcō Cicerōne factus, satis ōtiī habēbat carmina scrībendō.
8. Octāuiānus inimīcīs ignōscendō omnēs cīuēs sibi conciliāuit.
9. Pompēius Rōmam rediit ueniam petendī causā.
10. Horātius omnēs amīcōs conuocāuit ad Pompēiī reditum celebrandum.

EXERCISE 27.2

Translate into Latin

1. We have come to serve with Brutus (use **ad** + gerund).
2. For he is fighting to defend liberty (use gerund + **causā**).
3. Did you not hear the signal to advance (= of advancing)?
4. Do not try to save yourselves by delaying.
5. By fighting bravely we shall defeat the enemy and save the republic.
6. Horace was ordered to lead his legion against Antony's forces.
7. There was a fierce battle, but in the end Brutus was defeated.
8. Horace, throwing away his shield (= his shield having been thrown away), saved himself by running to the camp.
9. There it was announced that Brutus was dead.
10. All saved themselves by fleeing into the woods.

GRAMMAR

Gerundives

cēna paranda est.	Supper is to-be-prepared.
puerī monendī sunt.	The children are to-be-warned.
imperium regendum erat.	The empire was to-be-ruled.
magister audiendus est.	The master is to-be-listened-to.

Besides the *gerund* (an active verbal noun), Latin verbs have a passive verbal adjective called the *gerundive* which looks identical with the gerund:

parandus, -a, -um	to be prepared
monendus, -a, -um	to be warned
regendus, -a, -um	to be ruled
capiendus, -a, -um	to be taken
audiendus, -a, -um	to be heard

The gerundive is commonly used instead of a gerund:

Maecēnās poētās incitābat ad carmina compōnenda.

Maecenas used to encourage poets to compose poems.

Maecēnās amīcōs conuocāuit ad recitātiōnem audiendam.

Maecenas called together his friends to hear a recitation.

In these examples the nouns (**carmina, recitātiōnem**) are governed by the preposition **ad**, and the gerundives, being adjectives, agree with the nouns. The literal meaning of the examples is:

- Maecenas encouraged poets to poems to be composed.
- Maecenas called together his friends to a recitation to be heard.

But English verbs have no gerundive and the Latin idiom is so alien to English that it is better to grasp the gerundive phrase as a whole than to wrestle with the literal meaning. If you do this, such phrases are not difficult.

N.B. Deponent verbs, besides having a gerund, have a gerundive, passive in meaning, e.g. **cōnandus, -a, -um** to be tried; **uerendus, -a, -um** to be feared; **sequendus, -a, -um** to be followed.

EXERCISE 27.3

Translate

1. Maecēnās amīcōs conuocāuit ad poētās audiendōs.
2. inter aliōs Propertius uēnit carminis recitandī causā.
3. carmine optimē recitandō maximum plausum meruit.
4. Tibullus rūs recesserat ad carmina compōnenda.
5. Horātius Tibullum cōnsōlārī cōnātus est epistolā ad eum scrībendā.
6. Horātius ad aedēs Maecēnātis īre solēbat ad poētās optimōs audiendōs.
7. poētīs fouendīs Maecēnās exemplum patrōnī bonī sē praebuit.
8. domum Vergilī adībō carminis eius nouī audiendī causā.

9. Vergilius sē parābat ad opus maximum scrībendum.
10. Horātius magnopere dubitāuit num ipse satis ingeniōsus esset ad tantum opus suscipiendum.

GRAMMAR

Gerundives

Gerundives of Obligation

Tibullus omnī modō adiuuandus est.
Tibullus must be (is to be) helped in every way.
hoc carmen tibi scrībendum est.
This poem must be written by you, i.e. You must write this poem.

The gerundive is commonly used with *esse* expressing obligation (must/ought/have to). The person concerned (the agent) is in the dative.

As we have seen, the gerundive is a *passive* verbal adjective. This can be reflected in idiomatic English, e.g.

This film is on no account to be missed.
One thing remains to be done.

But far more often English prefers to make such sentences active in form with the person concerned (the agent) as the subject. Note the difference between the Latin and English expression in these sentences:

templum nōbīs aedificandum est.
We must build a temple.
multae recitātiōnes mihi audiendae erant.
I had to listen to many recitals.
ad aedēs Maecēnātis uōbīs festīnandum erit.
You will have to hurry to the palace of Maecenas.

The gerundive of intransitive verbs is used impersonally in such expressions, literally "it will have to be hurried by you."

> **EXERCISE 27.4**

Translate

1. Horātī carmina puerīs in lūdīs omnibus legenda sunt.
2. Tibullō rūs statim est abeundum ut Dēliam uīsat.
3. uīta Horātiō erat aureā mediocritāte agenda.
4. cotīdiē nōbīs bonīs poētīs ad aedēs Maecēnātis festīnandum erat.

5. librī omnibus legendī sunt quō sapientiōrēs in diēs fiant. (Translate *quō* as if it were *ut* and refer to p. 280 for this use of the relative plus the subjunctive.)
6. festīnāte, amīcī; statim proficīscendum est.
7. nox adest. sī morābimur, in montibus nōbīs tōtam noctem manendum erit.
8. pāstor quaerendus est quī nōs in casam suam accipiet.
9. nisi pāstōrem inuēnerimus, in siluīs dormiendum erit; sīc tūtī erimus.

GRAMMAR

The gerundive is sometimes found agreeing with the object of verbs such as **cūrō**, **mittō**, **dō** in expressing purpose or intent.

> **Maecēnās carmina Horatī recitanda cūrāuit.**
> Maecenas arranged for (cared for) Horace's poems to be recited.

EXERCISE 27.5

Translate:

1. Maecēnās epistolam cursōrī (*his runner*) trādidit in urbem ferendam.
2. Maecēnās multōs amīcos conuocandōs cūrāuit ad recitātiōnem audiendam.
3. Horātius carmen composuit amīcō suō Tibullō legendum.
4. Maecēnās, patrōnus clārissimus, multōs poētās fouendōs cūrābat.

EXERCISE 27.6

Translate into Latin using gerundives

1. Since I have met Virgil, I must cultivate his friendship.
2. Tibullus must avoid the city; he must stay in the country.
3. Propertius must love Cynthia until he dies.
4. Horace, a light(-hearted) lover must find another girl.
5. We shall have to listen to those songs which he has written about Pyrrha.

P.S. Alternative Verb and Noun Forms

1. A shortened form of the 3rd person plural of the perfect active is commonly used by the poets: **-ēre** for **-ērunt**, e.g. **parāuēre** for **parāuērunt**. So Horace's spring ode begins **diffūgēre niuēs** = **diffūgērunt niuēs** (the snows have fled away).

2. In the perfect active of the 4th conjugation verbs **u** is often omitted, e.g. **audiit = audīuit, audiērunt = audīuērunt, audierat = audīuerat.**
   In the perfect infinitive and pluperfect subjunctive, the forms are further shortened by the omission of one **i: audīsse = audīuisse** and **audīssem = audīuissem**, etc.
   So also from, e.g. **petō: petiit** for **petīuit**, and from **eō: iit** for **īuit**; compounds of **eō** always use this form, e.g. **rediit** (never **redīuit**).
   So also we find from 1st conjunction verbs **parāuisset** shortened to **parāsset**, and **parāuisse** shortened to **parāsse**.

3. Note carefully the alternative forms of the future infinitive of **esse: futūrus esse, fore.**

4. The active imperatives have alternative forms as follows: **parā/parātō, parā/parātōte**, but these are found commonly only in the following:

estō, estōte	be!
scitō, scitōte	know! be assured!
mementō, mementōte	remember!

5. the 2nd person singular of the future passive has alternative forms: **parābere** for **parāberis, monēbere** for **monēberis, regēre** for **regēris, capiēre** for **capiēris, audiēre** for **audiēris.**

6. 3rd declension nouns with stems in **-i** have an alternative ablative singular in **-ī**, e.g. **nāuī** for **nāue**; 3rd declension nouns and adjectives have an alternative accusative plural in **-īs**, e.g. **omnīs cīuīs** for **omnēs cīuēs**. (Note that the **i** is long.)

VIXI PUELLIS

Read these two translations of *Vīxī puellīs*. Which of them strikes you as the better?

In love's wars I have long maintained
Good fighting trim and ever gained
    Some glory. Now my lyre
    And veteran sword retire.

And the left wall in the temple of
The sea-born deity of love
    Shall house them. Come, lay here,
    Lay down the soldier's gear—

The crowbar, the far-blazing torch,
The bow for forcing past the porch.
    Here is my last request:
    Goddess, ruler of the blest

The so-called Ludovisi throne (because found in the Villa Ludovisi) is a lustrous masterpiece of the fifth century BC. It shows Venus rising from the sea to the embrace of a towel held by two women representing the seasons, who stand on the pebbled beach. The distinction between the three different types of drapery is just one fine feature of this superb sculpture. (Palazzo Altemps, Rome)

Cyprus and Memphis, shrine that knows
No shiver of Sithonian snows,
    Whose whip bends proud girls' knees—
    One flick for Chloe, please.
           James Michie (1965)

Till now I have lived my life without complaints
from girls, and campaigned with my share of honours.
Now my armour and my lyre—its wars are over—
    will hang on this wall

which guards the left side of Venus
of the sea. Here, over here, lay down my bright torches,
the crowbars and the bows that threatened
    opposing doors.

Paphos

O goddess, who rule the blessed isle of Cyprus.
and Memphis never touched by Sithonian snow,
lift high your whip, O Queen, and flick
    disdainful Chloe, just once.
           David West (1995)

Chapter 28

Horātius rūsticus fit

> **Grammar:** impersonal verbs; intransitive verbs in the passive; subjunctive in main clauses (jussive, deliberative, optative, potential)

PATTERN SENTENCES:

The impersonal verbs should be self-explanatory.

The meaning of the words jussive (from **iubeō** = I order), optative (from **optō** = I wish for) and potential should be clear from the sentences.

COMMENTARY

(a) Horātius rūsticus fit

l.7 *dormītum*: "to sleep": supine expressing purpose (see p. 194, note on l.20 in this book)

ll.11–12 *fūmus...strepitusque Rōmae*: cf. *Odes* 3.29.11–12:

omitte mīrārī beātae
 fūmum et opēs strepitumque Rōmae.
(Don't admire the smoke and riches and din of blessed Rome).

l.15 *calōre*: "from the heat." *uelim*: "I should like" (potential subjunctive).

[RV] **rūris tranquillitās:** this wall-painting of an orchard with pomegranates and quinces is from the Imperial Villa of Livia, the wife of Augustus, at Prima Porta. It was restored in 1952–3 and thus saved from falling into decay and is now in the Museo Nazionale Romano. Bernard Berenson wrote: "How dewy, how penetratingly fresh are grass and trees and flowers, how coruscating the fruit. Pomegranates as Renoir painted them. Bird songs charm one's ears.

The distance remains magically impenetrable." *See page 136 in* Oxford Latin Course, College Edition: Readings and Vocabulary.

l.31 *fōns aquae iūgis*: "a spring of ever-flowing water."
l.37 *numquam possim*: "I would never be able" (potential subjunctive).

RV **Horace's Sabine farm:** this villa in the Sabine hills may be the one that Maecenas gave to Horace. *See page 137 in* Oxford Latin Course, College Edition: Readings and Vocabulary.

(b) fōns Bandusiae

ō fōns Bandusiae: meter Asclepiad (see Metrical Appendix)
While the actual fons Bandusiae is almost certainly elsewhere, probably near Horace's birthplace, Venusia, we have taken the liberty of locating it at Horace's farm in the Sabine hills. He himself refers to a *iūgis aquae fōns* here (a spring of ever-flowing water—*Satires* 2.6.2). See Llewelyn Morgan, "The one and only *Fons Bandusiae*," *Classical Quarterly* 59.1, 132–41.

There is a stimulating discussion of the poem in David West, *Horace, Odes III, Dulce Periculum* (Oxford, 2002), 118–23.

RV **fōns Bandusiae:** this fountain is a short distance above the villa on p. 137 of RV. *See page 139 in* Oxford Latin Course, College Edition: Readings and Vocabulary.

GRAMMAR

Impersonal Verbs

A small number of verbs in English do not have a personal subject, e.g. "it rains," "it snows"; it makes no sense to ask "Who rains?" "Who snows?" Such verbs are called "impersonal," since they have no person as subject. In Latin there is a fair amount of such verbs, e.g.

pluit	it rains
ningit	it snows
tonat	it thunders
necesse est	it is necessary
fās est	it is right

Many Latin impersonal verbs are not used impersonally in English, e.g. with the accusative of the person:

(mē) oportet	it behooves me = I ought
(mē) pudet	it shames me = I am ashamed
(mē) iuuat	it delights me = I like to
(mē) taedet (+ gen.)	it wearies me = I am tired of
e.g. **(mē) taedet urbis**	I am tired of the city

with the dative of the person:

(mihi) licet	it is allowed to me = I may
(mihi) placet	it pleases me = I decide

They are often followed by an infinitive, e.g.

hoc facere mē oportet.	I ought to do this.
eī placuit domum redīre.	He decided to return home.
nōbīs licuit lūdōs spectāre.	We were allowed to watch the games.

EXERCISE 28.1

Translate

1. Horātiō placuit in fundō morārī.
2. sed Maecēnātī necesse fuit ad urbem redīre.
3. Horātium ualdē iuuābit prope fontem sedēre, carmina scrībentem.
4. fūmī strepitūsque urbis Horātium maximē taedēbat.
5. cum pluerat, Horātium in uīllam īre oportuit.
6. crās colōnīs haedum sacrificāre necesse erit.
7. omnibus licēbit ad fontem adīre.
8. fundī meī nunquam mē taedet.
9. cum seruīs colloquī Horātium nōn pudēbat.
10. tandem Horātium Rōmam inuītum redīre oportuit.

GRAMMAR

Intransitive Verbs in the Passive

Intransitive verbs must be used impersonally in the passive, e.g.

Antōniō nūntiātum est.   It was announced to Antony.

ferōciter pugnātum est.   It was fought fiercely, i.e. there was a fierce battle.

Sometimes verbs of motion are used impersonally in the passive; in such cases you must translate them in the active, supplying a person from the context, e.g.

prīmā lūce profectī sumus; merīdiē ad montem uentum est.

We set out at dawn; at midday we came (literally: it was come) to the mountain.

undique concurritur.

It is run together from all sides, i.e. people run together from all sides.

Verbs which take the dative are used impersonally in the passive:

captīuīs parcitur   It is spared to the captives, i.e. the captives are spared.

mihi persuāsum est.   I was persuaded.

EXERCISE 28.2

Translate

1. Brūtō nūntiātum est Antōnium omnibus cum cōpiīs in Graeciam prōgredī.
2. eī placuit prope Philippōs proelium committere.
3. cum proelium commīsissent, ab utrīsque fortiter pugnātum est; tandem tamen Brūtī cōpiae fūgērunt.
4. Brūtī cōpiae ē castrīs fūgerant; ubi ad siluās aduentum est, cubuērunt diemque trīstēs exspectābant.
5. Horātiō placuit Athēnās fugere. cum ad urbem aduēnisset, Theomnēstum petēbat.
6. Theomnēstus, "sī Octāuiānum ueniam rogāueris," inquit, "tibi ab eō parcētur."
7. Horātiō, cum ad Italiam rediisset, parentēs suōs quaerere placuit.
8. Horātiō ā Cicerōne persuāsum est ut in aerāriō labōrāret; sed eōs saepe iuuābat in tabernā sedēre, uīnum bibentēs.

EXERCISE 28.3

Translate the following sentences into Latin, using impersonal verbs for the phrases in bold

1. We set out at the first hour and hurried into the hills; before midday **we reached** the top of the mountain.
2. **We decided** to wait there for two hours.
3. But **we were not allowed** to rest for long.
4. For a shepherd warned us not to delay, and **we were persuaded** to descend at once.
5. It was a long and difficult journey, and before we reached home, **I was tired of** mountains.

GRAMMAR

Uses of the Subjunctive in Main Clauses

In main clauses the subjunctive has several uses: jussive (used in exhortations and 3rd person commands); deliberative questions; optative (wishes); potential.

1. Jussive (hortatory)

ad forum festīnēmus.	Let us hurry to the forum.
nē domum redeant.	Let them not return home.

You are already familiar with this usage. The negative is **nē**.

2. Deliberative Questions

quid faciāmus?	What are we to do?

The subjunctive (1st person singular or plural) is used in questions when the speaker is wondering what to do.

utrum hīc maneam an domum redeam?	Am I to stay here or return home?

EXERCISE 28.4

Translate

1. quid tibi dīcam?
2. quō eāmus?
3. utrum hostibus resistāmus an fugiāmus?
4. quōmodo molestum illum dīmittam?
5. quandō Rōmā discēdāmus?

GRAMMAR

3. Optative (Wishes)

(utinam) diū uīuās semperque ualeās.	May you live long and always be healthy!
(utinam) pater meus adesset.	I wish my father were here!
(utinam) nē pater meus Rōmam abiisset.	I wish my father had not gone away to Rome.

N.B.: 1 *utinam* (= I wish that) is often used in wishes to make the meaning clear.

   2 The tenses of the subjunctive are used as in "contrary to the fact" conditional clauses, i.e. the present subjunctive is used for a wish for the future, the imperfect for a wish for the present and the pluperfect for a wish for the past.

   3 The negative is **nē**:

   (utinam) nē perīculum incidāmus.   May we not fall into danger.

EXERCISE 28.5

Translate

1. uīuās et ualeās!
2. utinam dīues essem.
3. utinam nē mihi haec dīxissēs.
4. deī tē seruent.
5. utinam incolumis domum redeās.

GRAMMAR

4. Potential

uelim hoc facere.	I should like to do this.
nōn ausim pugnāre.	I would not dare to fight.

This use of the subjunctive is not common except with **uelim, nōlim, ausim** (an irregular present subjunctive form of **audeō**). It is a sort of conditional subjunctive with the "if" clause omitted, e.g. "I should like to help you (if I could)." The negative is **nōn**.

EXERCISE 28.6

Translate

1. quid faciam, amīcī? quōmodo Maecēnātī grātiās agam?
2. ad fundum eāmus. ibi multum uīnī bibēmus.
3. dē rēbus rūsticīs nihil sciō. quid uīlicō meō dīcam?
4. in fundō uelim plūrimōs diēs morārī.
5. utinam prope fontem semper maneāmus.
6. uīcīnus meus mē ad cēnam inuītāuit. nōn ausim recūsāre.
7. utinam Maecēnās rūrī adhūc manēret. dē carminibus uelim cum eō colloquī.
8. utinam nē Maecēnās ad urbem rediisset. mox ad fundum meum redīre eī placeat.

EXERCISE 28.7

Translate into Latin

1. Are we to stay here or hurry home?
2. Let us stay here; we cannot reach home before night.
3. I would not dare travel (= make the journey) by night.
4. I wish we had not set out late!
5. I wish we were now safe at home!
6. We are in great danger. May the gods preserve us!
7. Let us set out for home at first light.

P.S.
The following prepositions/adverbs form comparative and superlative adjectives:

		comparative	superlative	
extrā + acc.	outside	**exterior**	**extrēmus**	uttermost, extreme
intrā + acc.	inside	**interior**	**intimus**	innermost, most intimate
post + acc.	after	**posterior**	**postrēmus**	last
prae + acc.	before	**prior**	**prīmus**	first
suprā + acc.	above	**superior**	**suprēmus** **summus**	highest, latest highest, greatest
ultrā + acc.	beyond	**ulterior**	**ultimus**	furthest, last

PATRONS AND CLIENTS

A Roman who wanted to move up the social scale had to attach himself to a man of some eminence. He had in fact to become a client *(cliēns)* to a patron *(patrōnus).*

Soon after sunrise, during the first and second hours of the day, the great men of Rome held a *salūtātiō,* a ceremony of greeting when clients would gather outside their patron's house, eager to be admitted. It was not altogether a one-sided affair since the patron would gain prestige from the number of morning callers.

To begin with, the *salūtātiō* had been a meaningful business. The client asked for advice and help from his patron, and the patron planned political maneuvers and assessed the strength of his backing with his clients. Later, however, it became a matter simply of status, and callers were strictly graded.

Clients would often have to get up before daylight to make their way through the filthy streets to their patron's house. Here they would wait outside, hoping to give enough satisfaction at the *salūtātiō* to receive at least the *sportula,* originally a "little basket" containing food but now a kind of dole, a gift in money of 25 *asses* (6 ¼ sesterces), in the afternoon. They were forced to wear the toga, that expensive form of dress so ludicrously unsuited to the Italian climate. They were received with contempt by slaves whom they often had to bribe (Seneca, *Epistles* 4.10), and they might fail even to speak to their patron, as Seneca complains:

> How often will clients find themselves shoved out of the way because a patron is either asleep or amusing himself—or is just plain rude! How many patrons will inflict a long torture of waiting on their clients and then rush past them pretending to be in a great hurry! How many of them will avoid exiting through a hall crammed with clients and run off through a secret back-entrance—as if it were not more offensive to deceive them than to shut them out altogether! How many are still half-asleep with a stupefying hangover after the night before! Their poor clients have broken their own sleep to attend somebody else's, but the patrons can scarcely be bothered to raise their lips in an insolent yawn and only get the name right after it has been whispered to them a thousand times.
>
> (*Dē Breuitāte Vitae* 14.4)

If clients did make contact with their patron, they might be expected to escort him to the forum or the baths. And if they were invited to dinner—an invitation, writes Juvenal, that only comes once every two months or more (5.15–16)—they were only too likely to be placed apart from their patron and his real friends and served with inferior food and drink: while he has mullet and lamprey, you have eel and pike fed on sewage (Juvenal 5.92–106).

Yet the patron was uneasily aware that his clients did not necessarily have any affection for him as a person, As Seneca writes, "None of them is interested in you, just in what he can get out of you. It used to be friendship they were after; now it's plunder. If a lonely old man changes his will, next day the callers will make for another address." (*Epistles* 19.4)

Exactly how widespread this degrading ritual was we cannot know. Much of our evidence comes from the satirical poets Juvenal and Martial, and satirists are in the business of exaggeration. It is hard to believe that Maecenas expected Virgil or Horace to gyrate on this merry-go-round of greetings. Certainly from their perspective of more than a century later, the satirists looked back on Maecenas as a model of what a patron should be. Martial writes, "If you have a Maecenas, you'll have Virgils too." (8.56.5)

Further Reading

Still excellent on this subject is J. P. V. D. Balsdon, *Life and Leisure in Ancient Rome* (Bodley Head, 1969), 21–4.

> **Grammar:** clauses of fearing; connecting relative

COMMENTARY

(a) Actium

When Antony sent Octavia letters of divorce and formally married Cleopatra, Octavian embarked on a war of violent propaganda against him; Antony was represented as the slave of an eastern queen to whom he had given away large parts of the empire; it was even rumored that he intended to move the capital of the empire to Alexandria.

Octavian now prepared for war, first attempting to unite all Italy behind him in a "just" war that would save Rome from the menace of the East. In the summer his agents organized a sort of plebiscite, an oath of allegiance to him: *iurāuit in mea uerba tōta Italia sponte suā* ("the whole of Italy swore an oath of loyalty to me of its own accord"). This was followed by a declaration of war against Cleopatra. In point of fact, however, the two consuls as well as a significant number of senators fled to Antony.

l.5 *in uerba eius iūrāuit*: swore an oath (of loyalty) to him

ll.5–6 *eum ducem bellī poposcit*: demanded him as leader of the war, i.e. demanded that he should be leader.

R|V **Actium:** close to these white cliffs, some 200 feet high, the battle of Actium was fought. Cape Leucate takes its name from them (*leukos* is the Greek word for white). There are a few fragmentary remains of the temple of Apollo on top of the cape. The temple was restored by Octavian in gratitude for his victory. *See page 141 in* Oxford Latin Course, College Edition: Readings and Vocabulary.

R|V **Roman warship from Actium:** this relief of the first century BC from Praeneste may well date from the time of Cleopatra. Note the crocodile on the bow. The legionary soldiers stand on deck while invisible slaves work the oars below. (Museo Pio-Clementino, Rome) *See page 142 in* Oxford Latin Course, College Edition: Readings and Vocabulary.

l.12 *Maecēnāte Rōmae relictō*: it may in fact be the case that both Maecenas and Horace were present at the battle of Actium; see *The Cambridge Companion to Horace*, ed. S. Harrison (Cambridge, 2007), 11–12

l.15 *Agrippa*: M. Vipsanius Agrippa was an exact contemporary of Octavian. He was serving with Octavian when Julius Caesar was murdered, returned to Italy with him, and became his most successful general. It was he who defeated Sextus Pompeius in two naval battles and was responsible for the victory at Actium. He married Octavian's daughter Julia in 21 BC and was marked out to be his successor as emperor, but he died in 13 BC.

l.17 *famē*: from hunger

l.19 *aequō Marte pugnātum est*: it was fought with Mars equal, i.e. the battle was evenly balanced.

l.23 *minōris aestimāret*: valued less: *minōris* is genitive of value. We follow Plutarch's account in his *Life of Antony* 66. This may be basically accurate: see Carsten Hjort Lange, "The Battle of Actium: a reconsideration," *Classical Quarterly* 61.2 (2011), 608–23.

l.26 *clēmentiam*: Augustus made much of his *clēmentia*; in *Res Gestae* 3 he says "uictor omnibus ueniam petentibus cīuibus pepercī" (In victory I spared all citizens who asked for pardon).

(b) Bellum Alexandrīnum

RV **A coin commemorating the capture of Egypt by Octavian:** the inscription AEGYPT(O) CAPTA (after the capture of Egypt) on this gold coin is appropriately illustrated with a crocodile. (British Museum, London) *See page 143 in* Oxford Latin Course, College Edition: Readings and Vocabulary.

We follow the highly romantic account of Plutarch (*Life of Antony*, 69–86) followed by Shakespeare in *Antony and Cleopatra*.

l.4 *trānsfūgit*: fled across to = deserted to

l.20 *ut...sē dēderet*: to give herself up; in indirect commands the reflexive *sē* normally refers to the subject of the leading verb, but here, by sense, it refers to the subject of *dēderet*.

RV **calathus fīcīs plēnum:** a wall painting from the dining room of the villa at Oplontis near Pompeii. It was only in 1964 that systematic excavations began here. The villa may have belonged to Poppaea Sabina (died 65 AD), the wife of Nero. The property was unoccupied when it was buried beneath ash and pumice

from Vesuvius in 79 AD. *See page 144 in* Oxford Latin Course,
College Edition: Readings and Vocabulary.

Horace wrote a famous ode on the battle of Actium and the death of Cleopatra (*Odes* 1.37), which starts as a song of jubilant exultation, echoing Octavian's propaganda, but ends in admiration for Cleopatra's courage:

> Nunc est bibendum, nunc pede līberō
> pulsanda tellūs, nunc Saliāribus
>   ornāre puluīnar deōrum
>   tempus erat dapibus, sodālēs.....
>
>   ...quae generōsius
> perīre quaerēns nec muliebriter
>   expāuit ēnsem.....
>
> dēliberātā morte ferōcior,
> saeuīs Liburnīs scīlicet inuidēns
>   prīuāta dēdūcī superbō
>   nōn humilis mulier triumphō.

David West's translation reads:

> Now we must drink, now we must
> beat the earth with unfettered feet, now,
>   my friends, is the time to load the couches
>   of the gods with Salian feasts.
>
>   (a monster) who looked
> for a nobler death and did not have a woman's fear
>   of the sword...
>
> fiercer she was in the death she chose, as though
> she did not wish to cease to be a queen, taken to Rome
>   on the galleys of savage Liburnians
>   to be a humble woman in a proud triumph.

(c) Pāx et Prīnceps

R|V **Augustus as priest:** Augustus is represented as a pious citizen, performing a sacrifice or attending a religious ceremony, with part of the toga drawn up to veil his head. (Museo delle Terme, Rome)

See page 145 in Oxford Latin Course, College Edition: Readings and Vocabulary.

The deaths of Antony and Cleopatra marked the final end of the civil wars. Octavian, or Augustus as he was shortly to be called, was ready to embark on the work of reconstruction. He annexed Egypt, not as a province but as his personal possession, to be administered by a Prefect appointed by himself. He then proceeded to reestablish the old provinces in the East. He did not extend the territory ruled by the Romans but secured the frontiers by installing on their borders client kings loyal to Rome. After making arrangements which were to last for many years, he returned to Rome in summer 29 BC and celebrated triumphs for his victories in Illyricum, Actium and Alexandria.

Peace was now established throughout the Roman Empire. The army, swollen to nearly 70 legions, was reduced to 26 and the veterans settled on land partly paid for from the spoils of Egypt. In 28/27 BC Octavian made a constitutional settlement which he describes in *Res Gestae* (34) as transferring "the republic from my power into the control of the senate and people of Rome." (*Res Gestae* was a testament written by Augustus shortly before his death, in which he records his achievements. Copies of this were erected in Rome and in at least the eastern provinces of the empire; one copy survives in Ancyra, in the province of Galatia, modern Turkey). On January 13, 27 BC, he laid down all powers and resigned all provinces to the disposal of the senate and people. Pressed by the senators, he consented to assume a special commission consisting of proconsular authority over Gaul, Spain and Syria. The basis of his power was now the consulship, which he held repeatedly, and his imperium in those provinces, where a large proportion of the legions were stationed. The senate acclaimed the restitution of liberty and conferred on him the name Augustus. From then on he was known as Caesar Augustus. The title by which he preferred to be called and which he applied to himself was *prīnceps*; this was perhaps adapted from the title of the senior senator, *prīnceps senātūs*, and means no more than "leading citizen"; it implied no particular powers and had a civilian ring to it.

He then left Rome for a tour of the western provinces and was absent for three years. When he returned to Rome in 24 BC, a crisis supervened; there was a conspiracy led by discontented nobles and he fell seriously ill. He decided to revise the constitutional arrangements. He resigned the consulship, and to maintain his authority in the civilian sphere he assumed the *tribūnicia potestās*, which he held continuously. To keep his control over the army and the provinces he was granted *maius imperium prōcōnsulāre*, which enabled him to override the proconsuls in the provinces for which he was not directly responsible. Thus, while in theory the republic continued to function with annual elections, senatorial debates and the other machinery of republican government, in fact Augustus controlled the whole state both through the exceptional powers granted him and through his ever-growing *auctōritās*.

ll.9–10 *populō Rōmānō ōdiō esse*: "was for a hatred to the Roman people," i.e. was hated by the Roman people: *ōdiō* is predicative dative, to be learnt in the next chapter.

This monument to the German chieftain Hermann (Arminius in Latin) was begun in 1841 but not completed until 1875 following the unification of most of Germany under Bismarck. It stands on the southern side of the Teutoburg forest.

l.14 *potītus omnium rērum*: having obtained possession of all things, i.e. having won complete control—*potior* is one of the few verbs which takes the genitive.

ll.24–5 *bella multīs cum gentibus externīs*: Augustus added more territory to the Roman Empire than anyone else but his policy was essentially conservative, dictated not by a desire for military glory but to secure the safety of the frontiers of the empire. To achieve this he extended the boundaries to the Euphrates, the Danube, and the Rhine, creating four new provinces (see map on page 147 of RV). He also planned to advance the frontier in the north from the Rhine to the Elbe; in a series of campaigns between 12 BC and 9 AD the Roman armies advanced to the Elbe but all these gains were lost when the German chief Arminius raised a successful rebellion and destroyed the Roman general Varus and three legions in an ambush in the Teutoburg forest. Augustus then gave up the project of conquering Germany and bequeathed to his successors *cōnsilium coercendī intrā terminōs imperiī* (the policy of not extending the boundaries of the empire—Tacitus, *Annals* 1.11).

RV **Caesar Augustus:** this noble statue from Prima Porta near Rome shows Augustus wearing his general's cloak (*palūdāmentum*). (Vatican Museums, Rome) *See page 146 in* Oxford Latin Course, College Edition: Readings and Vocabulary.

GRAMMAR

Clauses of Fearing

1. **Antōnius timēbat nē in manūs hostium caderet.**
   Antony feared lest/that he might fall into the hands of the enemy.
   Cleopātra uerēbātur nē Octāuiānō prōderētur.
   Cleopatra was afraid she would/might be betrayed to Octavian.
   timēmus nē hostēs nōs capiant.
   We are afraid the enemy may catch us.

Fears for the future are expressed by **nē** + subjunctive: present subjunctive if the leading verb is present or future; imperfect subjunctive if the leading verb is past.

English introduces such clauses by either "lest," or "that," or without any connecting conjunction.

2. **timēmus nē puerī domum ante noctem nōn redeant.**
   We are afraid the children may not return home before night.

If the clause of fearing is negative **nē nōn** (or **ut**) is used.

3. **timēbāmus longius prōgredī.**
   We were afraid to advance further.

Latin, like English, uses an infinitive when the meaning is "I am afraid to do something." Thus **hoc facere timeō** = I am afraid to do this, but **timeō nē hoc faciat** = I am afraid he may do this.

EXERCISE 29.1

Translate
1. Maecēnās timēbat nē ad fundum ante noctem nōn aduenīrent.
2. "festīnā, Quīnte," inquit; "timeō nē sērō adueniāmus."
3. Quīntus "equus meus fessus est; timeō celerius equitāre."
4. puerī, ueritī nē magister sibi īrāscerētur, dīligenter labōrābant.
5. timēbat nē magister sē nōn dīmitteret.
6. puellae, ueritae nē puerī sē sequantur, domum festīnant.

GRAMMAR

N.B.: 1. the reflexives **sē** and **suus** refer back to the leading verb (see numbers 4, 5, and 6 above).

(You will notice that **sē** and **suus** refer to the subject of the leading verb not only in indirect statement, question and command, but also in clauses of purpose introduced by **ut** or **nē** (since purpose is a thought in one's head), and in clauses of fearing introduced by **nē** (since the fear is a feeling in one's heart).

2. **ueritī**, **ueritae** (numbers 4 and 6); these are perfect participles, "having feared," but the English idiom is to use the present, "fearing."

EXERCISE 29.2

Translate the following sentences, in each of which the perfect participle could be translated by an English present (English is less precise in its uses of tenses than Latin)

1. ducem secūtī ad urbem mox aduēnimus.
2. prīmā lūce profectus domum ante noctem rediī.
3. Cleopātra, uerita nē Octāuiānō prōderētur, turrem relinquere nōluit.
4. Cleopātra, Antōnium intuita, sciēbat eum moritūrum esse.
5. senex carcerem ingressus custōdēs salūtāuit.

EXERCISE 29.3

Translate into Latin

1. Let us hurry; I am afraid we may arrive late.
2. Fearing that the master might be angry with them, the boys waited outside the door of the school.
3. The girls were not afraid to enter for they knew the master would not be angry with them.
4. Fearing that Antony would be defeated, Cleopatra fled with her ships.
5. Antony was not afraid to fight, but overcome by his love for (= of) Cleopatra he followed her.

GRAMMAR

The Connecting Relative

Apollō lyram Horātiō trādidit; quō factō ēuānuit.

Apollo handed his lyre to Horace; after doing this he vanished (literally: which having done he vanished)

Antōnius Cleopātram uxōrem suam esse prōnūntiāuit. quae cum cognōuissent senātōrēs, statim bellum Cleopātrae indīxērunt.

Antony proclaimed that Cleopatra was his wife. When the senators learned this (literally: which things when the senators learned), they at once declared war on Cleopatra.

The relative pronoun is often used at the beginning of a sentence instead of a demonstrative. In the first example above, **quō factō = eō factō**, in the second example, **quae cum cognōuissent = cum ea cognōuissent**.

An English relative pronoun will not work in a translation into English. You must use a demonstrative, as we have done in our examples.

EXERCISE 29.4

Translate

1. Cleopātra classem suam in fugam dūxit. quae cum uīdisset Antōnius, eam secūtus est.
2. Antōnius Cleopātram uīdit fugientem. quam adeō amāuit ut ipse quoque ē proeliō fūgerit.
3. quibus uīsīs Agrippa Antōniī classem etiam ferōcior oppugnāuit.
4. tandem sē dēdidērunt Antōniī mīlitēs. quōs Octāuiānus hūmānē tractātōs in exercitum suum accēpit.
5. quibus cognitīs Antōnius dēspērāuit.

P.S. The Genders of 3rd Declension Nouns

These have to be learned in every instance, but the following general rules will be of some help.

1. Nouns ending **-er** in the nominative are masculine, e.g. **pater**, **imber**, except for: **mulier** (woman), **māter** (mother), **linter** (boat), which are feminine; and **iter** (journey) and **uēr** (spring), which are neuter.
2. All nouns ending **-or/-ōs** in the nominative are masculine, e.g. **honor**, **flōs**, except for: **soror** (sister), **uxor** (wife), **arbor** (tree), which are feminine; and **cor** (heart) and **aequor** (sea), which are neuter.

3. All nouns ending in **-iō** in the nominative are feminine, e.g. **īnscrīptiō**, except for **centuriō** (centurion) and **decuriō** (town councillor).
4. All nouns ending **-ās** in the nominative, e.g. **aetās** (age), are feminine, with a few rare exceptions, e.g. **gigās** (giant).
5. All nouns ending **-ūdō** in the nominative, e.g. **magnitūdō** (greatness, size), are feminine.
6. All nouns ending **-e**, **-us**, **-en** in the nominative, e.g. **mare** (sea), **genus** (race), **flūmen** (river), are neuter.

CLEOPATRA

Cleopatra: this striking bust is in the Antiken-saummlung in Berlin.

Cleopatra was born in 69 BC. She was to be the last ruler of Egypt descended from Alexander's general Ptolemy. She was lively, charming, intelligent, civilized and a brilliant linguist. Such a combination of qualities proved irresistible.

When she was 14, her elder sister seized the throne of Egypt from her father. The Roman army regained it for him, the sister was executed and Cleopatra was now joint heir to the kingdom. When she was 17, her father died and she succeeded to his throne together with her brother Ptolemy, who was only ten. They were forced to marry, following their family's custom, but they heartily detested each other. Cleopatra's brother's supporters drove her out of Egypt three years later.

She fled to Syria, gathered an army and returned to Egypt to regain her kingdom. Ptolemy's advisers made a bid for the good will of Julius Caesar, but when Caesar arrived in Alexandria, he quarreled with them and soon found himself besieged in the palace by an angry mob. Meanwhile Cleopatra, who wished to put her case to him in person, had herself smuggled to him rolled up in a carpet. Caesar was captivated by the enchanting queen who crawled from the bundle at his feet. They became lovers, he gave her back the throne of Egypt, and before long she bore him a child, known as Caesarion.

Then in 41 BC Mark Antony called her to meet him at Tarsus (in Cilicia in modern Turkey). It was a fateful occasion, and Shakespeare describes the magic of Cleopatra as she arrived on her elaborate barge:

> The barge she sat in, like a burnish'd throne,
> Burn'd on the water; the poop was beaten gold,
> Purple the sails, and so perfumed, that
> The winds were love-sick with them; the oars were silver,
> Which to the tune of flutes kept stroke, and made
> The water which they beat to follow faster,
> As amorous of their strokes. For her own person,
> It beggar'd all description; she did lie
> In her pavilion—cloth-of-gold of tissue—,
> O'er-picturing that Venus where we see
> The fancy outwork nature.
>   (*Julius Caesar* 2.3.195–205)

The next year (46 BC) Caesar, now back in Rome, summoned Cleopatra and Caesarion to the city and installed them in a villa near the Tiber. He went so far as to have a golden statue of her set up in the temple of Venus. But he did not divorce his wife, and when he was assassinated in 44 BC, Cleopatra found herself without a friend in Rome. She returned to Egypt.

Once again Cleopatra must have felt herself close to real political power. She soon became Antony's mistress and they passed the winter in a round of wild parties and lively pranks. She bore him twins, but it is impossible to say how deep their feelings were for each other at this stage. As we have seen, Antony returned to Italy in 40 BC and married Octavian's sister. Cleopatra did not see him again for nearly four years.

However, in 37 BC Antony abandoned Octavia and renewed his affair with Cleopatra. It remains in doubt how passionately he was in love with her. Their relationship was certainly valuable to him for the important financial and military support it gave him. They conducted a marriage ceremony—which had no validity under Roman law—and soon had a third child.

Antony was responsible for the Eastern provinces of the empire and his absence from Italy enabled Octavian to promulgate hostile propaganda about him. Antony, he declared, was "bewitched by that accursed Egyptian." Quite possibly true. But was it also true, as Dio claims (49.41.1–4), that he gave away Roman provinces to her children by Caesar and himself? Just as damaging was the fiction which circulated in Italy that, if he conquered Octavian, Antony would present Rome to Cleopatra and make Alexandria the center of the empire (Dio 50.4.1, 5.4; cf. Horace, *Odes* 1.37.6–12). From the speech that Dio puts into Octavian's mouth on the eve of the inevitable battle (50.24.6–7), we get some impression of the propaganda: the contemptible and cowardly Egyptians worship reptiles and other beasts, and, worst of all, are slaves to a woman.

Public opinion in Italy rallied behind Octavian and late in 32 BC he declared war on Cleopatra. You have read the rest of the story earlier in Latin. Cleopatra died on August 10 at the age of 39. Octavian killed Caesarion. It was not safe to allow a possible rival to live.

Further Reading

A valuable book on Cleopatra is S. Walker and P. Higgs, *Cleopatra of Egypt* (British Museum, 2003), with especially good chapters by A. Meadows and C. Pelling. There are some excellent essays in Jean Bingen, *Hellenistic Egypt: Monarchy, Society, Economy, Culture* (Edinburgh University Press, 2007), a collection of translated articles by the world's leading Ptolemaic scholar.

Chapter 30
Horātius amīcus fit prīncipis

Grammar: predicative dative; relative with the subjunctive

COMMENTARY

(a) Horātius amīcus fit prīncipis

R̄V̄ **Augustus:** this fine bronze, dating from the emperor's lifetime, was found in Meroe, Sudan. (British Museum, London) *See page 148 in* Oxford Latin Course, College Edition: Readings and Vocabulary.

1.4 *sufficiēbam scrībendīs epistolīs*: I was sufficient for writing letters, i.e. I was able to write letters on my own.

(b) mors Vergilī

ll.3–4 *Augustō...ab Oriente redeuntī*: Augustus was in the East from 22 to 19 BC settling the eastern frontiers of the empire (during his stay there he made a treaty with the Parthians and recovered the standards lost at Carrhae in the defeat suffered by Crassus in 53 BC).

R̄V̄ **The tomb of Virgil:** the so-called tomb of Virgil in Naples is a *columbārium* (literally a dovecote, in which the compartments could be used for storing the ashes of the dead). It was restored in 1927. *See page 149 in* Oxford Latin Course, College Edition: Readings and Vocabulary.

l.6 *cūrāuit eum Neapolī sepeliendum*: saw that he was buried at Naples. Virgil had lived at Naples for the last years of his life. On his tomb was an inscription attributed to Virgil himself:

Mantua mē genuit, Calabrī rapuēre, tenet nunc
    Parthenopē; cecinī pascua, rūra, ducēs.

(Mantua gave me birth; Calabria carried me off; Parthenope [=Naples] is now my home. I sang of shepherds [the *Eclogues*], the country [the *Georgics*], and leaders [the *Aeneid*].)

The *Aeneid* was unfinished when he died, and, according to Aelius Donatus, before setting off to Greece, he asked his literary executors, Varius and Tucca, to burn it if he died. Augustus countermanded this request and ordered them to publish it in its unfinished state.

l.7 *animae dīmidium meae*: see *Odes* 1.3.5–8; Horace prays for Virgil's safe return when he is embarking on a voyage to Greece:

nāuis quae tibi creditum
    dēbēs Vergilium, fīnibus Atticīs
reddās incolumem precor
    et seruēs animae dīmidium meae.

("Ship, which owes [me] Virgil, entrusted to you, bring him safe to the shores of Attica, I pray, and save the half of my soul.")

(c) Horātius rūsticus

R|V **Bringing in the vintage:** this vault mosaic from Santa Costanza in Rome dates from the fourth century AD and shows *putti* (young cupids) gathering and treading the vintage. *See page 151 in* Oxford Latin Course, College Edition: Readings and Vocabulary.

R|V **mūrēs Rōmānī:** these small bronzes of mice are from the British Museum. *See page 152 in* Oxford Latin Course, College Edition: Readings and Vocabulary.

l.14 *mūrī rūsticō persuādētur*: a country mouse is persuaded; intransitive verbs are used impersonally in the passive.

The fable, in which animals are given human characteristics, had a long history, going back to Archilochus (at his prime 650 BC) and best known from the collection attributed to Aesop (6th century BC?).

GRAMMAR

The Predicative Dative (Dative of Purpose)

uīlicus Horātiō magnō auxiliō erat.

His farm manager was a great help to Horace.

fūmus strepitusque urbis Horātiō odiō erant.

The smoke and racket of the city were hateful to Horace.

In certain phrases Latin uses a noun in the dative after the verb **esse** instead of a complement in the nominative; thus the first example above means literally: "The farm manager was *for a great help* to Horace." The second means literally: "The smoke and racket of the city were *for a hatred* to Horace."

The commonest of such phrases are:

auxiliō esse	to be a help to
cordī esse	to be dear to (**cor, cordis**, n. heart)
cūrae esse	to be a care to, a cause of anxiety to
exemplō esse	to be an example of
exitiō esse	to be a cause of destruction to
odiō esse	to be hateful to
salūtī esse	to be a cause of safety to
ūsuī esse	to be useful to

EXERCISE 30.1

Translate

1. segetēs Horātiō magnae cūrae erant.
2. grandinēs (*hailstones*) nōnnumquam ūuīs exitiō fuērunt.
3. fundus Horātiō semper cordī erat.
4. Līuia, Augustī uxor, exemplō erat mātrōnīs Rōmānīs.
5. fēminae dissolūtae (*licentious*) eī odiō erant.
6. Līuia Augustō magnō auxiliō fuit.
7. "nōnne uīs hunc canem emere? magnō ūsuī tibi erit."
8. "canem iam habeō quī mihi cordī est ouēsque bene custōdit."
9. "sed tuus canis īnfirmus est; sine dubiō hic canis auxiliō tibi erit."
10. "ille canis saeuus esse mihi uidētur; timeō nē exitiō ouibus sit."

GRAMMAR

The Relative with the Subjunctive

Horātius seruōs ēmīsit <u>quī</u> segetēs <u>meterent</u>, puerōs dēsignāuit <u>quī</u> ouēs <u>custōdīrent</u>.
Horace sent out slaves <u>to reap</u> the corn, he appointed boys <u>to guard</u> the sheep.

The relative with the subjunctive can be used to express purpose; in the example above, **quī...meterent** means literally "who might reap"; **quī...custōdīrent** means "who might guard."

> **prīmā lūce profectī sumus quō celerius domum aduenīrēmus.**
> We set out at first light to reach (so that we might reach) home more quickly.

quō celerius literally means "by which the more quickly"; purpose clauses containing a comparative are usually introduced by **quō** not **ut**.

EXERCISE 30.2

Translate

1. Augustus quīnque legiōnēs in Oriente relīquit quae fīnēs prōuinciārum custōdīrent.
2. quattuor classēs īnstrūxit quae praedōnibus (*pirates*) exitiō essent mercātōribusque salūtī.
3. in urbe Rōmā uigiliās (*watches*) īnstituit quae cīuēs ā latrōnibus (*robbers*) incendiīsque tuērentur.
4. uiās pūblicās per Italiam custōdīuit quō tūtius uiātōrēs iter facerent.
5. Horātius nūntium ad Maecēnātem mīsit, quī eī dīceret sē mox Rōmam reditūrum esse.

EXERCISE 30.3

Translate into Latin

1. This dog was a great help to the shepherd.
2. For he was very useful in defending the sheep.
3. And so he was dear to the heart of the shepherd.
4. When he was wounded by a wolf, the shepherd was very concerned for him (= he was a great care to the shepherd).
5. The shepherd's wife looked after (use **foueō**) the dog with the greatest care but did no good (= achieved nothing).
6. The shepherd summoned the doctor to cure him (= the dog) but he could not save him.

7. The shepherd's wife said he must buy another dog.
8. But the new dog was no use to the shepherd in guarding sheep.
9. The shepherd asked his master to give him a good dog to guard sheep.
10. The master sent a messenger to say that he would soon give him an excellent dog.

EXERCISE 30.4

Translate into Latin

Dear Maecenas,

When I left Rome, I promised to return in five days. But I am still here on my farm. I ask you to forgive me. I cannot bear the heat (**calor, calōris,** m.) of summer in the city; I must stay in the hills until autumn comes. If I returned to Rome now, I would without doubt be ill, and you would be sad if you heard I had died of fever (**febris, febris**, f.).

Besides, I am very busy. I am writing a poem about the art of poetry (**ars poētica**), which is very long and difficult. When summer is over (**praetereō**), I shall go down to Naples and spend the winter there. But as soon as spring returns and I see the first swallow (**hirundō, hirundinis**, f.), I shall hurry to Rome and hope to see you there.

Your loving friend, Quintus.

(This passage is based on Horace, *Epistles* 1.7.1–13.)

P.S. *Memorābilia*: Famous Lines from Virgil

1. omnia uincit Amor: et nōs cēdāmus Amōrī.
   (*Eclogues* 10.69)
2. fēlīx quī potuit rērum cognōscere causās.
   (*Georgics* 2.490)
   (of Lucretius, poet, philosopher and scientist)
3. fortūnātus et ille deōs quī nōuit agrestēs.
   (*Georgics* 2.493)
   deōs agrestēs   the gods of the country
4. tantae mōlis erat Rōmānam condere gentem.
   (*Aeneid* 1.33)
   tantae mōlis erat   so great a task it was

5.   equō nē crēdite, Teucrī.

quidquid id est, timeō Danaōs et dōna ferentēs.

(*Aeneid* 2.48–9)

et   even

6.   reuocāte animōs maestumque timōrem

mittite; forsan et haec ōlim meminisse iuuābit.

(*Aeneid* 1.202–3)

forsan ... iuuābit   perhaps it will be a pleasure

7. uīxī et quem dederat cursum Fortūna perēgī.

(Dido speaks, just before her suicide)

(*Aeneid* 4.653)

8. Trōs Anchīsiadēs, facilis dēscēnsus Auernō:

noctēs atque diēs patet ātrī iānua Dītis;

sed reuocāre gradūs superāsque ēuadere ad aurās,

hoc opus, hic labor est.

(The Sibyl warns Aeneas of the dangers of attempting to go down to the underworld (*Auernus*))

(*Aeneid* 6.126–9)

patet   is open

ātrī ... Dītis   of black Death

9. stābant ōrantes prīmī trānsmittere cursum

tendēbantque manūs rīpae ulteriōris amōre.

(Aeneas sees the souls of the dead waiting to cross the river Styx into the underworld)

(*Aeneid* 6.313–14)

trānsmittere   to cross

SOME GLIMPSES OF AUGUSTUS

Some hundred years after the death of Augustus, his biography was written by Suetonius, who was for some time the secretary to the emperor Hadrian and thus had the enormous advantage of access to the imperial archives. The following passages are excerpts from this biography.

As Marcus Cicero escorted Gaius Caesar to the Capitol, he happened to tell his friends a dream he had had the night before. He had dreamed that a boy of noble features had been let down from the sky by a golden chain, had stood at the doors of the temple and been given a whip by Jupiter.

Then he suddenly caught sight of Augustus who had been unknown to most people before his uncle Caesar had summoned him to the ceremony. "That," he said, "is the very youth whose image appeared to me in my dream."

(Life of Augustus 94.9)

When he was 16, after receiving his *toga uirilis,* he was awarded military prizes at Caesar's African triumph although he had been too young to take part in the war. Not much later, when his uncle went to Spain to fight against Pompey's sons, though he had only just recovered from a serious illness, he followed him with a tiny escort along roads held by the enemy, even suffering shipwreck, and won great favor with Caesar who quickly formed a high opinion of his character over and above the keen commitment with which he had made the journey.

(8.1)

When he joined with Antony and Lepidus in the Second Triumvirate, he finished the Philippi war, weakened with illness though he was, in two battles. In the first of these he was driven out of his camp and barely managed to escape to Antony's wing. He showed no moderation after the victory but sent Brutus' head to Rome to be thrown before the statue of Caesar and used violent language to the most distinguished captives, not even sparing them insulting taunts. For instance, when one of them asked humbly for burial, he is said to have replied, "That will be up to the carrion birds!" When two others, a father and a son, begged for their lives, he is said to have ordered them to cast lots to decide which of them should be spared, and in fact to have seen both of them die since the father was killed because he had offered his own life for his son, and the latter then committed suicide.

(13.1–2)

There are many great illustrations of his mercy and moderation. It would be tedious if I were to give the full list of political enemies whom he not only pardoned but even allowed to hold high office.

(51.1)

If any cohorts broke in battle, he ordered every tenth man to be killed and fed the rest on barley instead of wheat.

(24.2)

Since the city was not adorned as befitted the grandeur of its empire and was liable to flooding and fires, he so improved it that he could justifiably boast that he had found it brick and left it marble.

(28.3)

For more than 40 years he stayed in the same bedroom in his house on the Palatine hill both in winter and in summer: Although he found that the city was bad for his health in the winter, he continued to spend that season there. If ever he planned to do something on his own or without interruption, he had a private room at the top of his house which he called "Syracuse"— Archimedes of Syracuse [the great scientist] had had a similar study—or his "little workshop." He used to hide away here or in the house of one of his freedmen in the suburbs. However, if he fell ill, he would sleep at Maecenas' house.

(72.1–2)

One can tell how simple his furniture and household goods were from the couches and tables which still exist. Most of these are scarcely grand enough for a private citizen. They say that he always slept on a low bed with a plain covering.

(73)

He was a very light eater and generally ate plain food. He was particularly fond of coarse bread, tiny fishes, fresh hand-pressed cheese and green figs of the second crop. He would eat even before dinner, whenever and wherever he felt hungry. Here are some quotations from his own letters: "I ate some bread and dates in my carriage" and "While I was on my way back from King Numa's Palace in my litter, I ate an ounce of bread with a few hard-skinned grapes."

(76.1–2)

He was also by nature a very abstemious drinker. The historian Cornelius writes that he never drank more than three units over dinner at Mutina. In later life, when he indulged himself more generously, he would not exceed a pint, or if he did, he would vomit it up.

(77)

He always wrote down his more important statements to individuals, even to his wife Livia, and read them out from a notebook. He was afraid that he would say either too much or too little if he spoke off the cuff.

(84.2)

On the last day of his life, he repeatedly asked whether talk of his illness was causing any public disturbance. Then he called for a mirror and ordered his hair to be combed and his sagging jaws to be set straight. Next he summoned his friends and asked them if they thought that he had played his part in the comedy of life with a good enough grace. And he added the tag:

> If I have pleased you kindly signify
> Appreciation with a warm goodbye.

(99.1)

Chapter 31
Indomita mors

COMMENTARY

ll.5–6 *uiuōrum meminerat*: he remembered the living; *meminī* is a defective verb, i.e. it only has perfect stem tenses. Like *coepī* and *ōdī*, it has a present meaning despite its perfect form. If a past meaning is required, the pluperfect form is used (as here). It usually takes the genitive, as does *oblīuīscor*.

l.6 Pompeius, whom we last met during the Philippi campaign, had returned safely to Italy. Horace celebrated his homecoming in *Odes* 2.7.

R V **The three Graces:** a detail from the famous *Primavera* (Spring) by Sandro Botticelli (1444–1510). (Uffizi Gallery, Florence) *See page 156 in* Oxford Latin Course, College Edition: Readings and Vocabulary.

Diffugēre niuēs: *Odes* 4.7

The poet and classical scholar A. E. Housman surprised his class with a rare outburst of emotion after he had dissected this Ode "with the usual display of brilliance, wit, and sarcasm. Then for the first time in two years he looked up at us, and in quite a different voice said: 'I should like to spend the last few minutes considering this Ode simply as poetry.' …He read the Ode aloud with deep emotion first in Latin and then in an English translation of his own. 'That,' he said hurriedly, almost like a man betraying a secret, 'I regard as the most beautiful poem in ancient literature'" (from a letter to *The Times* from Dora Pym, a former student of Housman, quoted by Grant Richards, *Housman 1897–1936*, p. 289).

We append his translation (the only Ode of Horace he translated):

The snows are fled away, leaves on the shaws
    And grasses in the mead renew their birth,
The river to the river-bed withdraws,
    And altered is the fashion of the earth.

The Nymphs and Graces three put off their fear
    And unapparelled in the woodland play.
The swift hour and the brief prime of the year
    Say to the soul, Thou wast not born for aye.

Thaw follows frost; hard on the heel of spring
    Treads summer, sure to die, for hard on hers
Comes autumn, with his apples scattering;
    Then back to wintertide, where nothing stirs.

But, oh, whate'er the sky-led seasons mar,
    Moon upon moon rebuilds it with her beams:
Come we where Tullus and where Ancus are,
    And good Aeneas, we are dust and dreams.

Torquatus, if the gods in heaven shall add
    The morrow to the day, what tongue has told?
Feast then thy heart, for what thy heart has had
    The fingers of no heir shall ever hold.

When thou descendest once the shades among,
    The stern assize and equal judgement o'er,
Not thy lineage nor thy golden tongue,
    No, nor thy righteousness, shall friend thee more.

Night holds Hippolytus the pure of stain,
    Diana steads him nothing, he must stay;
And Theseus leaves Perithous in the chain
    The love of comrades cannot take away.

RV **puluis et umbra sumus:** containing the ashes of a cremated body, this glass funeral urn dates from the first or second century AD. (Old Speech Room Gallery, Harrow School, UK) *See page 157 in* Oxford Latin Course, College Edition: Readings and Vocabulary.

1.19 (RV p. 158) *mortuus est Maecēnās.* Maecenas died a few months before Horace, who himself died on November 22, 8 BC.

EXERCISE 31.1

Translate into Latin

Horace said that on his farm he could enjoy leisure for composing poems. He liked to read the books of the ancients and lie idle in the shade. But in fact whenever he returned to his farm, he always had to work hard. He called his farm manager and arranged for the fields to be plowed; he sent out boys to guard the sheep; he himself with his own hands used to move stones from the fields. The grapes had to be picked and the wine had to be made. When evening came, he often used to ask his neighbors to dinner; after they had dined modestly, they sat in the garden drinking wine and talking about philosophy. You could scarcely say that Quintus was an idle (**ignāuus, -a, -um**) man, but he was content with his life and was always sad when he had to return to Rome.

P.S. *Memorābilia*: Famous Lines from Horace

1. nātūram expellās furcā, tamen usque recurret.
   (*Epistles* 1.10.24)
   furcā   with a pitchfork
   usque   always
2. caelum nōn animum mūtant quī trāns māre currunt.
   (*Epistles* 1.11.27)
3.   dum loquimur, fūgerit inuida
   aetās: carpe diem, quam minimum crēdula posterō.
   (*Odes* 1.11.7)
   inuida aetās   jealous time
   quam minimum crēdula posterō   trusting as little as possible in tomorrow
4. multīs ille bonīs flēbilis occidit.
   (*Odes* 1.24.9)
5. aequam mementō rēbus in arduīs
   seruāre mentem.
   (*Odes* 2.3.1)
   rēbus in arduīs   in difficult things/in a crisis
6. omnēs eōdem cōgimur
   (*Odes* 2.3.25)
   eōdem   the same way, i.e. to death

DEATH

There was a high rate of infant mortality in the Roman world and those who survived childhood would die on average between the ages of 40 and 50. Scholars suggest that the closest modern equivalent is the life table of a developing country in the mid to late twentieth century. Death was a threat that was constantly present.

At, or just before, the moment of death the body may have been laid on the bare earth, perhaps to symbolize that at death humanity returned to the earth. A close relative of the dead, preferably a mother or spouse, would catch their final breath with a kiss, then close their eyes and call out their name loudly, either to recall the soul or to reawaken its powers. Next came the preparation of the body. It was washed with warm water, dressed in its best clothes and laid out on public display in the *atrium*. A small coin was placed under its tongue to pay Charon, the ferryman who would carry it across the river of the dead to a kind of rest in the shadowy afterlife in the underworld. The women of the house would mourn loudly. They might pour ashes over their hair, pull at it and even cut it, beat their breasts and scratch their cheeks. And a branch of pine or cypress was put in front of the house to warn passersby that a corpse lay inside. If they could be afforded, undertakers (*libitīnāriī*) would oversee the arrangements. Theirs was a profitable profession but they were held in such contempt that their civil rights were reduced.

This funeral scene from a sarcophagus of the first century BC or AD shows musicians, pall-bearers and mourners. Artistic license has allowed the sculptor of the relief to raise the pall which would have covered the dead man, who is seen reclining rather than lying on his back as a dead person would. (Museo Aquilano, Abruzzi)

Roman funerals varied greatly according to the age and status of the deceased. Our evidence tends to refer to the death of wealthy people who had lived well into adult life and fulfilled their social obligations. In such cases the ritual would be something like the following. Pipers would lead the funeral procession which moved to the sound of flutes and brass instruments. Torch-bearers may have accompanied it; possibly all funerals had originally taken place at night but it may equally well be the case that the torches were intended to light the way to the next world or to ward off evil spirits. Hired female mourners would howl noisily, together with the dead person's family. There was an element of mockery too. Dancers and clowns capered through the processions, singing ballads in which they jeered at the dead. When the emperor Vespasian died, the chief clown dressed up to look like him and joked about his famous stinginess (Suetonius, *Vespasian* 19).

However, the overall impression of an important man's funeral was profoundly serious, as Polybius, a Greek who lived in the second century BC, conveys in this description:

> Whenever one of their famous men dies, he is carried at his funeral to the so-called *rōstra* in the forum. Sometimes he is displayed in an upright posture, more rarely he reclines. When all the people are standing around, a grown-up son, if one is still alive and happens to be present, or, if not, some other relative, goes up onto the *rōstra* and speaks about the virtues of the dead man and the successful achievements of his life. As a result of this the crowd recalls these deeds to their minds and recreates them before their eyes, and this applies not only to those who shared in those achievements but to everyone. They are moved to such sympathy that the loss seems not to belong to the mourners alone but to the whole people.
>
> Afterwards they bury the corpse and perform the usual customs and then they place the image of the dead man in the most conspicuous place in the house, enclosing it in a wooden shrine. The image is a mask which looks exactly like the dead man in features and complexion. At public sacrifices they display these images and decorate them with the utmost care, and when any distinguished member of the family dies, they bring them to the funeral, putting them on those who seem to be most like the originals in stature and appearance. These wear togas with a purple border if the deceased was a consul or praetor, an entirely purple one if he was a censor, and one embroidered with gold if he had celebrated a triumph or achieved something similar. They ride in chariots preceded by the *fascēs,* the axes and the other insignia appropriate to the original's status in his life and when they reach the *rōstra* they all sit down in rank on chairs of ivory. You could not easily find a finer sight for a young man who is eager for fame or virtue. For who could fail to be inspired by the sight of the images of men famous for their virtue all sitting together as if alive and breathing? What spectacle could be finer than this?
>
> (Polybius, 6.53–4)

The rich were likely to be cremated on a pyre. Offerings of clothes, ornaments, weapons and even food were thown onto the flames. When the pyre had burnt down, the ashes were cooled with wine and a relative or friend would collect the bones and put them in an urn. The urn was then placed in one of the fine tombs which lined the streets leading into the city. The urns containing the ashes of less wealthy citizens were placed in a *columbārium,* literally a pigeon nesting-box but generally used of a niche in a tomb. The corpses of the poorest citizens or of slaves would either be buried in cheap coffins in public cemeteries or thrown unceremoniously into communal pits.

This statue of a Roman nobleman carrying the busts of his ancestors is from the first century BC. (Capitoline Museum, Rome)

Further Reading

V. M. Hope, *Roman Death: The Dying and the Dead in Ancient Rome* (Continuum, 2009), Chapters 2 & 3; M. Harlow and R. Laurence, *Growing Up and Growing Old in Ancient Rome* (Routledge, 2002), Chapter 10; and H. I. Flower, *Ancestor Masks and Aristocratic Culture in Ancient Rome* (Oxford, 1996), Chapter 4.

COMPREHENSION EXERCISE

Read the following and then answer the questions below:
The Roman legions' successes in Germany seem to be a cause for rejoicing, but Quintilius Varus' false sense of security leads to disaster.

breue fuit id gaudium: Germānī uictī magis quam
domitī erant, mōrēsque nostrōs magis quam arma
suspiciēbant. postquam Drūsus mortuus est,
Quīntilius Vārus imperātor factus est, cuius su-
perbiam barbarī ōdisse coepērunt. duce Arminiō
arma corripiunt; sed tanta erat Vārō pācis fīdūcia
ut, quamquam dē coniūrātiōne ā prīncipe quōdam
Germānōrum monitus erat, nōn commouērētur.
itaque imprōuidum eum et nihil timentem undique aggrediuntur. castra rapiunt, trēs legiōnēs
opprimunt. summā ferōcitāte pugnātum est.

nihil illā caede quae per palūdēs perque
siluās facta est fuit cruentius, nihil crūdēlitāte
barbarōrum saeuius, praecipuē in lēgātōs. aliīs
oculōs, aliīs manūs amputābant: ūnīus excīsa est
lingua, quam in manū tenēns barbarus quīdam,
"tandem," inquit, "uīpera, sībilāre dēsine!"
ipsīus quoque Vārī corpus, quod mīlitēs in terrā
cēlāuerant, effossum est. signa nostra barbarī
adhūc tenent iamque sunt nōbīs recipienda. hāc
clāde factum est ut imperium Rōmānōrum in rīpā
Rhēnī flūminis stāret.

id gaudium i.e. the rejoicing over the apparent conquest of the Germans.

5 **domitī erant** had been tamed
suspiciēbant respected
fīdūcia (+ gen) confidence in

10 **imprōvidum** off his guard
opprimunt overwhelm
caede massacre
palūdēs marshes

15 **cruentius** more bloody
praecipuē especially
excīsa est was cut out
lingua tongue
sībilāre to hiss

20 **effossum est** was dug up
signa standards

Florus: 4.12 (adapted)

1. Translate the first paragraph.
2. What do we find out about the terrain where the massacre took place?
3. Who especially suffered from the brutality of the barbarians?
4. Give three examples of the barbarians' brutality.
5. Who is the *uīpera* (l. 17)? What case is the word in? What does the barbarian mean by his exclamation? And how does the sound of this exclamation reflect its meaning?
6. What two things are we told happened to Varus after his death?

7. What happened to the Roman standards and what now remains to be done with them?
8. What are we told in the last sentence was the consequence of the disaster?
9. *stāret* (l. 22): what subjunctive of what verb is this? What is the first person singular of the perfect indicative active of this verb?
10. Explain the following case usages: *duce Arminiō* (l. 5); *aliīs oculōs, aliīs manūs* (ll. 14–15).
11. Explain the following constructions: *pugnātum est* (l. 11); *signa…sunt nōbīs recipienda* (ll. 19–20)

Appendix 1
Continuous Indirect Speech

Indirect statements are expressed by the accusative and infinitive; if there is more than one indirect statement, the subject of the second and subsequent infinitives is often omitted, if it is the same as that of the first:

Horātius ad fundum suum Rōmā discessūrus Maecēnātī <u>dīxit sē</u> quīnque diēbus tantum <u>mānsūrum esse</u>; deinde Rōmam <u>regressum eum</u> <u>reuīsūrum</u> <u>esse</u>.

When Horace was about to leave Rome for his farm, <u>he said</u> to Maecenas that <u>he would stay</u> for only five days; then <u>he would return</u> to Rome and <u>revisit</u> him.

The reflexives **sē** and **suus** always refer to the subject of the introductory verb:

Horātius ad Maecēnātem scrīpsit sē cōnstituisse rūrī manēre; <u>ueniam sibi daret</u>; reditūrum esse cum uēr uēnisset. sī anteā in urbem redīret, sine dubiō aegrōtātūrum esse.

Horace wrote to Maecenas that he had decided to stay in the country; <u>he (Maecenas) must forgive him</u>; he would return when spring came. If he returned to the city before that, he would undoubtedly be ill.

Indirect commands (or requests) are in the subjunctive *without ut*; if negative, they are introduced by **nē.**

All subordinate clauses are in the subjunctive, following the sequence of tenses, i.e. present or perfect subjunctive if the introductory verb is present, future or perfect with have; imperfect or pluperfect subjunctive if the introductory verb is past.

Indirect questions are introduced by an interrogative word and have verbs in the subjunctive, following the sequence of tenses.

Maecēnās ad Horātium rescrīpsit sē eum ualdē dēsīderāre. nē diūtius rūrī morārētur. quandō Rōmam reditūrus esset?

Maecenas wrote back to Horace that he missed him a lot. He must not (let him not) delay any longer in the country. When would he come back to Rome?

Appendix 2

Uses of the Indicative and the Subjunctive

The *indicative* is used in statements and questions in main clauses.

In subordinate clauses, the verb is in the indicative in:
1. definite relative clauses
2. causal clauses when the cause is stated as a fact*
3. temporal clauses*
4. open and future more vivid conditional clauses
5. concessive (although) clauses introduced by **quamquam** (= although)

*for the uses of **cum** with subjunctive, see below

The *subjunctive* is used in all types of clause which are not expressing facts:

1. in main clauses
   (a) jussive subjunctive (negative **nē**):

domum redeāmus.	Let us return home.
nē domum redeat.	Let him not return home.
nē hoc fēcerīs/ nē hoc faciās	Do not do this.

   (b) deliberative subjunctive:

   utrum domum redeāmus an hīc maneāmus?
   Are we to return home or stay here?

   (c) wishes (negative **nē**):

deī nōs seruent.	May the gods preserve us.
utinam nē domī mānsissem.	I wish I had not stayed at home.

   (d) potential subjunctive (negative **nōn**), e.g. **uelim** (I should like to), **nōlim** (I shouldn't like to), **mālim** (I should prefer to), **ausim** (I should dare to):

nōn ausim hoc facere.	I should not dare to do this.

(e) in contrary to fact and future-less-vivid conditional clauses:

sī domī mānsissēs, incolumis fuissēs.
If you had stayed at home, you would have been safe.

sī domī iam essēs, incolumis essēs.
If you were now at home, you would be safe.

sī domī maneās, in perīculum nōn cadās.
If you were to stay at home, you would not fall into danger.

2. in subordinate clauses
  (a) clauses of purpose, introduced by **ut/nē**
  (b) indirect commands, introduced by **ut/nē**
  (c) indirect questions
  (d) clauses of fearing, introduced by **nē/nē nōn** or **ut**
  (e) (i) causal clauses introduced by **cum** = since
      (ii) causal clauses where the cause is not stated as a fact:

  condemnātus est quod senem occīdisset.
  He was condemned for killing the old man/on the grounds that he had killed the old man.

  (f) (i) temporal clauses introduced by **cum** (= when) in past time (see Chapter 25)
      (ii) temporal clauses expressing purpose as well as time:

  in forō manēbat dum pater redīret.
  He was waiting in the forum for his father to return.
  (Compare: **in forō manēbat dum pater rediit.** He waited in the forum until his father returned.)
  in Italiam redī antequam ā mīlitibus capiāris.
  Return to Italy before you are caught by the soldiers.
  (Here the **antequam** clause expresses both time and purpose, which we cannot do in English.)
  (g) concessive (although) clauses introduced by **cum** (= although) and **quamuīs** (= however much):

  quamuīs dīues esset, nihil pauperibus dābat.
  Although he was rich, he gave nothing to the poor.

(h) relative clauses expressing purpose or consequence:

nūntium mīsit quī patrī omnia dīceret.
He sent a messenger to tell his father everything.
seruus dignus est quī praemium accipiat.
The slave is worthy to receive a reward.

quō is used instead of **ut** in purpose clauses which contain a comparative:

ad forum cucurrī quō celerius eō aduenīrem.
I ran to the forum in order to get there faster.

(i) relative clauses expressing a type or kind (generic):

ea est quae pauperēs semper cūret.
She is the sort of woman who is always looking after the poor.
sunt quī Graecōs meliōrēs quam Rōmānōs putent.
There are people who consider Greeks better than Romans.

(j) all subordinate clauses in indirect speech (see Appendix 1 above)

In all types of clause listed above, except for those introduced by **cum**, the subjunctive is used because they are not expressing facts (e.g. a purpose is an idea in someone's head; indirect speech is not an expression of fact but a report by someone who may be wrong or lying).

(k) clauses of result or consequence introduced by **ut/ut nōn** have their verbs in the subjunctive although they often express facts:

tam fessus erat ut diū dormīret.
He was so tired that he slept a long time.

Appendix 3
Quīn and *quōminus*

QUĪN

I do not doubt that she is a respectable woman.
Nothing will prevent me from coming to your birthday party.

The English verbs "doubt," "deny," "hinder" and "prevent" are followed by a number of different expressions. Latin often uses **quīn** followed by the subjunctive (the tense depending on the sequence of tenses, see p. 170) after a negative main verb with one of these meanings (e.g. **nōn dubitō** (1) "I do not doubt," **nōn negō** (1) "I do not deny," **nōn impediō** (4) "I do not hinder, prevent"). The Latin for the sentences above could be:

> **nōn dubitō quīn pudīca sit**.
> **nihil mē impediet quīn nātālī tuō adsim**.

The word **quīn** causes English speakers problems because it does not translate into idiomatic English. Literally, it means "by which not." The old-fashioned "but that" may be useful as a first stage in translation:

> I do not doubt <u>but that</u> she is a respectable woman.

> **nōn dubitāuit quīn Germānī oppugnātūrī essent**.
> He did not doubt that the Germans were going to attack.
> **nōn negāuit quīn ipse scelus admīsisset**.
> He did not deny that he himself had committed the crime.
> **nōn tē impediam quīn proficīscāris**.
> I shall not prevent you from setting out.

As we have seen, the main verb before **quīn** will be negative. Sometimes the words **uix** or **aegrē** (scarcely) are found instead of a plain negative (they are known as "virtual negatives"). A question expecting the answer "no" (**num** . . .?) or implying the answer "no" (who doubts that . . .? *can imply* no one doubts that . . .) may also come before **quīn**.

> **uix quisquam dubitāre potest quīn stultus sīs**.
> Scarcely anyone can doubt that you are a fool.

num quisquam dubitāre potuit quīn sapiēns essēs?
Surely no one could have doubted that you were wise.

Note the following common expressions:

- **haud (nōn) dubium est quīn . . .**
  there is no doubt that . . .
- **haud dubitārī potest quīn . . .**
  it cannot be doubted that . . .
- **haud multum (or minimum) āfuit quīn. . .**
  almost (*literally*, it was not much (*or* very little) distant but that . . .)

    haud multum āfuit quīn interficerer. (impersonal)
    I was almost killed.

or

    haud multum āfuī quīn interficerer.
    Literally, I was not much distant . . . (personal).
- **nōn possum facere quīn. . .**
  I cannot help . . .
- **nōn potest fierī quīn. . .**
  it is impossible that . . . not
- **nēmō est quīn. . .**
  there is nobody who . . . not

    nēmō est quīn hoc sciat.
    Everybody knows this.

QUŌMINUS

quōminus is used with much the same meaning as **quīn** ("but that" in old-fashioned English) after verbs of *hindering* and *preventing* whether negatived or not. As with **quīn**, the main problem here for English-speakers is that **quōminus**, which literally means "by which the less," does not translate into idiomatic English.

    (nōn) mē impedīuit quōminus in urbem inīrem.
    He prevented (didn't prevent) me from going into the city.

Note the following common idioms:

- **per mē stat quōminus . . .**
  it is due to me that . . . not

per mē stetit quōminus rēs pūblica ēuerterētur.
It was due to me that the republic was not overthrown.

- **per mē stetit <u>ut</u>** . . .

it was due to me that . . .

per mē stetit ut rēs pūblica cōnseruārētur.

It was due to me that the republic was saved.

Note that **prohibeō** (2) (I prevent) can be followed simply by the infinitive.

prohibuī eum Rōmā ēgredī.

I prevented him from leaving Rome.

It can also be followed by **nē** or **quōminus** or, when negative, **quīn**, all with the subjunctive.

PRACTICE SENTENCES

Translate into English or Latin as appropriate:

1. **nōn dubitārī dēbet quīn fuerint ante Homērum poētae.** (Cicero, *Brutus*, 71)
2. **nōn dēterret sapientem mors quōminus in omne tempus reī pūblicae cōnsulat.** (Cicero, *Tusculan Disputations*, 1.91)
3. **facere nōn possum quīn litterās cotīdiē ad tē mittam.** (Cicero, *ad Atticum*, 12.27.2)
4. **nihil abest quīn sim miserrimus.** (Cicero, *ad Atticum*, 11.15.3)
5. **impedīuit eam coniūnx quōminus amātōrem uīseret.**
6. I almost died laughing (use **quīn**—for "laughing" use the ablative of the gerund).
7. Who can prevent me from leaving Rome?
8. I could not help admiring your poems.
9. It is due to me that you are so rich.
10. Everyone knows that Homer was the greatest of poets (use **quīn**).

Glossary of Grammatical Terms

ablative	a case with the basic meanings of "by," "with," "from," "at," "in" or "on"; some prepositions take the ablative.
accusative	the usual case of a direct object; many prepositions take the accusative.
active	the form of a verb used when the subject of the sentence is the doer of the action: we saw = uīdimus.
adjective	a word describing a noun, with which it agrees in gender, number and case: a *happy* girl = puella *laeta*.
adverb	a word that describes or changes the meaning of a verb, an adjective or another adverb: he walks *slowly* = *lentē* ambulat.
agree	are in the same case and number as
antecedent	the noun or pronoun to which a relative pronoun refers back.
cardinals	see numerals.
case	the form of a noun, pronoun, adjective, or article that shows the part it plays in a sentence; there are six cases: nominative, genitive, dative, accusative, ablative and vocative.
clause	a self-contained section of a sentence in which there are at least a subject and a verb.
common	either masculine or feminine according to meaning.
comparative	the form of an adjective or adverb that makes it mean *more*, *rather*, or *too*: more old (older), rather old, too old = *senior*.
complement	a word or phrase which describes the subject of the verb; it is used with verbs such as "I am" and "I become" which cannot take an object: my sister is *intelligent* = soror mea *sapiēns* est.

compound verb	a verb formed by adding a prefix to a simple verb: I propose = *prōpōnō*.
concessive clause	a clause usually beginning with the word "although" or "though."
conditional clause	a clause usually beginning with the words "if," "if not" or "unless."
conjugate	give the different forms of the verb, e.g. amā*s* = *you* love; āmā*uērunt* = *they* loved.
conjugation	there are four main patterns according to which most Latin verbs change their endings; we call these "conjugations."
conjunction	a word used to join clauses, phrases or words together: pāx *et* imperium = peace *and* empire.
consonant	a letter representing a sound that can only be used together with a vowel, such as b, c, d: see vowel.
dative	the case of an indirect object, among its many meanings are "to" and "for."
declension	there are five main patterns according to which most Latin nouns change their endings; we call these "declensions."
decline	go through the different cases of a noun, adjective or pronoun, in order.
definite article	in English, "the." There is no definite article in Latin, though the pronoun *is*, *ea*, *id* often serves the same purpose.
deliberative	showing that a process of decision is going on: What am I to do?
deponent verb	a verb which is passive in form but active in meaning.
direct object	the noun or pronoun directly affected by the verb: he killed *the king* = *rēgem* interfēcit.
direct speech	the words actually used by a speaker.
distributives	see numerals.
ending	letters added to the stem of verbs, nouns, and adjectives, according to tense, case, etc.
feminine	one of the three genders: fēmina = a woman and arbor = a tree.
finite verb	a verb in a tense, as opposed to infinitives and participles.
future perfect tense	the tense of a verb that refers to something in the future at a stage after it has happened: I *shall have* done this: hoc *fēcerō*.

future tense	the tense of a verb that refers to something that will happen in the future.
gender	the class in which a noun or pronoun is placed in a grammatical grouping; in both English and Latin, these classes are masculine, feminine, neuter and common (i.e. either masculine or feminine according to meaning).
genitive	the case that shows possession; among its many meanings the dominant one is "of."
gerund	a verbal noun: the art of *ruling* = ars *regendī*.
gerundive	a verbal adjective, frequently expressing the idea of obligation: this *must-be-done* = hoc *faciendum* est.
imperative	the part of the verb that expresses a command: hurry up! = festīnā!
imperfect tense	the tense which expresses continuous or repeated or incomplete action in the past: I *was* walking = ambulā*bam*.
impersonal verb	a verb introduced in English by the word "it," and in Latin found only in the 3rd person singular: it rains = pluit.
indeclinable	refers to a noun or adjective which never varies.
indefinite article	in English, "a" or "an." There is no indefinite article in Latin, though the function of the indefinite article is frequently performed by the pronoun quīdam.
indicative	refers to a verb when it makes a statement or asks a question: he said this = hoc dīxit. In Latin grammar, the main use of this word is to indicate that the verb is not in the subjunctive.
indirect command	the reporting of an actual command: e.g. "Do this" (direct speech, direct command). She instructed him *to do this* (indirect command).
indirect object	the noun or pronoun indirectly affected by the verb at which the direct object is aimed: I gave *him* the book = librum *eī* dedī.
indirect question	the reporting of an actual question: e.g. "What are you doing?" (direct speech, direct question). I asked/told her *what she was doing* (indirect question).
indirect statement	the reporting of someone's actual words, e.g. "I have done this" (direct speech). He said *that he had done this* (indirect speech).

infinitive	a verbal noun, the basic part of a verb: to love = amāre.
inflection	see under ending.
interjection	a sound, word, or phrase standing outside the grammatical structure of the sentence and expressing an emotion such as anger, fear, distress or joy: alas! = ēheu!
intransitive verb	a verb which does not take a direct object: e.g. "go," "come."
irregular verb	a verb that does not follow one of the set patterns (i.e. is not one of the four conjugations) and has its own individual forms.
jussive	giving an order.
locative	the case which tells us where something is happening, e.g. domī = at home.
main clause	the clause which is the basic grammatical unit of the sentence. "Although I hate him, he still chases me." "He still chases me" makes sense on its own, while "although I hate him" does not. Thus "He still chases me" is the main clause, and "although I hate him" is a subordinate clause.
masculine	one of the three genders: uir = a man and liber = a book.
mood	the grammatical form of a verb which shows whether it is in the indicative, subjunctive or imperative.
negative	expressing denial, refusal or prohibition. The words "no" or "not" are generally used.
neuter	one of the three genders: animal = an animal.
nominative	the case of the subject of a sentence or of the complement of a verb: *the* king is *angry* = rēx īrātus est.
noun	a word that names a person or thing: war = bellum.
number	a state of being either singular or plural.
numerals	numbers: in Latin these are either "cardinals" (1, 2, 3, etc.), "ordinals" (1st, 2nd, 3rd, etc.), "distributives" (one each, two each, three each, etc.), or adverbs (once, twice, three times, etc.).
object	a noun or its equivalent acted upon by a transitive verb: the dog bit the *boy*; canis *puerum* momordit.
ordinals	see numerals.

part of speech	a grammatical term for the function of a word: noun, adjective, pronoun, verb, adverb, preposition, conjunction, interjection.
participle	an adjective formed from a verb. In Latin these are either present (a *loving* wife = uxor *amāns*), future (*about to love* her husband = uirum *amātūra*), or past (the *murdered* king = rēx *interfectus*).
passive	the form of a verb used when the subject does not perform the action but experiences it: the king *was killed* = rēx *interfectus est.*
perfect tense	the tense of a verb that refers to a completed action. In English the word "have" or "has" is often used: they *have lived* = *uīxērunt.*
person	a term that refers to the subject of a verb: 1st person – I (singular), we (plural); 2nd person—you (both singular and plural); 3rd person—he, she, it (singular), they (plural).
personal pronoun	a pronoun that refers to a person: e.g. I, you = ego, tū.
phrase	a distinct group of words which does not contain a finite verb: I swam *in the sea.*
pluperfect tense	the tense that means "had," referring to an action already completed in the past: I *had* come to Rome = Rōmam *aduēneram.*
plural	of nouns, etc., referring to more than one: the trees = arborēs.
positive	not negative.
possessive pronoun	a pronoun that shows possession, belonging to someone or something: my, mine = meus, mea, meum.
prefix	a syllable or word added to the beginning of another word: *prōcēdō* = I *proceed.*
preposition	a word that stands in front of a noun or pronoun to produce an adverbial phrase. In Latin it will be followed by the accusative or ablative: *ante* merīdiem = *before* midday.
present tense	the tense of a verb that refers to something happening now: I am walking, I walk = ambulō.
principal parts	in Latin, the principal parts of active verbs generally consist of four elements, 1. the present tense, 2. the present infinitive, 3. the perfect tense, 4. the supine. For deponent and passive

verbs, we give, 1. the present tense, 2. the present infinitive, 3. the perfect tense.

pronoun   a word that stands instead of a noun or thing: e.g. he, she, this, that = is, ea, hoc, illud.

pronunciation   the way of pronouncing, or speaking, words.

reflexive pronoun   a word referring back to the subject of the verb, in which the action of the verb is performed on its subject: he washed *himself*: *sē lāuit.*

regular verb   a verb that follows a set pattern (i.e. that of one of the four conjugations) in its forms.

relative pronoun   a pronoun that introduces a subordinate clause, relating to the person or thing mentioned in the main clause: the man *who* loves me = uir *quī* mē amat.

sentence   a group of words, with a subject and a verb, that can stand on its own to make a statement, ask a question or give a command.

sequence of tenses   the process by which the use of a certain tense in the main clause determines the tense of the subjunctive used in a subordinate clause. If the tense in the main clause is present or future, the sequence is *primary*; if it is a past tense, the sequence is *historic.*

singular   of nouns, etc., referring to just one: the tree = arbor.

stem   the part of a noun or verb to which endings are added: *bell-* is the stem of *bell*um = war; *am-* is the stem of *amō* = I love.

subject   in a clause or sentence, the noun or pronoun that causes the action of the verb: the *queen* killed the king = *rēgīna* rēgem interfēcit.

subjunctive   a verb form that is used, among many other functions, to express doubt or unlikelihood. Words such as *may, might, would, should* and *could* can indicate a subjunctive in English.

subordinate clause   a clause which depends on another clause (usually the main clause) of the sentence. In the sentence "This is a book which is hard to follow," "which is hard to follow" describes the book. The clause would not make sense on its own. Thus it is subordinate.

superlative	the form of an adjective or adverb that makes it mean "most" or "very": *most* small (small*est*), *very* small = minimus.
supine	a part of the verb (fourth of the principal parts) from which other forms of the verb, especially the passive, can be predicted.
syllable	part of a word that forms a spoken unit, usually a vowel sound with consonants before and/or after: mi-ni-mus.
tense	the form of a verb that shows when the action takes place: present, future, perfect, etc.
transitive verb	a verb used with a direct object either expressed or understood, e.g. *pick* apples or *pick till you are tired* (but not *he picked at the scab*—here "picked" is intransitive).
verb	a word or group of words that describes an action: the children *had set* out= līberī *profectī erant.*
vocative	the case by which you address or call to someone: *Quīntus,* come here = *Quīnte,* uenī hūc.
voice	the set of forms of a verb that show the relation of the subject to the action, i.e. active or passive.
vowel	a letter representing a vowel that can be spoken by itself: a, e, i, o, u, y.

Metrical Appendix

QUANTITY

The scansion of Latin verse of the classical period is quantitative, not accentual as in English. Syllables are either light or heavy, regardless of where the accent falls on any given word.

(a) All syllables are heavy which contain a long vowel or dipthong, e.g. **lāetī, sōlēs, Rōmānī**. For the purposes of scansion heavy syllables are marked with a macron ‾, light syllables with the symbol ˘. This convention sometimes results in a syllable containing a short vowel being marked with a macron; see below.

(b) If a short vowel is followed by two consonants, whether in the same or in different words, the syllable is heavy, e.g.

t̲a̲ntāē | mōlĭs ĕ|r̲a̲t Rō|mānā̲m̲ | c̲ō̲ndĕrĕ | gēntĕm.

In this line the syllables underlined are heavy although in each case the vowel is short.

(c) Exceptions to rule (b): if a short vowel is followed by a combination of mute (**p, t, c, b, d, g**) and liquid (**r** and less commonly **l**) in that order, the syllable may be scanned either light or heavy, e.g. **pătris, uolŭcris, latĕbrae**. This is really a question of pronunciation; such syllables can be pronounced either **pāt-ris** or **pă-tris** (**tr** making one sound).

ELISION

A final open vowel followed by a vowel or an h in the next word is elided, as in the French *c'est*, but in Latin the elision is not written, e.g.

cōntĭcŭ|ēr(e) ōm|nēs īn|tentīqu(e) |ōră tĕ|nēbānt

The final **e** of **conticuēre** elides before the following **o** of **omnia**, and the final **e** of **que** elides before the following **ō** of **ōra**.

$$\text{hūc sē} \mid \text{prōuēc|tī dē|sērt(ō) īn} \mid \text{lītŏrĕ} \mid \text{cōndūnt}$$

The final **ō** in **dēsertō** elides before the following **i** of **in.**

More surprisingly, a final syllable ending in **-m** elides before a following vowel, e.g.

$$\text{pārs stŭpĕt} \mid \text{īnnūp|tāē dōn(um)} \mid \text{ĕxĭtĭ|ālĕ Mĭ|nēruāē}$$

The **-um** of **dōnum** elides before the **e** of **exitiāle.**

In reading Latin verse the elided vowel or syllable should be lightly sounded.

THE METERS

An iambic metron (measure) consists of two iambic feet: ⌣‾⌣‾ A spondee (‾ ‾) may be substituted for an iamb in the first foot of each metron:

$$\overline{\underset{\smile}{}} = \smile \ -$$

The last syllable in the line in all types of meter may be long or short (anceps).

The commonest iambic line is the iambic trimeter; this scans, counting in feet as follows:

1	2	3	4	5	6
⌣̄ ̄	⌣ ‾	⌣̄ ∧ ‾	⌣∧‾	⌣̄ ‾	⌣ ⌣̄

There is a caesura, i.e. a rhythmical pause between words, halfway through the third or fourth foot, marked ∧. The only example of iambics in RV is Horace: *Epode* 2 (Chapter 24), where iambic trimeters alternate with iambic dimeters:

$$\text{bĕā|tŭs īl|lĕ } _\wedge \text{ quī} \mid \text{prŏcūl} \mid \text{nĕgōtĭ īs}$$
$$\text{ūt prīs|că gēns} \mid \text{mōrtā|lĭūm}$$

DACTYLIC HEXAMETERS

The dactylic hexameter consists of six dactylic feet (‾ ⌣ ⌣). A spondee (‾ ‾) may be substituted for a dactyl in any of the first four feet; the fifth foot is nearly always a dactyl and the sixth is always a spondee or ‾ ⌣. There is usually a strong caesura (a break between words after the first long syllable of the foot) in the middle of the third foot:

$$\text{ārmă uĭ|rūmquĕ că|nō, } _\wedge \text{ Trōī|āē quī} \mid \text{prīmŭs ăb} \mid \text{ōrīs}$$

(3rd foot strong caesura)

If there is a weak caesura (a break between words after – �‿) or there is no caesura in the third foot there are usually strong caesuras in the second or fourth feet:

quĭduĕ dŏ|lēns ‸ rē|gīnă dĕ|ūm ‸ tōt | uōluĕrĕ | cāsūs
(3rd foot weak caesura; strong caesuras in 2nd and 4th feet)

īndĕ tŏ|rō ‸ pătĕr | A̅enēās ‸ sīc | ōrsŭs ăb | āltō
(no 3rd foot caesura; strong caesuras in 2nd and 4th feet)

This is the meter used by Homer and all subsequent epic poets. Virgil uses it in his *Eclogues, Georgics* and *Aeneid*. Horace uses it in all the *Satires* and *Epistles*.

ELEGIAC COUPLETS

These consist of a dactylic hexameter followed by the first half of the same (up to the third foot strong caesura) repeated. We call this shorter line a pentameter. In this book they are used only in the lines of Propertius quoted in Chapter 27:

mīrā|bār quīd|nām ‸ rīs|īssēnt | mānĕ Că|mēnāē,
āntĕ mĕ|ūm stān|tēs ‸ sōlĕ rŭ|bēntĕ tŏ|rŭm.

LYRIC METERS

There is a wide variety of lyric meters, which first appear in the (Greek) poems of Sappho and Alcaeus, who wrote in the Aeolic dialect about 600 BC. Horace claims to have been the first to adapt these meters to Latin poetry (*Odes* 3.30.13–14):

dīcār …
prīnceps Aeolium carmen ad Ītalōs
dēdūxisse modōs.

But Catullus had in fact led the way in the previous generation.

In these meters, which are dance rhythms, we cannot speak of feet or metra; the unit is the line and many systems are constructed in four-line stanzas. Most Aeolic meters contain a unit called the choriamb (– �‿ �‿ –) and the lines are built up round one or more of these. They usually consist of a base (e.g. ––, �‿ –), choriamb(s), clausula (a closing cadence which can take various forms). Thus the line quoted above scans:

prīncēps | A̅eŏlĭūm | cārmĕn ăd Ī|tălōs

i.e. base (– –), two choriambs (– ˘ ˘ – – ˘ ˘ –) and clausula (˘ –).

The lyric meters illustrated in this book are:

Asclepiads

All Asclepiad meters, of which there are several forms, consist of base (– –), one or more choriambs, clausula. Horace, *Odes* 3.13 is the only example in this book:

ō fōns | Bāndŭsĭǣ, | splēndĭdĭōr | uītrō
dūlcī | dīgnĕ mĕrō | nōn sĭnĕ flō|rĭbŭs,
  crās dō|nābĕrĭs hǣ|dō
    cuī frōns | tūrgĭdǎ cōr|nĭbŭs

Sapphics

This is the favorite meter of Sappho. It is composed in four-line stanzas, of which the first three are the same:

  – ˘ – ≍ (extended base), – ˘ ˘ – (choriamb), ˘ – ≍ (extended clausula)

The fourth line consists of:

  – ˘ ˘ – (choriamb). ≍ (abbreviated clausula).

In this book the lines quoted in Chapter 30 (*uīle potābis…*) form the beginning of a Sapphic stanza (*Odes* 1.20). The following stanza begins Horace's *Carmen Saeculāre*:

Phoēbĕ sīluā|rūmquĕ pŏtēns | Dǐānǎ
lūcǐdūm cāē|lī dĕcŭs, ō | cŏlēndī
sēmpĕr ēt cūl|tī, dǎtĕ quāē | prĕcāmŭr
  tēmpŏrĕ sāc|rō.

Alcaics

This is the favorite meter of both Alcaeus and Horace, used in this book in *Odes* 3.26 (Chapter 27). Alcaics consist of four-line stanzas in which lines 1 and 2 are the same:

  ≍ – ˘ – – ‿|– ˘ ˘ –|˘ ≍
  ≍ – ˘ – – ‿|– ˘ ˘ –|˘ ≍
    ≍ – ˘ – – – ˘ ≍
      – ˘ ˘ – ˘ ˘ –|˘ – ≍
  uīxī pŭēllīs ‿|nūpĕr ǐdō|nĕŭs

ēt mīlĭtāuī ∧|nōn sĭnĕ glō|rĭă;
   nūnc ārmă dēfūnctūmquĕ bēllō
     bārbĭtŏn hīc părĭēs | hăbēbĭt.
          (*Odes* 3.26.1–4)

There is a caesura after the fifth syllable of the first two lines; the second half of the line consists of a choriamb + clausula. The third line starts like the first two but there is no caesura and no choriamb in the second half; it is a very heavy line. The last line moves fast; it consists of an expanded choriamb (–◡◡–◡◡–) followed by a clausula (◡–◡̆).

N.B. When the principles of scansion have been learned, it is important to emphasize that Latin verse should be read with attention not only to scansion but also to the natural pronunciation of the Latin words; the stress accent natural to every word of two or more syllables should not be distorted. There are two rhythms being sounded at once, and the reader has to acknowledge both.

   In the hexameters of Virgil there is usually a clash between the stress of the scansion and that of the word accent (marked ´) which is usually resolved in the last two feet of the line, where they coincide, e.g.

ármă uī́|rūmquĕ cắ|nō, Trōī́|āē quī|prī́mŭs ăb | ṓrīs
Ītắlĭ|ām fắ|tō prŏ́fŭ|gūs Lā|uī́nĭăquĕ | uḗnĭt

Reference Grammar

NOUNS

	1st declension	2nd declension		3rd declension	
	stems in -a	*stems in -o*		*stems in consonants*	
	feminine	*masculine*	*neuter*	*masc. & fem.*	*neuter*
singular					
nom	puell-a	colōn-us	bell-um	rēx	lītus
gen.	puell-ae	colōn-ī	bell-ī	rēg-is	lītor-is
dat.	puell-ae	colōn-ō	bell-ō	rēg-ī	lītor-ī
acc.	puell-am	colōn-um	bell-um	rēg-em	lītus
abl.	puell-ā	colōn-ō	bell-ō	rēg-e	lītor-e
plural					
nom	puell-ae	colōn-ī	bell-a	rēg-ēs	lītor-a
gen.	puell-ārum	colōn-ōrum	bell-ōrum	rēg-um	lītor-um
dat.	puell-īs	colōn-īs	bell-īs	rēg-ibus	lītor-ibus
acc.	puell-ās	colōn-ōs	bell-a	rēg-ēs	lītor-a
abl.	puell-īs	colōn-īs	bell-īs	rēg-ibus	lītor-ibus

	3rd declension		4th declension		5th declension
	stems in -i		*stems in -u*		*stems in -e*
	masc. & fem.	*neuter*	*masc.*	*neuter*	*feminine*
singular					
nom.	nāu-is	mare	grad-us	corn-ū	r-ēs
gen.	nāu-is	mar-is	grad-ūs	corn-ūs	r-eī
dat.	nāu-ī	mar-ī	grad-uī	corn-ū	r-eī
acc.	nāu-em	mare	grad-um	corn-ū	r-em
abl.	nāu-e	mar-ī	grad-ū	corn-ū	r-ē

plural					
nom	nāu-ēs	mar-ia	grad-ūs	corn-ua	r-ēs
gen.	nāu-ium	mar-ium	grad-uum	corn-uum	r-ērum
dat.	nāu-ibus	mar-ibus	grad-ibus	corn-ibus	r-ēbus
acc.	nāu-ēs	mar-ia	grad- ūs	corn-ua	r-ēs
abl.	nāu-ibus	mar-ibus	grad-ibus	corn-ibus	r-ēbus

NOTES

1. The vocative is the same as the nominative for all nouns of all declensions except for 2nd declension masculine nouns in **-us**, e.g. **colōn-us**, which form the vocative singular **-e**, e.g. **colōn-e**, and in **-ius**, e.g. **fīli-us**, which form vocative singular **-ī**, e.g. **fīl-ī**.

2. All nouns of the first declension are feminine except for a few which are masculine by meaning, e.g. **nauta** a sailor, **agricola** a farmer.

3. 2nd declension masculine nouns with nominative singular **-er**, e.g. **puer, ager**: some keep **-e** , e.g. **puer, puer-ī**; others drop it, e.g. **ager, agr-ī**.
   The genitive singular of masculine nouns ending **-ius** and neuter nouns ending **-ium** in the nominative is often contracted from **-iī** to **-ī**, e.g. **fīlī, ingenī**.

4. The following 2nd declension nouns have minor irregularities: **deus;** a god has nominative plural **deī** or **dī**, genitive plural **deōrum** or **deum**, ablative plural **deīs** or **dīs**; **uir**, or **uirī** man has genitive plural **uirōrum** or **uirum**.

5. 3rd declension. The gender of all 3rd declension nouns has to be learned. Genitive plural: the general rule is that nouns with stems in **-i** have genitive plural **-ium**, those with stems in consonants have genitive plural **-um**. All nouns with nominative **-is**, e.g. **nāuis**, have stems in **-i**. And so do nouns the nominative of which ends in two consonants, e.g. **fōns, urbs,** genitive plural **fontium, urbium** (their original nominative was, e.g., **urbis**).
   Nouns with stems in **-i** have alternative forms for ablative singular, e.g. **nāue** or **nāuī**, for accusative plural, e.g. **nāuēs** or **nāuīs.**

6. Most 4th declension nouns are masculine; **manus** is the only common noun which is feminine. There are very few neuter nouns; the only common one is **cornū** horn or the wing of an army.

7. All 5th declension nouns are feminine except for **diēs**, which is usually masculine.

ADJECTIVES

masculine & neuter 2nd declension; feminine 1st declension

singular	m.	f.	n.
nom.	bon-us	bon-a	bon-um
gen.	bon-ī	bon-ae	bon-ī
dat.	bon-ō	bon-ae	bon-ō
acc.	bon-um	bon-am	bon-um
abl.	bon-ō	bon-ā	bon-ō

plural			
nom.	bon-ī	bon-ae	bon-a
gen.	bon-ōrum	bon-ārum	bon-ōrum
dat.	bon-īs	bon-īs	bon-īs
acc.	bon-ōs	bon-ās	bon-a
abl.	bon-īs	bon-īs	bon-īs

NOTE:

Similarly, **miser, misera, miserum** (keeping -e- like **puer**) and **pulcher, pulchra, pulchrum** (dropping the -e- like **ager**).

3rd declension

singular	consonant stems		stems in -i	
	m. & f.	n.	m. & f.	n.
nom.	pauper	pauper	omnis	omn-e
gen.	pauper-is	pauper-is	omn-is	omn-is
dat.	pauper-ī	pauper-ī	omn-ī	omn-ī
acc.	pauper-em	pauper	omn-em	omn-e
abl.	pauper-e	pauper-e	omn-ī	omn-ī

plural	consonant stems		stems in -i	
	m. & f.	n.	m. & f.	n.
nom.	pauper-ēs	pauper-a	omn-ēs	omn-ia
gen.	pauper-um	pauper-um	omn-ium	omn-ium
dat.	pauper-ibus	pauper-ibus	omn-ibus	omn-ibus
acc.	pauper-ēs	pauper-a	omn-ēs	omn-ia
abl.	pauper-ibus	pauper-ibus	omn-ibus	omn-ibus

	alter (one or the other of two)			**uter** (which of two?)		
	m.	*f.*	*n.*	*m.*	*f.*	*n.*
nom.	alter	altera	alterum	uter	utra	utrum
gen.	alterīus	alterīus	alterīus	utrīus	utrīus	utrīus
dat.	alterī	alterī	alterī	utrī	utrī	utrī
acc.	alterum	alteram	alterum	utrum	utram	utrum
abl.	alterō	alterā	alterō	utrō	utrā	utrō

Plural like that of **bon-ī, bon-ae, bon-a**. Similarly: **uterque, utraque, utrumque** (each of two): **utrīque, utraeque, utraque**

NOTES

1. Most 3rd declension adjectives have stems in **-i**. Other types of adjective with stems in **-i** are: **ingēns** (neuter **ingēns**), genitive **ingent-is**; **ferōx** (neuter **ferōx**), genitive **ferōc-is**; **celer** (f. **celeris**, n. **celere**), genitive **celer-is**.
2. 3rd declension adjectives with stems in consonants are few, e.g. **dīues, dīuit-is**, **pauper, pauper-is; uetus, ueter-is**; and the comparative adjective, e.g. **fortior** (*n.* **fortius**), genitive **fortiōr-is**. The ablative singular ends in **-e**.

The following adjectives have the same characteristic as **alter** and **uter**, e.g. gen. sing. **-īus**, dat. sing. **-ī**:

alius, alia, aliud	other	*gen. sing.*	**alīus**	*dat.sing.*	**aliī**
nūllus, nūlla, nūllum	no		**nūllīus**		**nūllī**
ūllus, ūlla, ūllum	any		**ūllīus**		**ūllī**
sōlus, sōla, sōlum	only		**sōlīus**		**sōlī**
tōtus, tōta, tōtum	whole		**tōtīus**		**tōtī**
ūnus, ūna, ūnum	one		**ūnīus**		**ūnī**

Comparison of adjectives

Most adjectives add **-ior** to the stem to form the comparative and **-issimus** to form the superlative:

positive	*comparative*	*superlative*
longus	**longior**	**longissimus**
long	longer	longest, very long
trīstīs	**trīstior**	**trīstissimus**
sad	sadder	saddest, very sad

The comparative declines as a 3rd declension adjective (consonant stem):

| | singular | | plural | |
singular	m. & f.	n.	m. & f.	n.
nom.	longior	longius	longiōrēs	longiōra
gen.	longiōris	longiōris	longiōrum	longiōrum
dat.	longiōrī	longiōrī	longiōribus	longiōribus
acc.	longiōrem	longius	longiōrēs	longiōra
abl.	longiōre	longiōre	longiōribus	longiōribus

The superlative declines like **bonus, bona, bonum**.

The following common adjectives have irregular comparison:

positive	comparative	superlative
bonus	melior	optimus
malus	peior	pessimus
magnus	maior	maximus
multus	plūs*	plūrimus
paruus	minor	minimus

*plūs in the singular is a neuter noun, declining: **plūs, plūris, plūrī, plūs, plūre.**

So **plūs cibī** = more (of) food.

In the plural it is an adjective: **plūrīs, plūra,** etc. So **plūrīs puellae** = more girls.

Adjectives ending in **-er** in the nominative double the **-r-** in the superlative, e.g.

miser, miserior, miserrimus
pulcher, pulchrior, pulcherrimus
celer, celerior, celerrimus

Six adjectives with nominative **-ilis** double the **-l-** in the superlative:

facilis (easy), **facilior, facillimus**
difficilis (difficult), **difficilior, difficillimus**
gracilis (slender), **gracilior, gracillimus**
humilis (low), **humilior, humillimus**
similis (like), **similior, simillimus**
dissimilis (unlike), **dissimilior, dissimillimus**

Other adjectives with nominative **-ilis** form regular superlatives, e.g. **amābilis** (lovable), **amābilior, amābilissimus**.

ADVERBS

1. From **bonus** type adjectives, adverbs are usually formed by adding **-ē** to the stem, e.g. **lent-us** slow: **lent-ē** slowly; **miser** miserable: **miser-ē** miserably. A few add **-ō**, e.g. **subit-us** sudden: **subit-ō** suddenly.

2. From 3rd declension adjectives, adverbs are usually formed by adding **-ter** to the stem, e.g. **fēlīx** fortune: **fēlīci-ter** fortunately; **celer** quick: **celeri-ter** quickly. A few 3rd declension adjectives use the accusative neuter singular as an adverb, e.g. **facilis** easy, **facile** easily.

3. There are many adverbs which have no corresponding adjectival form, e.g. **diū, quandō? iam, semper.**

4. Comparison of adverbs. The comparative adverb is the same as the neuter accusative singular of the comparative adjective: the superlative adverb is formed by changing the nominative ending **-us** to **-ē**, e.g.

adjective	adverb	comparative adverb	superlative adverb
longus	longē	longius	longissimē
fortis	fortiter	fortius	fortissimē

Note the following irregular adverbs:

adjective	adverb	comparative adverb	superlative adverb
bonus	bene	melius	optimē
malus	male	peius	pessimē
facilis	facile	facilius	facillimē
magnus	magnopere	maius	maximē
multus	multum	minus	minimē
paruus	paulum	plūs	plūrimum
prīmus	prīmum	—	—

NUMERALS

cardinals		
1	ūnus	I
2	duo	II
3	trēs	III
4	quattuor	IV
5	quīnque	V
6	sex	VI

7	septem	VII
8	octō	VIII
9	nouem	IX
10	decem	X
11	ūndecim	XI
12	duodecim	XII
13	tredecim	XIII
14	quattuordecim	XIV
15	quīndecim	XV
16	sēdecim	XVI
17	septendecim	XVII
18	duodēuīgintī	XVIII
19	ūndēuīgintī	XIX
20	uīgintī	XX
30	trīgintā	XXX
40	quadrāgintā	XL
50	quīnquāgintā	L
100	centum	C
200	ducentī, -ae, -a	CC
300	trecentī, -ae, -a	CCC
400	quadringentī, -ae, -a	CCCC
1,000	mīlle	M
2,000	duo mīlia	MM

NOTES

1. the numbers 4–100 do not decline; 200–900 decline like **bonī, -ae, -a.**
2. **mīlle** does not decline; **mīlia** is a 3rd declension noun, so:
   mīlle passūs = 1,000 paces (a mile)
   duo mīlia passuum = 2,000 (of) paces (2 miles)
3. Adverbial numbers: **semel, bis, ter** (once, twice, three times, etc.); **centiēs/ centiēns** 100 times, **mīliēs/ mīliēns** 1,000 times.

ordinals	
1st	prīmus, -a, -um
2nd	secundus, -a, -um/alter, -a, -um
3rd	tertius, -a, -um
4th	quārtus, -a, -um
5th	quīntus, -a, -um

6th	sextus, -a, -um
7th	septimus, -a, -um
8th	octāuus, a, um
9th	nōnus, -a, -um
10th	decimus, -a, -um
20th	uīcēsimus, -a, -um
100th	centēsimus, -a, -um
1,000th	mīllēsimus

Declension of **ūnus, duo, trēs**

	m.	*f.*	*n.*	*m.*	*f.*	*n.*	*m.*	*f.*	*n.*
nom.	ūnus	ūna	ūnum	duo	duae	duo	trēs	trēs	tria
gen.	ūnīus	ūnīus	ūnīus	duōrum	duārum	duōrum	trium	trium	trium
dat.	ūnī	ūnī	ūnī	duōbus	duābus	duōbus	tribus	tribus	tribus
acc.	ūnum	ūnam	ūnum	duōs	duās	duo	trēs	trēs	tria
abl.	ūnō	ūnā	ūnō	duōbus	duābus	duōbus	tribus	tribus	tribus

PRONOUNS

singular	*personal pronouns*			
nom.	ego (I)	tū (you)		Possessive adjectives:
gen.	meī	tuī	suī	
dat.	mihi	tibi	sibi	meus, -a, -um (my)
acc.	mē	tē	sē (himself, herself)	tuus, -a, -um (your)
abl.	mē	tē	sē	suus, -a, -um (his/her own)

plural				
nom.	nōs (we)	uōs (you)		noster, nostra, nostrum (our)
gen.	nostrum, nostrī	uestrum, uestrī	suī	uester, uestra, uestrum (your)
dat.	nōbīs	uōbīs	sibi	suus, -a, -um (their own)
acc.	nōs	uōs	sē (themselves)	All decline like **bonus, -a, -um**
abl.	nōbīs	uōbīs	sē	but the vocative of **meus** is **mī**

singular	*demonstrative pronouns*								
	m.	*f.*	*n.*	*m.*	*f.*	*n.*	*m.*	*f.*	*n*
nom.	hic	haec	hoc (this)	ille	illa	illud (that)	is	ea	id (he, she, it; that)
gen.	huius	huius	huius	illīus	illīus	illīus	eius	eius	eius
dat.	huic	huic	huic	illī	illī	illī	eī	eī	eī
acc.	hunc	hanc	hoc	illum	illam	illud	eum	eam	id
abl.	hōc	hāc	hōc	illō	illā	illō	eō	eā	eō

plural									
	m.	*f.*	*n.*	*m.*	*f.*	*n.*	*m.*	*f.*	*n*
nom.	hī	hae	haec	illī	illae	illa	eī	eae	ea
gen.	hōrum	hārum	hōrum	illōrum	illārum	illōrum	eōrum	eārum	eōrum
dat.	hīs	hīs	hīs	illīs	illīs	illīs	eīs	eīs	eīs
acc.	hōs	hās	haec	illōs	illās	illa	eōs	eās	ea
abl.	hīs	hīs	hīs	illīs	illīs	illīs	eīs	eīs	eīs

singular								*relative pronoun*	
	m.	*f.*	*n.*	*m.*	*f.*	*n.*	*m.*	*f.*	*n*
nom.	ipse	ipsa	ipsum (self)	īdem	eadem	idem (same)	quī	quae	quod (who, which)
gen.	ipsīus	ipsīus	ipsīus	eiusdem	eiusdem	eiusdem	cuius	cuius	cuius
dat.	ipsī	ipsī	ipsī	eīdem	eīdem	eīdem	cui	cui	cui
acc.	ipsum	ipsam	ipsum	eundem	eandem	idem	quem	quam	quod
abl.	ipsō	ipsā	ipsō	eōdem	eādem	eōdem	quō	quā	quō

plural								*relative pronoun*	
	m.	*f.*	*n.*	*m.*	*f.*	*n.*	*m.*	*f.*	*n*
nom.	ipsī	ipsae	ipsa	eīdem	eaedem	eadem	quī	quae	quae
gen.	ipsōrum	ipsārum	ipsōrum	eōrundem	eārundem	eōrundem	quōrum	quārum	quōrum
dat.	ipsīs	ipsīs	ipsīs	eīsdem	eīsdem	eīsdem	quibus	quibus	quibus
acc.	ipsōs	ipsās	ipsa	eōsdem	eāsdem	eadem	quōs	quās	quae
abl.	ipsīs	ipsīs	ipsīs	eīsdem	eīsdem	eīsdem	quibus	quibus	quibus

quidam (a certain, a) declines like the relative pronoun with the suffix **-dam**:

nom.	quīdam	quaedam	quoddam	
acc.	quendam	quandam	quoddam	etc.

The interrogative pronoun **quis?** (who? what?):

nom.	quis?	quis?	quid?	
acc.	quem?	quam?	quid?	(The rest is exactly like the relative pronoun.)

The interrogative adjective **quī?** (which? what?):

nom.	quī?	quae?	quod?	(The rest is exactly like the relative pronoun.)

The indefinite pronoun **aliquis** (someone, something) declines like **quis?** with the prefix **ali-** with the exception of the nominative singular feminine:

nom.	aliquis	aliqua	aliquid	etc.

quisquam, quicquam (anyone, anything, after a negative) declines like **quis** with the suffix **-quam**:

nom.	quisquam	quisquam	quicquam

Interrogatives and demonstratives

quis? quī?	who? which?	**is, ille, iste**	that
uter?	which of two?	**alter**	one or the other of two
quālis?	of what kind?	**tālis**	of such kind, such
quantus?	how great?	**tantus**	so great
ubi?	where?	**ibi, illīc, istīc**	there
unde?	from where?	**inde**	from there
quō?	where to?	**eō, illō**	to there
quā?	by what way?	**eā**	by that way
quam?	how?	**tam**	so
quandō?	when?	**tum**	then
quotiēns?	how often?	**totiēns**	so often

VERBS

Active
Indicative

		1st conjugation	2nd conjugation	3rd conjugation	3rd **-iō** conjugation	4th conjugation
		stems in **-a**	stems in **-e**	consonant stems		stems in **-i**
present						
singular	1	par-ō	mone-ō	reg-ō	capi-ō	audi-ō
	2	parā-s	monē-s	reg-is	capi-s	audī-s
	3	para-t	mone-t	reg-it	capi-t	audi-t
plural	1	parā-mus	monē-mus	reg-imus	capi-mus	audī-mus
	2	parā-tis	monē-tis	reg-itis	capi-tis	audī-tis
	3	para-nt	mone-nt	reg-unt	capi-unt	audi-unt
future						
singular	1	parā-bō	monē-bō	reg-am	capi-am	audi-am
	2	parā-bis	monē-bis	reg-ēs	capi-ēs	audi-ēs
	3	parā-bit	monē-bit	reg-et	capi-et	audi-et
plural	1	parā-bimus	monē-bimus	reg-ēmus	capi-ēmus	audi-ēmus
	2	parā-bitis	monē-bitis	reg-ētis	capi-ētis	audi-ētis
	3	parā-bunt	monē-bunt	reg-ent	capi-ent	audi-ent
imperfect						
singular	1	parā-bam	monē-bam	regē-bam	capiē-bam	audiē-bam
	2	parā-bās	monē-bās	regē-bās	capiē-bās	audiē-bās
	3	parā-bat	monē-bat	regē-bat	capiē-bat	audiē-bat
plural	1	parā-bāmus	monē-bāmus	regē-bāmus	capiē-bāmus	audiē-bāmus
	2	parā-bātis	monē-bātis	regē-bātis	capiē-bātis	audiē-bātis
	3	parā-bant	monē-bant	regē-bant	capiē-bant	audiē-bant
perfect						
singular	1	parāu-ī	monu-ī	rēx-ī	cēp-ī	audīu-ī
	2	parāu-istī	monu-istī	rēx-istī	cēp-istī	audīu-istī
	3	parāu-it	monu-it	rēx-it	cēp-it	audīu-it
plural	1	parāu-imus	monu-imus	rēx-imus	cēp-imus	audīu-imus
	2	parāu-istis	monu-istis	rēx-istis	cēp-istis	audīu-istis
	3	parāu-ērunt	monu-ērunt	rēx-ērunt	cēp-ērunt	audīu-ērunt

		1st conjugation	2nd conjugation	3rd conjugation	3rd -iō conjugation	4th conjugation
		stems in **-a**	stems in **-e**	consonant stems		stems in **-i**
future perfect						
singular	1	parāu-erŏ	monu-erŏ	rĕx-erŏ	cĕp-erŏ	audīu-erŏ
	2	parāu-eris	monu-eris	rĕx-eris	cĕp-eris	audīu-eris
	3	parāu-erit	monu-erit	rĕx-erit	cĕp-erit	audīu-erit
plural	1	parāu-erimus	monu-erimus	rĕx-erimus	cĕp-erimus	audīu-erimus
	2	parāu-eritis	monu-eritis	rĕx-eritis	cĕp-eritis	audīu-eritis
	3	parāu-erint	monu-erint	rĕx-erint	cĕp-erint	audīu-erint
pluperfect						
singular	1	parāu-eram	monu-eram	rĕx-eram	cĕp-eram	audīu-eram
	2	parāu-erās	monu-erās	rĕx-erās	cĕp-erās	audīu-erās
	3	parāu-erat	monu-erat	rĕx-erat	cĕp-erat	audīu-erat
plural	1	parāu-erāmus	monu-erāmus	rĕx-erāmus	cĕp-erāmus	audīu-erāmus
	2	parāu-erātis	monu-erātis	rĕx-erātis	cĕp-erātis	audīu-erātis
	3	parāu-erant	monu-erant	rĕx-erant	cĕp-erant	audīu-erant

Subjunctive

		1st conjugation	2nd conjugation	3rd conjugation	3rd -iō conjugation	4th conjugation
present						
singular	1	par-em	mone-am	reg-am	capi-am	audi-am
	2	par-ēs	mone-ās	reg-ās	capi-ās	audi-ās
	3	par-et	mone-at	reg-at	capi-at	audi-at
plural	1	par-ēmus	mone-āmus	reg-āmus	capi-āmus	audi-āmus
	2	par-ētis	mone-ātis	reg-ātis	capi-ātis	audi-ātis
	3	par-ent	mone-ant	reg-ant	capi-ant	audi-ant
imperfect						
singular	1	parār-em	monēr-em	reger-em	caper-em	audīr-em
	2	parār-ēs	monēr-ēs	reger-ēs	caper-ēs	audīr-ēs
	3	parār-et	monēr-et	reger-et	caper-et	audīr-et
plural	1	parār-ēmus	monēr-ēmus	reger-ēmus	caper-ēmus	audīr-ēmus
	2	parār-ētis	monēr-ētis	reger-ētis	caper-ētis	audīr-ētis
	3	parār-ent	monēr-ent	reger-ent	caper-ent	audīr-ent

		1st conjugation	*2nd conjugation*	*3rd conjugation*	*3rd -iō conjugation*	*4th conjugation*
perfect						
singular	1	parāu-erim	monu-erim	rēx-erim	cēp-erim	audīu-erim
	2	parāu-erīs	monu-erīs	rēx-erīs	cēp-erīs	audīu-erīs
	3	parāu-erit	monu-erit	rēx-erit	cēp-erit	audīu-erit
plural	1	parāu-erīmus	monu-erīmus	rēx-erīmus	cēp-erīmus	audīu-erīmus
	2	parāu-erītis	monu-erītis	rēx-erītis	cēp-erītis	audīu-erītis
	3	parāu-erint	monu-erint	rēx-erint	cēp-erint	audīu-erint
pluperfect						
singular	1	parāu-issem	monu-issem	rēx-issem	cēp-issem	audīu-issem
	2	parāu-issēs	monu-issēs	rēx-issēs	cēp-issēs	audīu-issēs
	3	parāu-isset	monu-isset	rēx-isset	cēp-isset	audīu-isset
plural	1	parāu-issēmus	monu-issēmus	rēx-issēmus	cēp-issēmus	audīu-issēmus
	2	parāu-issētis	monu-issētis	rēx-issētis	cēp-issētis	audīu-issētis
	3	parāu-issent	monu-issent	rēx-issent	cēp-issent	audīu-issent

Imperative

singular	parā	monē	rege	cape	audī
plural	parāte	monēte	regite	capite	audīte

Infinitives

present	parāre	monēre	regere	capere	audīre
perfect	parāuisse	monuisse	rēxisse	cēpisse	audīuisse
future	parātūrus esse	monitūrus esse	rēctūrus esse	captūrus esse	audītūrus esse

Participles

present	parāns	monēns	regēns	capiēns	audiēns
future	parātūrus	monitūrus	rēctūrus	captūrus	audītūrus
Gerund	parandum	monendum	regendum	capiendum	audiendum
Supine	parātum	monitum	rēctum	captum	audītum

Passive
Indicative

		1st conjugation	2nd conjugation	3rd conjugation	3rd -iō conjugation	4th conjunction
		stems in **-a**	stems in **-e**	consonant stems		stems in **-i**
present						
singular	1	par-or	mone-or	reg-or	capi-or	audi-or
	2	parā-ris	monē-ris	reg-eris	cap-eris	audī-ris
	3	parā-tur	monē-tur	reg-itur	cap-itur	audī-tur
plural	1	parā-mur	monē-mur	reg-imur	cap-imur	audī-mur
	2	parā-minī	monē-minī	reg-iminī	cap-iminī	audī-minī
	3	para-ntur	mone-ntur	reg-untur	capi-untur	audi-untur
future						
singular	1	parā-bor	monē-bor	reg-ar	capi-ar	audi-ar
	2	parā-beris	monē-beris	reg-ēris	capi-ēris	audi-ēris
	3	parā-bitur	monē-bitur	reg-ētur	capi-ētur	audi-ētur
plural	1	parā-bimur	monē-bimur	reg-ēmur	capi-ēmur	audi-ēmur
	2	parā-biminī	monē-biminī	reg-ēminī	capi-ēminī	audi-ēminī
	3	parā-buntur	monē-buntur	reg-entur	capi-entur	audi-entur
imperfect						
singular	1	parā-bar	monē-bar	reg-ēbar	capi-ēbar	audi-ēbar
	2	parā-bāris	monē-bāris	reg-ēbāris	capi-ēbāris	audi-ēbāris
	3	parā-bātur	monē-bātur	reg-ēbātur	capi-ēbātur	audi-ēbātur
plural	1	parā-bāmur	monē-bāmur	reg-ēbāmur	capi-ēbāmur	audi-ēbāmur
	2	parā-bāminī	monē-bāminī	reg-ēbāminī	capi-ēbāminī	audi-ēbāminī
	3	parā-bantur	monē-bantur	reg-ēbantur	capi-ēbantur	audi-ēbantur
perfect						
singular	1	parātus sum	monitus sum	rēctus sum	captus sum	audītus sum
	2	parātus es	etc.	etc.	etc.	etc.
	3	parātus est				
plural	1	parātī sumus				
	2	parātī estis				
	3	parātī sunt				

		1st conjugation	2nd conjugation	3rd conjugation	3rd -iō conjugation	4th conjunction
		stems in **-a**	stems in **-e**	consonant stems		stems in **-i**
future perfect						
singular	1	parātus erō	monitus erō	rēctus erō	captus erō	audītus erō
	2	parātus eris	etc.	etc.	etc.	etc.
	3	parātus erit				
plural	1	parātī erimus				
	2	parātī eritis				
	3	parātī erunt				
pluperfect						
singular	1	parātus eram	monitus eram	rēctus eram	captus eram	audītus eram
	2	parātus erās	etc.	etc.	etc.	etc.
	3	parātus erat				
plural	1	parātī erāmus				
	2	parātī erātis				
	3	parātī erant				

Subjunctive

		1st conjugation	2nd conjugation	3rd conjugation	3rd -iō conjugation	4th conjugation
present						
singular	1	par-er	mone-ar	reg-ar	capi-ar	audi-ar
	2	par-ēris	mone-āris	reg-āris	capi-āris	audi-āris
	3	par-ētur	mone-ātur	reg-ātur	capi-ātur	audi-ātur
plural	1	par-ēmur	mone-āmur	reg-āmur	capt-āmur	audī-āmur
	2	par-ēminī	mone-āminī	reg-āminī	capi-āminī	audī-āminī
	3	par-entur	mone-antur	reg-antur	capi-antur	audi-antur
imperfect						
singular	1	parār-er	monēr-er	reger-er	caper-er	audīr-er
	2	parār-ēris	monēr-ēris	reger-ēris	caper-ēris	audīr-ēris
	3	parār-ētur	monēr-ētur	reger-ētur	caper-ētur	audīr-ētur
plural	1	parār-ēmur	monēr-ēmur	reger-ēmur	caper-ēmur	audīr-ēmur
	2	parār-ēminī	monēr-ēminī	reger-ēminī	caper-ēminī	audīr-ēminī
	3	parār-entur	monēr-entur	reger-entur	caper-entur	audīr-entur

		1st conjugation	2nd conjugation	3rd conjugation	3rd -**iō** conjugation	4th conjugation
perfect						
singular	1	parātus sim	monitus sim	rēctus sim	captus sim	audītus sim
	2	parātus sīs	etc.	etc.	etc.	etc.
	3	parātus sit				
plural	1	parātī sīmus				
	2	parātī sītis				
	3	parātī sint				
pluperfect						
singular	1	parātus essem	monitus essem	rēctus essem	captus essem	audītus essem
	2	parātus essēs	etc.	etc.	etc.	etc.
	3	parātus esset				
plural	1	parātī essēmus				
	2	parātī essētis				
	3	parātī essent				

Imperative

	1st conjugation	2nd conjugation	3rd conjugation	3rd -iō conjugation	4th conjugation
singular	parāre	monēre	regere	capere	audīre
plural	parāminī	monēminī	regiminī	capiminī	audīminī

Infinitives

	1st conjugation	2nd conjugation	3rd conjugation	3rd -iō conjugation	4th conjugation
present	parārī	monērī	regī	capī	audīrī
perfect	parātus esse	monitus esse	rēctus esse	captus esse	audītus esse
future	parātum īrī	monitum īrī	rēctum īrī	captum īrī	audītum īrī

Participle

	1st conjugation	2nd conjugation	3rd conjugation	3rd -iō conjugation	4th conjugation
perfect	parātus	monitus	rēctus	captus	audītus
Gerundive	parandus	monendus	regendus	capiendus	audiendus

Deponent verbs

	indicative	subjunctive
present	cōnor	cōner
future	cōnābor	—
imperfect	cōnābar	cōnārer
perfect	cōnātus sum	cōnātus sim
future perfect	cōnātus erō	—
pluperfect	cōnātus eram	cōnātus essem

Imperative		
singular cōnāre	*plural* cōnāminī	

Infinitives		
present cōnārī	*perfect* cōnātus esse	*future* cōnātūrus esse

Participles		
present cōnāns	*perfect* cōnātus	*future* cōnātūrus

Gerund	cōnandum
Gerundive	cōnandus

Irregular Verbs

			sum: I am	**possum:** I am able	**eō:** I go
present					
singular		1	sum	possum	eō
		2	es	potes	īs
		3	est	potest	it
plural		1	sumus	possumus	īmus
		2	estis	potestis	ītis
		3	sunt	possunt	eunt
future					
singular		1	erō	pot-erō	ī-bō
		2	eris	pot-eris	ī-bis
		3	erit	pot-erit	ī-bit
plural		1	erimus	pot-erimus	ī-bimus
		2	eritis	pot-eritis	ī-bitis
		3	erunt	pot-erunt	ī-bunt

imperfect				
singular	1	eram	pot-eram	ī-bam
	2	erās	pot-erās	ī-bās
	3	erat	pot-erat	ī-bat
plural	1	erāmus	pot-erāmus	ī-bāmus
	2	erātis	pot-erātis	ī-bātis
	3	erant	pot-erant	ī-bant

perfect stem		*fu-*	*potu-*	*i-*
singular	1	fu-ī	potu-ī	i-ī
	2	fu-istī	potu-istī	īstī
	3	fu-it	potu-it	i-it
plural	1	fu-imus	potu-imus	i-imus
	2	fu-istis	potu-istis	īstis
	3	fu-ērunt	potu-ērunt	i-ērunt

future perfect	fu-erō etc.	potu-erō etc.	ī-erō etc.
pluperfect	fu-eram etc.	potu-eram etc.	ī-eram etc.

imperative			
singular	es, estō	—	ī
plural	este	—	īte

Infinitives			
present	esse	posse	īre
perfect	fuisse	potuisse	īsse
future	futūrus esse, fore	—	itūrus esse

Participles			
present	—	(potēns)	iēns, euntis
future	futūrus	—	itūrus

| *Gerund* | — | — | eundum |

uolō, uelle, uoluī I wish, I am willing
nōlō, nōlle, nōluī I am unwilling, I refuse
mālō, mālle, māluī I prefer
ferō, ferre, tulī, lātum I carry, I bear

present					active	passive
singular	1	uolō	nōlō	mālō	ferō	feror
	2	uīs	nōn uīs	māuīs	fers	ferris
	3	uult	nōn uult	māuult	fert	fertur
plural	1	uolumus	nōlumus	mālumus	ferimus	ferimur
	2	uultis	nōn uultis	māuultis	fertis	feriminī
	3	uolunt	nōlunt	mālunt	ferunt	feruntur
future						
singular	1	uolam	nōlam	mālam	feram	ferar
	2	uolēs	nōlēs	mālēs	ferēs	ferēris
	3	uolet etc	nōlet etc.	mālet etc.	feret etc.	ferētur etc
imperfect		uolēbam etc.	nōlēbam etc.	mālēbam etc.	ferēbam etc.	ferēbar etc.
perfect		uoluī etc.	nōluī etc.	māluī etc	tulī etc.	lātus sum etc.
future perfect		uoluerō etc.	nōluerō etc.	māluerō etc	tulerō etc.	lātus erō etc.
pluperfect		uolueram etc.	nōlueram etc.	mālueram etc.	tuleram etc.	lātus eram etc.
Imperative		—	nōlī	—	fer	ferre
		—	nōlīte	—	ferte	feriminī
Infinitives						
present		uelle	nōlle	mālle	ferre	ferrī
perfect		uoluisse	nōluisse	māluisse	tulisse	lātus esse
future		—	—	—	lātūrus esse	lātum īrī
participles						
present		uolēns	nōlēns	—	ferēns	—
perfect		—	—	—	—	lātus
future		—	—	—	lātūrus	—
Gerund		—	—	—	ferendum	—
Gerundive		—	—	—	—	ferendus

Principal Parts of Verbs
Regular verbs of 1st, 2nd and 4th conjugations

	present	infinitive	perfect	supine
1st	parō	parāre	parāuī	parātum
2nd	moneō	monēre	monuī	monitum
4th	audiō	audīre	audīuī	audītum

The following are irregular:
1st conjugation
1. Perfect **-uī**
cubō, cubāre, cubuī, cubitum	I lie down
ueto, uetāre, uetuī, uetitum	I forbid

2. Perfect with lengthened vowel
iuuō, iuuāre, iūuī, iūtum	I help
lauō, lauāre, lāuī, lautum	I wash

3. Reduplicated perfect
dō, dare, dedī, datum	I give
stō, stāre, stetī, statum	I stand

2nd conjugation
1. Perfect **-uī**, supine **-tum**
doceō, docēre, docuī, doctum	I teach
teneō, tenēre, tenuī, tentum	I hold

2. Perfect **-uī**
dēleō, dēlēre, dēlēuī, dēlētum	I destroy
fleō, flēre, flēui, flētum	I weep

3. Perfect **-sī**
augeō, augēre, auxī, auctum	I increase
ardeō, ardēre, arsī, arsum	I burn, am on fire
iubeō, iubēre, iussī, iussum	I order
maneō, manēre, mānsī, mānsum	I stay, remain
rīdeō, rīdēre, rīsī, rīsum	I laugh
suādeō, suādēre, suāsī, suāsum + dat.	I persuade

4. Perfect with lengthened vowel

caueō, cauēre, cāuī, cautum	I beware
faueō, fauēre, fāuī, fautum + dat.	I favor
foueō, fouēre, fōuī, fōtum	I cherish, look after
moueō, mouēre, mōuī, mōtum	I move
sedeō, sedēre, sēdī, sessum	I sit
uideō, uidēre, uīdī, uīsum	I see

5. Perfect with no change

respondeō, respondēre, respondī, respōnsum	I answer

4th conjugation

1. Perfect in **-uī**

aperiō, aperīre, aperuī, apertum	I open

2. Perfect with lengthened vowel

sentiō, sentīre, sēnsī, sēnsum	I feel
ueniō, uenīre, uēnī, uentum	I come

3rd conjugation

1a Perfect **-sī**, supine **-tum**

carpō, carpere, carpsī, carptum	I pick
dīcō, dīcere, dīxī, dictum	I say, tell
dūcō, dūcere, dūxī, ductum	I lead
gerō, gerere, gessī, gestum	I carry, wear
nūbō, nūbere, nūpsī, nūptum	I marry
regō, regere, rēxī, rēctum	I rule
scrībō, scrībere, scrīpsī, scrīptum	I write
sūmō, sūmere, sūmpsī, sūmptum	I take
surgō*, surgere, surrēxī, surrēctum	I rise up, get up (**sub-regō**)
tegō, tegere, tēxī, tēctum	I cover
trahō, trahere, trāxī, tractum	I drag (**traghō**)
uehō*, uehere, uēxī, uectum	I carry (**ueghō**)
uīuō*, uīuere, uīxī, uīctum	I live (**uiguō**)

1b Perfect **-sī**, supine **-sum**

cēdō, cēdere, cessī, cessum	I yield ("go" in compounds)
claudō, claudere, clausī, clausum	I shut
ēuādō, ēuādere, ēuāsī, ēuāsum	I escape

lūdō, lūdere, lūsī, lūsum	I play
mittō, mittere, mīsī, missum	I send
plaudō, plaudere, plausī, plausum	I clap, applaud

NOTE

1. verbs marked*: the forms in parentheses are the original form of the verb.
2. **regō, surgō, mittō** lengthen the vowel of the stem in the perfect.
3. Compound verbs usually form the perfect in the same way as the simple verb, e.g. **prōcēdō, prōcēdere, prōcessī, prōcessum; remittō, remittere, remīsī, remissum.**

2a Perfect stem the same as the present, supine **-tum**

cōnstituō, cōnstituere, cōnstituī, cōnstitūtum	I decide
contendō, contendere, contendī, contentum	I march, hurry
induō, induere, induī, indūtum	I put on
soluō, soluere, soluī, solūtum	I loosen

2b Perfect stem the same as the present, supine **-sum**

accendō, accendere, accendī, accēnsum	I light (a fire)
ascendō, ascendere, ascendī, ascēnsum	I climb
dēscendō, dēscendere, dēscendī, dēscēnsum	I climb down
dēfendō, dēfendere, dēfendī, dēfēnsum	I defend
uertō, uertere, uertī, uersum	I turn
uīsō, uīsere, uīsī, uīsum	I go to see, visit

2c Perfect stem the same as the present but no supine

bibō, bibere, bibī	I drink
metuō, metuere, metuī	I fear

3a Verbs lengthening stem vowel in the perfect, supine **-tum**

agō, agere, ēgī, āctum	I do, I drive
cōgō, cōgere, coēgī, coāctum	I drive together, compel
emō, emere, ēmī, ēmptum	I buy
legō, legere, lēgī, lēctum	I read, I gather
frangō*, frangere, frēgī, frāctum	I break
relinquō*, relinquere, relīquī, relictum	I leave
rumpō*, rumpere, rūpī, ruptum	I burst open
uincō*, uincere, uīcī, uictum	I conquer

NOTE

Verbs marked * insert **n** (**m** before **p**) in the present, which is dropped in perfect and supine, e.g. **fra-n-gō,** original stem **fragō,** hence **frēgī, frāctum.**

4a Verbs with reduplicated perfect, supine **-tum**

addō, addere, addidī, additum	I add (so all compounds of **dō**)
canō, canere, cecinī, cantum	I sing
(cōn)sistō, (cōn)sistere, (cōn)stitī, (cōn)stitum	I stand, stop, halt
tangō, tangere, tetigī, tāctum	I touch

4b Verbs with reduplicated perfect, supine **-sum**

cadō, cadere, cecidī, cāsum	I fall
caedō, caedere, cecīdī, cāesum	I beat, kill
currō, currere, cucurrī, cursum	I run
discō, discere, didici	I learn
parcō, parcere, pepercī, parsum + dat.	I spare
pellō, pellere, pepulī, pulsum	I drive
poscō, poscere, poposci	I demand

NB: Compounds of **cadō, caedō, currō** and **pellō** do not have reduplicated perfects, e.g.

occidō, occidere, occidī, occāsum	I fall down, die
occīdō, occīdere, occīdī, occīsum	I kill
occurrō, occurrere, occurrī, occursum	I run to meet, meet
expellō, expellere, expulī, expulsum	I drive out

5 Verbs forming perfect **-uī,** or **īuī**

arcessō, arcessere, arcessīuī, arcessītum	I summon
colō, colere, coluī, cultum	I cultivate
petō, petere, petīuī, petītum	I seek
pōnō, pōnere, posuī, positum	I place
quaerō, quaerere, quaesīuī, quaesītum	I ask, seek
sinō, sinere, sīuī, situm	I allow
dēsinō, dēsinere, dēsiī, dēsitum	I cease

6 Inceptive verbs

cōgnōscō, cōgnōscere, cōgnōuī, cognitum	I get to know, learn
crēscō, crēscere, crēuī, crētum	I grow
nōscō, nōscere, nōuī, nōtum	I get to know
quiēscō, quiēscere, quiēuī, quiētum	I rest

7   3rd **-iō** conjugation

capiō, capere, cēpī, captum	I take
cupiō, cupere, cupīuī, cupītum	I desire
faciō, facere, fēcī, factum	I make, do
fugiō, fugere, fūgī, fugitum	I flee
iaciō, iacere, iēcī, iactum	I throw
rapiō, rapere, rapuī, raptum	I seize
(īn)spiciō, (īn)spicere, (īn)spexī, (īn)spectum	I look at

Deponent verbs

1st conjugation (all regular)

cōnor, cōnārī, cōnātus sum	I try

2nd conjugation

cōnfitērī, cōnfitērī, cōnfessus sum	I confess
uereor, uerērī, ueritus sum	I fear

3rd conjugation

fruor, fruī, (frūctus sum) + abl.	I enjoy
loquor, loquī, locūtus sum	I speak
queror, querī, questus sum	I complain
sequor, sequī, secūtus sum	I follow
īrāscor, īrāscī, īrātus sum + dat.	I am angry
nancīscor, nancīscī, nactus sum	I obtain
nāscor, nāscī, nātus sum	I am born
oblīuīscor, oblīuīscī, oblītus sum + gen.	I forget
proficīscor, proficīscī, profectus sum	I set out
amplector, amplectī, amplexus sum	I embrace
lābor, lābī, lāpsus sum	I slip
reuertor, reuertī, reuersus sum	I return
ūtor, ūtī, ūsus sum + abl.	I use

4th conjugation

experior, experīrī, expertus sum	I try
orior, orīrī, ortus sum	I arise

3rd -io (mixed) conjugation

gradior, gradī, gressus sum	I walk
morior, morī, mortuus sum (fut. part. **moritūrus**)	I die
patior, patī, passus sum	I suffer
prōgredior, prōgredī, prōgressus sum	I advance

Semi-deponent verbs
2nd conjugation

audeō, audēre, ausus sum	I dare
gaudeō, gaudēre, gāuīsus sum	I rejoice
soleō, solēre, solitus sum	I am accustomed

3rd conjugation

cōnfīdō, cōnfīdere, cōnfīsus sum + dat.	I trust

Irregular

fīō, fierī, factus sum	I am made, I become

PREPOSITIONS

The following take the accusative		The following take the ablative	
ad	to, towards	**ā/ab**	from, by
ante	before	**cum**	with
apud	at	**dē**	down from; about
circum	around	**ē/ex**	out of
contrā	against	**in**	in, on
extrā	outside	**prō**	in front of, on behalf of
in	into, onto, to, against	**sine**	without
inter	among	**sub**	under
per	through		
post	after, behind		
prope	near		
propter	on account of		
secundum	along		
sub	up to; towards (of time)		
super	above		
trāns	across		
ultrā	beyond		

CONJUNCTIONS

Coordinating		Subordinating	
atque	and	**antequam**	before
aut	or	**cum**	when, since, although
aut...aut	either...or	**dōnec**	until
enim*	for	**dum**	while, until
ergō	and so	**nē**	lest, that not
et	and	**nisi**	unless
et...et	both...and	**priusquam**	before
igitur*	therefore, and so	**postquam**	after
itaque	and so	**quamquam**	although
nam	for	**quod**	because
nec/neque	and not, nor	**sī**	if
nec/neque...nec/neque	neither...nor	**ubi**	when
-que	and	**ut** + indicative	as, when
sed	but	**ut** + subjunctive	1. (so) that (purpose, command)
tamen*	but, however		2. that (result)

* These come second in their sentences.

English–Latin Vocabulary

Regular verbs are given with infinitive only.

about   dē + abl.

Academy   Acadēmīa, -ae, *f.*

accept, I   accipiō, accipere, accēpī, acceptum

accustomed, I am   soleō, solēre, solitus sum

achieve, I   prōficiō, prōficere, prōfēcī, prōfectum

admiration   admīrātiō, admīrātiōnis, *f.*

admire   admīror, admīrārī, admīrātus sum

advance, I   prōgredior, prōgredī, prōgressus sum

Aeneas   Aenēās, Aenēae, *m.*

affair   rēs, reī, *f.*

afraid, I am   timeō, timēre, timuī; uereor, uerērī, ueritus sum

after   post + acc.

again   iterum

against   contrā + acc.; in + acc.

Agamemnon   Agamemnōn, Agamemnonis, *m.*

age   aetās, aetātis, *f.*; **new age**   nouum saeculum

all   omnis, omne

allowed, I am   mihi licet, licēre, licuit

alone   sōlus, -a, -um

already   iam

also   quoque

always   semper

am, I   sum, esse, fuī

I am there   adsum, adesse, adfuī, affuī

ancient   uetus, ueteris

and   et, -que

and so   itaque, igitur

anger   īra, īrae, *f.*

angry   īrātus, -a, -um

angry, I become (with)   īrāscor, īrāscī, īrātus sum + dat.

announce, I   nūntiō, nūntiāre

another   alius, alia, aliud

answer, I   respondeō, respondēre, respondī, respōnsum

anxious   ānxius, -a, -um

Apollo   Apollō, Apollinis, *m.*

approach, I   accēdō, accēdere, accessī, accessum (ad)

army   exercitus, -ūs, *m.*

arrange for, I   cūrō, cūrāre

arrive, I   adueniō, aduenīre, aduēnī, aduentum

ask, ask for, I   rogō, rogāre

astonished   attonitus, -a, -um

at last   tandem

at once   statim

Athens   Athēnae, -ārum, *f. pl.*

attack, I   oppugnō, oppugnāre

autumn   autumnus, -ī, *m.*

avoid, I   uītō, uītāre

bad   malus, -a, -um

badly   male

battle   proelium, proeliī, *n.*

bear, I   ferō, ferre, tulī, lātum

because   quod

become, I   fīō, fierī, factus sum

before (adverb)   anteā

before (conjunction)   antequam

before (preposition)   ante + acc.

begin   incipiō, incipere, incēpī,
   inceptum

besides   praetereā

better   melior, melius

big   magnus, -a, -um

bigger   maior, maius

board (a ship), I   cōnscendō,
   cōnscendere, cōnscendī, cōnscēnsum

book   liber, librī, *m.*

born, I am   nāscor, nāscī, nātus sum

both...and   et...et

boy   puer, puerī, *m.*

brave   fortis, forte

bring, I (= carry)   ferō, ferre, tulī, lātum
   (= lead)   dūcō, dūcere, dūxī, ductum

build, I   aedificō, aedificāre

burn, I (= I am on fire)   ardeō, ardēre,
   arsī, arsum

burn, I (= I set on fire)   incendō,
   incendere, incendī, incēnsum

busy   rēbus occupātus, -a, -um

but   sed

buy, I   emō, emere, ēmī, ēmptum

by   ā/ab + abl.

call, I   uocō, uocāre

calm   tranquillus, -a, -um

calmly   aequō animō

camp   castra, -ōrum, *n. pl.*

can, I   possum, posse, potuī

captain (of ship)   magister, magistrī, *m.*

care   cūra, -ae, *f.*

care for, I   cūrō, cūrāre

carry, I   portō, portāre; ferō, ferre, tulī,
   lātum

cast off, I   soluō, soluere, soluī, solūtum

catch sight of, I   cōnspiciō, cōnspicere,
   cōnspexī, cōnspectum

celebrate, I   celebrō, celebrāre

centurion   centuriō, centuriōnis, *m.*

certain, a   quīdam, quaedam,
   quoddam

cheerfully   hilare

child   puer, puerī, *c.*

children (*both girls and boys*)   puerī,
   -ōrum, *m. pl.*

chorus   chorus, -ī, *m.*

Cicero   Cicerō, Cicerōnis, *m.*

citizen   cīuis, cīuis, *c.*

city   urbs, urbis, *f.*

civil   cīuīlis, cīuīle

climb, I   ascendō, ascendere, ascendī,
   ascēnsum

come, I   ueniō, uenīre, uēnī, uentum

come back, I   redeō, redīre, rediī,
   reditum

come in, I   intrō, intrāre

comfort, I   cōnsōlor, cōnsōlārī,
   cōnsōlātus sum

companion   comes, comitis, *c.*

compel, I   cōgō, cōgere, coēgī, coāctum

compose, I   compōnō, compōnere,
   composuī, compositum

comrade   comes, comitis, *c.*

content (with)   contentus, -a, -um + abl.

country (*as opposed to town*)   rūs, rūris, *n.*

  in the country   rūrī

country (*native country*)   patria, -ae, *f.*

courage   uirtūs, uirtūtis, *f.*

courtyard   aula, -ae, *f.*

criticize, I   reprehendō, reprehendere, reprehendī, reprehēnsum

cross, I   trānseō, trānsīre, trānsiī, transitum

crowd   turba, -ae, *f.*

cultivate, I   colō, colere, coluī, cultum

Cyclops   Cyclōps, Cyclōpis, *m.*

danger   perīculum, -ī, *n.*

dare, I   audeō, audēre, ausus sum

daughter   fīlia, fīliae, *f.*

day   diēs, diēī, *m.* (sometimes f.)

  every day   cotīdiē

dead   mortuus, -a, -um

dear   cārus, -a, -um

Dear (*at start of letter*)   salūtem plūrimam dīcō + dat.

death   mors, mortis, *f.*

  meet my death, I   mortem obeō, obīre, obiī

decide, I   cōnstituō, cōnstituere, cōnstituī, cōnstitūtum; mihi placet, placēre, placuit

defeat, I   uincō, uincere, uīcī, uictum

defend, I   defendō, defendere, defendī, defēnsum

delay   mora, -ae, *f.*

delay, I   moror, morārī, morātus sum

delight, I   dēlectō, dēlectāre

Delphi   Delphī, Delphōrum, *m. pl.*

deny, I   negō, negāre

descend, I   dēscendō, dēscendere, dēscendī, dēscēnsum

despise, I   contemnō, contemnere, contempsī, contemptum

Dido   Dīdō, Dīdōnis, *f.*

die, I   morior, morī, mortuus sum

difficult   difficilis, difficile

dine, I   cēnō, cēnāre

dinner   cēna, -ae, *f.*

dismiss, I   dīmittō, dīmittere, dīmīsī, dīmissum

disturb, I   turbō, turbāre

do, I   faciō, facere, fēcī, factum

doctor   medicus, -ī, *m.*

dog   canis, canis, *c.*

don't!   nōlī, nōlīte! (+ inf.)

door   iānua, -ae, *f.*

doubtful   dubius, -a, -um;   **without doubt**   sine dubiō

drag, I   trahō, trahere, trāxī, tractum

drink, I   bibō, bibere, bibī

duty   officium, officiī, *n.*

each (of two)   uterque, utraque, utrumque

early   māne

earn, I   mereō, merēre

easily   facile

easy   facilis, facile

eat, I   edō, ēsse, ēdī ēsum

emperor   prīnceps, prīncipis, *m.*

end, in the   tandem

enemy   hostēs, hostium, *m. pl.*

enjoy, I   gaudeō, gaudēre, gāuīsus sum + abl.; fruor, fruī, frūctus sum + abl.

enough   satis + gen.

enter, I   intrō, intrāre; ineō, inīre, iniī, initum; ingredior, ingredī, ingressus sum

evening   uesper, uesperis, *m.*

ever umquam

  for ever semper; in perpetuum

every day cotīdiē

everything (= all things) omnia, omnium, *n. pl.*

excellent optimus, -a, -um

excuse excūsātiō, excūsātiōnis, *f.*

exercise, I exerceō, exercēre

explore, I explōrō, explōrāre

expression uultus, -ūs, *m.*

eye oculus, -ī, *m.*

fact, in rē uērā

fame fāma, fāmae, *f.*

family genus, generis, *n.;* (= household) familia, -ae, *f.*

farm fundus, -ī, *m.*

farm manager uīlicus, -ī, *m.*

farmer colōnus, -ī *m.*

father pater, patris, *m.*

fear, I timeō, timēre, timuī; uereor, uerērī, ueritus sum

few paucī, -ae, -a

field ager, agrī, *m.*

fierce ferōx, ferōcis

fifty quīnquāgintā

fight, I pugnō, pugnāre

find, I inueniō, inuenīre, inuēnī, inuentum

finish, I cōnficiō, cōnficere, cōnfēcī, cōnfectum

finished cōnfectus, -a, -um

fire ignis, ignis, *m.*

flee, I fugiō, fugere, fūgī, fugitum

follow, I sequor, sequī, secūtus sum

food cibus, -ī, *m.*

foolish stultus, -a, -um

for nam

for (= on behalf of) prō + abl.

forces cōpiae, -ārum, *f. pl.*

forgive, I ignōscō, ignōscere, ignōuī, ignōtum + dat.

forum forum, -ī, *n.*

fountain fōns, fontis, *m.*

fourth quārtus, -a, -um

freedman lībertus, -ī, *m.*

freedom lībertās, lībertātis, *f.*

friend amīcus, -ī, *m.*

friendship amīcitia, amīcitiae, *f.*

from ā/ab + abl.

full (of) plēnus, -a, -um (+ abl.)

game lūdus, -ī, *m.*

garden hortus, -ī, *m.*

gate porta, portae, *f.*

get up, I surgō, surgere, surrēxī, surrēctum

girl puella, -ae, *f.*

give, I dō, dare, dedī, datum

glad laetus, -a, -um

glory glōria, glōriae, *f.*

go, I eō, īre, iī/īuī, itum

go away, I abeō, abīre, abiī

go into, I intrō, intrāre

go out, I exeō, exīre, exiī, exitum; ēgredior, ēgredī, ēgressus sum

good bonus, -a, -um; **very good** optimus, -a, -um

goodbye, I say ualēre iubeō, iubēre, iussī

grape ūua, ūuae, *f.*

great magnus, -a, -um; **so great** tantus, -a, -um

greatest maximus, -a, -um

greatly magnopere; ualdē

Greece Graecia, -ae, *f.*

Greeks Graecī, Graecōrum, *m. pl.*

greet, I salūtō, salūtāre

guard, I custōdiō, custōdīre, custōdīuī, custōdītum

hand manus, -ūs, *f.*

hand over, I trādō, trādere, trādidī, trāditum

happens, it accidit, accidere, accidit

happy laetus, -a, -um

harbor portus, -ūs, *m.*

hard (adv.) (= diligently) dīligenter

have, I habeō, habēre

hear, I audiō, audīre

heart cor, cordis, *n.*

Hector Hector, Hectoris, *m.*

help auxilium, auxiliī, *n.*

help, I (ad)iuuō, (ad)iuuāre, (ad)iūuī, (ad)iūtum

here hīc; **to here** hūc

here, I am adsum, adesse, adfuī, affuī

hide, I cēlō, cēlāre

high altus, -a, -um

highly (of value) magnī

hill collis, collis, *m.*

himself, herself, itself (emphatic) ipse, ipsa, ipsum; (reflexive) sē

his/her/its own suus, sua, suum

home domūs, -ūs, *f.*; **at home** domī; **to home** domum

honor honor, honōris, *m.*

hope spēs, speī, *f.*

hope, I spērō, spērāre

Horace Horātius, Horātī, *m.*

horse equus, equī, *m.*

hour hōra, -ae, *f.*

house casa, -ae, *f.*, **(= grand house)** aedēs, aedium, *f. pl.*

huge ingēns, ingentis

hurry, I festīnō, festīnāre

idle ōtiōsus, -a, -um; ignāuus, -a, -um

if sī

ill, I am aegrōtō, aegrōtāre

in in + abl.

increase, I augeō, augēre, auxī, auctum

into in + acc.

invite, I inuītō, inuītāre

Italy Italia, -ae, *f.*

join, I (battle) proelium committō, committere, commīsī, commissum

journey iter, itineris, *n.*

joy gaudium, gaudiī, *n.*

kind benignus, -a, -um

king rēx, rēgis, *m.*

know, I sciō, scīre, scīuī, scītum

know, I don't nesciō, nescīre, nescīuī, nescītum

known nōtus, -a, -um

land terra, -ae, *f.*

last, at last tandem

late (adv.) sērō

laugh, I rīdeō, rīdēre, rīsī, rīsum

lead, I dūcō, dūcere, dūxī, ductum

leader dux, ducis, *c.*

learn, I discō, discere, didicī

leave, I (= go away from) discēdō, discēdere, discessī, discessum
(= leave behind) relinquō, relinquere, relīquī, relictum

lecture schola, -ae, *f.*

legion legiō, legiōnis, *f.*

leisure ōtium, -ī, *n.*

lest nē

letter (= of alphabet)   littera, -ae, *f.*;
   (= written communication)   epistola,
   -ae, *f.*

liberty   lībertās, lībertātis, *f.*

lie, I   iaceō, iacēre, iacuī

life   uīta, -ae, *f.*

light   lūx, lūcis, *f.*

light (adj.)   leuis, leue

like, I (= it pleases me)   mē iuuat,
   iuuāre, iūuit

like, I (= feel friendly towards)   amō,
   amāre

listen to, I   audiō, audīre

live, I   uīuō, uīuere, uīxī, uīctum
   (= inhabit)   habitō, habitāre

long   longus, -a, -um

for a long time   diū; **longer**   diūtius

long for, I   dēsīderō, dēsīderāre

look!   ecce

look after, I   cūrō, cūrāre

look at, I   spectō, spectāre; īnspiciō,
   īnspicere, īnspexī, īnspectum

look back, I   respiciō, respicere, respexī,
   respectum

look for, I   quaerō, quaerere, quaesīuī,
   quaesītum

loud (of voice)   magnus, -a, -um

love   amor, amōris, *m.*

love, I   amō, amāre

lover   amātor, amātōris, *m.*

Maecenas   Maecēnās, Maecēnātis, *m.*

make, I   faciō, facere, fēcī, factum

man   uir, uirī, *m.*

many   multī, -ae, -a

marry, I   nūbō, nūbere, nūpsī, nūptum
   + dat.

master (= schoolmaster; master of a
   ship)   magister, magistrī, *m.*
   (= master of slaves)   dominus, -ī, *m.*

me   mihi (dat.), mē (acc.)

meet, I   occurrō, occurrere, occurrī,
   occursum + dat.

messenger   nūntius, nūntiī, *m.*

midday   merīdiēs, merīdiēī, *m.*

miserable   miser, misera, miserum

mistress   domina, -ae, *f.*

modest   modestus, -a, -um

money   argentum, -ī, *n.*

month   mēnsis, mēnsis, *m.*

more   plūs, plūris; (= more
   greatly)   magis

mother   māter, mātris, *f.*

mountain, mount   mōns, montis, *m.*

move, I   moueō, mouēre, mōuī, mōtum

moved   commōtus, -a, -um

much, many   multus, -a, -um

much (*with comparative*)   multō

must, I   dēbeō, dēbēre, dēbuī, dēbitum

name   nōmen, nōminis, *n.*

Naples   Neāpolis; acc. Neāpolim, f.

near   prope + acc.

need, I   opus est mihi + abl.

neighbor   uīcīnus, -ī, *m.*

neither...nor   nec...nec

never   numquam

ninth   nōnus, -a, -um

noble   nōbilis, nōbile

no one   nēmō, (gen.) nūllīus, (dat.)
   nēminī, (acc.) nēminem, (abl.) nūllō, *c.*

not   nōn

nothing   nihil, nihilī, *n.*

now   iam; nunc

obey, I   pāreō, pārēre, pāruī, paritum +
   dat.

occupied   occupātus, -a, -um

often saepe

old uetus, ueteris

on in + abl.

once, at once statim

one ūnus, -a, -um; **one (of two)** alter, altera, alterum

one day diē quōdam, quondam

open apertus, -a, -um

oracle ōrāculum, -ī, n.

order, I iubeō, iubēre, iussī, iussum; imperō, imperāre + dat.

other alius, alia, aliud; **the other (of two)** alter, altera, alterum; **the others (= the rest)** cēterī, -ae, -a

ought, I dēbeō, dēbēre, dēbuī, dēbitum; mē oportet, oportēre, oportuit

our noster, nostra, nostrum

outside extrā + acc.

overcome, I superō, superāre

pardon uenia, -ae, f.

parent parēns, parentis, c.

passenger uiātor, uiātōris, m.

peace pāx, pācis, f.

people populus, -ī, m.

persuade, I persuādeō, persuādēre, persuāsī, persuāsum + dat.

philosopher philosophus, -ī, m.

philosophy philosophia, -ae, f.

pick, I carpō, carpere, carpsī, carptum

play, I lūdō, lūdere, lūsī, lūsum

please, I dēlectō, dēlectāre; placeō, placēre + dat.

plow, I arō, arāre

poem carmen, carminis, n.; poēma, poēmatis, n.

praise, I laudō, laudāre

prepare, I parō, parāre

preserve, I seruō, seruāre; cōnseruō, cōnseruāre

prince prīnceps, prīncipis, m.

proceed, I prōcēdō, prōcēdere, prōcessī, prōcessum

promise, I prōmittō, prōmittere, prōmīsī, prōmissum

pub taberna, -ae, f.

punish, I pūniō, pūnīre

pupil discipulus, -ī, m.

quaestor quaestor, quaestōris, m.

queen rēgīna, -ae, f.

quickly celeriter

race cursus, -ūs, m.

reach, I peruenīo, peruenīre, peruēnī, peruentum (ad +acc.)

read, I legō, legere, lēgī, lēctum

ready parātus, -a, -um

recall, I reuocō, reuocāre

receive, I accipiō, accipere, accēpī, acceptum

recite, I recitō, recitāre

recommend, I commendō, commendāre

rejoice, I gaudeō, gaudēre, gāuīsus sum

remove, I remoueō, remouēre, remōuī, remōtum

reply, I respondeō, respondēre, respondī, respōnsum

republic rēspūblica, reīpūblicae, f.

rest, I quiēscō, quiēscere, quiēuī, quiētum

return, I (= go back) redeō, redīre, rediī, reditum
(= **give back**) reddō, reddere, reddidī, redditum

riot tumultus, -ūs, *m.*

road uia, uiae, *f.*

rock saxum, saxī, *n.*

Roman Rōmānus, -a, -um

Rome Rōma, -ae, *f.*

rouse, I excitō, excitāre

row, I rēmigō, rēmigāre

run, I currō, currere, cucurrī, cursum

run back, I recurrō, recurrere, recurrī, recursum

run up to, run towards, I accurrō, accurrere, accurrī, accursum

sad trīstis, trīste

safe incolumis, incolume

sail, I nāuigō, nāuigāre

sailor nauta, -ae, *m.*

save, I seruō, seruāre

say, I dīcō, dīcere, dīxī, dictum; inquam

he/she says *or* **said** inquit

scarcely uix

school lūdus, -ī, *m.*

sea mare, maris, *n.*

see, I uideō, uidēre, uīdī, uīsum

seem, I uideor, uidērī, uīsus sum

self (himself, herself, itself) (emphatic) ipse, ipsa, ipsum; (reflexive) sē

send, I mittō, mittere, mīsī, missum

send for, I arcessō, arcessere, arcessīuī, arcessītum

sensible prūdēns, prūdentis

serve (as a soldier), I mīlitō, mīlitāre

set out, I proficīscor, proficīscī, profectus sum

severe seuērus, -a, -um

shade umbra, -ae, *f.*

sheep ouis, ouis, *f.*

shepherd pāstor, pāstōris, *m.*

shield scūtum, -ī, *n.*

ship nāuis, nāuis, *f.*

shore lītus, lītoris, *n.*

shout clāmor, clāmōris, *m.*

shout, I clāmō, clāmāre

show, I ostendō, ostendere, ostendī, ostentum/ostēnsum

show, I (*of qualities*) praebeō, praebēre, praebuī, praebitum (e.g. uirtūtem praebeō = I show courage)

shut, I claudō, claudere, clausī, clausum

Sibyl Sibylla, Sibyllae *f.*

signal signum, -ī, *n.*

silent tacitus, -a, -um

sing, I cantō, cantāre

sister soror, sorōris, *f.*

sit, I sedeō, sedēre, sēdī, sessum

sky caelum, caelī, *n.*

sleep, I dormiō, dormīre

slowly lentē

small paruus, -a, -um; **very small** minimus, -a, -um

smile subrīdeō, subrīdēre, subrīsī, subrīsum

so (with adj. or adv.) tam; (with verb) adeō

so great tantus, -a, -um

so much tantopere

soldier mīles, mīlitis, *m.*

someone, something aliquis, aliqua, aliquid

son fīlius, fīliī, *m.*

soon mox; **as soon as** cum prīmum

as soon as possible quam prīmum

sound sonus, sonī, *m.*

speak, I loquor, loquī, locūtus sum; for, fārī, fātus sum

speed celeritās, celeritātis, *f.*

spend, I (time) agō, agere, ēgī, āctum

spring uēr, uēris, *n.*

stand, I stō, stāre, stetī, statum
stay, I maneō, manēre, mānsī, mānsum
step gradus, -ūs, *m.*
still adhūc
stone saxum, -ī, *n.*
story fābula, fābulae, *f.*
street uia, -ae, *f.*
study studium, studiī, *n.*
suddenly subitō
suffering labor, labōris, *m.*
summer aestās, aestātis, *f.*
summon, I arcessō, arcessere, arcessīuī, arcessītum
supper cēna, cēnae, *f.*
sure certus, -a, -um
sure, I am prō certō habeō, habēre
surely not? num?

tablet (= writing tablet) tabula, tabulae, *f.*
talk, I dīcō, dīcere, dīxī, dictum; loquor, loquī, locūtus sum
tavern taberna, -ae, *f.*
teach, I doceō, docēre (someone (in acc.) something (in acc.))
tell, I (= inform) (aliquem) certiōrem faciō, facere, fēcī, factum
  (= narrate) nārrō, nārrāre
  (= order) iubeō, iubēre, iussī, iussum; imperō, imperāre + dat.
  (= say) dīcō, dīcere, dīxī, dictum
temple templum, -ī, *n.*
ten decem
terrified territus, -a, -um
than quam
that ille, illa, illud
theater theātrum, theātrī, *n.*
their own suus, -a, -um
then (= next) deinde

there ibi; **to there** eō
there, I am adsum, adesse, adfuī, affuī
thing rēs, reī, *f.*
this hic, haec, hoc
three trēs, trēs, tria
through per + acc.
throw away, I abiciō, abicere, abiēcī, abiectum
time tempus, temporis, *n.;* **for some time** aliquamdiū
tired fessus, -a, -um
tired of, I am mē taedet, taedēre, taeduit + gen.
to ad + acc.
today hodiē
toga toga, -ae, *f.*
top (= highest, greatest) summus, -a, -um
travel, I iter faciō, facere, fēcī, factum
treasury aerārium, aerāriī, *n.*
tree arbor, arboris, *f.*
Trojans Trōiānī, Trōiānōrum, *m. pl.*
true uērus, -a, -um
trust (in), I cōnfīdō, cōnfīdere, cōnfīsus sum + dat.; crēdō, crēdere, crēdidī, crēditum + dat.
truth uērum, -ī, *n.;* **to speak the truth** uēra dīcere
try, I cōnor, cōnārī, cōnātus sum
turn, I uertō, uertere, uertī, uersum
turn round, I mē uertō

under sub + abl.
until dum
unwilling inuītus, -a, -um
unwilling, I am nōlō, nōlle, nōluī
us nōbīs (dat.), nōs (acc.)
use ūsus, -ūs, *m.*

use, I   ūtor, ūtī, ūsus sum + abl.

useful, to be   ūsuī esse

value, I   aestimō, aestimāre

verse   uersus, -ūs, *m.*

very   ualdē

Virgil   Vergilius, Vergilī, *m.*

visit, I   uīsō, uīsere, uīsī, uīsum

voice   uōx, uōcis, *f.*

wait, I (= stay)   maneō, manēre, mānsī, mānsum

   (= wait for)   exspectō, exspectāre

walls (city walls)   moenia, moenium, *n. pl.*

wake up, I   ēuigilō, ēuigilāre (intr.); excitō, excitāre (trans.)

walk, I   ambulō, ambulāre; contendō, contendere, contendī, contentum

want, I   cupiō, cupere, cupīuī, cupītum

war   bellum, -ī, *n.*

warn, I   moneō, monēre

watch, I   spectō, spectāre

water   aqua, aquae, *f.*

wave   unda, -ae, *f.*

way   uia, uiae, *f.*

wedding   nūptiae, -ārum, *f. pl.*

weep, I   fleō, flēre, flēuī, flētum

well   bene

what?   quid?

when   ubi, cum

when?   quandō?

where   ubi, quā

where?   ubi? **where to?**   quō?

whether   num

whether ... or   utrum ... an

which   quī, quae, quod

which (of two)?   uter, utra, utrum?

while   dum

wife   uxor, uxōris, *f.*

who?   quis?

why?   cūr?

willing, I am   uolō, uelle, uoluī

wine   uīnum, -ī, *n.*

winter   hiems, hiemis, *f.*

wish, I   cupiō, cupere, cupīuī, cupītum; uolō, uelle, uoluī

with   cum + abl.

without   sine + abl.

wolf   lupus, -ī, *m.*

woman   fēmina, -ae, *f.*

wood   silua, -ae, *f.*

wool   lāna, -ae, *f.*

word   uerbum, -ī, *n.*

work, I   labōrō, labōrāre

work (= job)   negōtium, negōtiī, *n.*

worse   peior, peius

worthy (of)   dignus, -a, -um (+ abl.)

wound, I   uulnerō, uulnerāre

write, I   scrībō, scrībere, scrīpsī, scrīptum

year   annus, -ī, *m*

you   (sing.) tū, (pl.) uōs

young man   iuuenis, iuuenis, *m.*

your   (sing.) tuus, tua, tuum, (pl.) uester, uestra, uestrum

Index of Grammar

Credits